M

Henry Hemming is the author of five ~~books~~
including *Misadventure in the Middle East* ~~and~~ ~~Churchill's~~
Iceman. He has written for, among others, the *Economist*, *The Times*,
FT Magazine and the *Washington Post*. He lives in London with his
wife and daughter.

Praise for *M*

'Fascinating . . . Hemming has done a superb job'
Ben Macintyre, *The Times*

'Compelling . . . a gripping portrait' *Daily Telegraph*

'Excellent . . . Fluently written and highly entertaining'
Max Hastings, *Sunday Times*

'A fascinating portrait of a complex man. Espionage writing
at its best' Charles Cumming (Author of *A Divided Spy*)

'A rattling good read that is also a major piece of
revisionist history' *Wall Street Journal*

'Has everything you'd want from a great espionage story'
Matt Charman, Oscar-nominated screenwriter of *Bridge of Spies*

'Engaging and suspenseful' *Financial Times*

'Excellent . . . [Hemming] has a honed ability to fathom
the mysteries of his unusual subjects' *The Spectator*

'A read worthy of Le Carré himself' *Daily Express*

'Vivid and gripping . . . a cracking read, which both informs
and entertains in equal measure' *Country Life*

'A lively contribution to a maverick literature' *Observer*

Also available by Henry Hemming

Offscreen
Misadventure in the Middle East
In Search of the English Eccentric
Together
Churchill's Iceman

M

Maxwell Knight,
MI5's Greatest Spymaster

Henry Hemming

arrow books

1 3 5 7 9 10 8 6 4 2

Arrow Books
20 Vauxhall Bridge Road
London SW1V 2SA

Arrow Books is part of the Penguin Random House group of companies
whose addresses can be found at global.penguinrandomhouse.com.

Copyright © Henry Hemming 2017

Henry Hemming has asserted his right to be identified
as the author of this Work in accordance with the Copyright,
Designs and Patents Act 1988.

First published by Preface Publishing in 2017
First published in paperback by Arrow Books in 2018

www.penguin.co.uk

A CIP catalogue record for this book is available from the British Library.

ISBN 9781784752040

Printed and bound by Clays Ltd, St Ives plc

Penguin Random House is committed to a sustainable future
for our business, our readers and our planet. This book is made
from Forest Stewardship Council® certified paper.

For Matilda,
My M

If I had to choose between betraying my country and betraying my friend, I hope I should have the guts to betray my country.

– E. M. Forster, 'What I Believe', in *Two Cheers for Democracy*

CONTENTS

AUTHOR'S NOTE

This book is based on recently declassified MI5 files, conversations with former officers from MI5 and MI6, and the relatives of Maxwell Knight and the agents he ran, as well as diaries, memoirs, newspaper reports and contemporary accounts. References for most quotations can be found at the back of the book.

Maxwell Knight may have been the greatest spymaster ever employed by MI5, Britain's counterespionage agency, yet technically he never worked for it. The organisation that we all know today as MI5 was quietly renamed 'the Security Service' several weeks before Knight began to work there, but the new title took years to catch on in Whitehall. For most people today the Security Service is better known as MI5, the name I have used in this book. Maxwell Knight also worked at one point for MI5's foreign counterpart, originally known as MI1(c) or C's Organisation, later MI6 and today SIS, which I have referred to throughout as MI6. (Just to help tell them apart: the TV series *Spooks* is set in MI5, whereas James Bond works for MI6.)

The most complex relationship in espionage, as well as the most fraught and dramatically compelling, is usually between the operative out in the field who gathers information and the man or woman to whom that operative reports. There are all sorts of terms to describe the two roles. The individual collecting intelligence might be a *contact, source, informant, spy* or *agent* (and if this agent takes on his or her own informants, they are *subagents*), while the person they report to could be the *agent runner, agent handler, officer, case officer, operations officer* or *spymaster*. A further source of confusion is that an American intelligence officer can sometimes be referred to as an agent. In this book I have generally referred to the people who gather intelligence as agents, and those who look after them as either officers or spymasters. For clarification on this, or any other question, feel free to get in touch. My email address can be found at henryhemming.com

Henry Hemming
January 2017

PROLOGUE

Early on Monday, 20 May, 1940, at a point in the Second World War when the threat of a Nazi invasion of Britain feels unmistakably real, a police car pulls up outside a boarding house in central London. Five men pile out of the vehicle and make for the building. The door is opened by a maid. One of the men explains that they are looking for an American. His name is Tyler Kent. She asks them to wait and goes to fetch her employer. There follows a pause, probably no more than a few seconds, before the five men rush into the building.

One goes after the maid, while the others make a dash for the stairs. Two of the four men now haring up the staircase of No. 47 Gloucester Place are seasoned, solid-looking police detectives from Special Branch. The third is an official from the United States Embassy. The last is a broad-shouldered thirty-nine-year-old with a beaky nose and a gait that speaks of long country walks. His name is Maxwell Knight. To his friends, he is Max. To most of his colleagues in MI5, Britain's counterespionage agency, and to his sprawling family of undercover agents, he is better known as 'M'.

This is M's raid. It is based on his analysis of intelligence from his operatives, a web of men and women that he personally recruited to his maverick wing of MI5 known as 'M Section'. His speciality is getting agents inside extremist political groups. One of M's under-cover operatives, a middle-aged single mother who made a living before the war doing cooking demonstrations, recently provided her spymaster with the intelligence that led to this raid.

After the first flight of stairs, the four men are confronted by the landlady. One of the detectives produces his search warrant and asks for the whereabouts of Kent. She gestures at the door behind them.

Tyler Kent is an American embassy official that M believes to be a Nazi spy. If the man from MI5 is wrong about this, there will be a diplomatic incident. If he is right, but has left it too late, classified communications may have already been dispatched to Rome and from there to Berlin. In the spy films this spymaster loves to watch the plot usually centres on an enemy agent trying to steal secret papers – the 'MacGuffin', as Alfred Hitchcock calls them. It rarely matters what is on those papers. This is different. The documents that M hopes to find, and that the alleged Nazi spy has stolen, contain secret correspondence between Winston Churchill, the new British Prime Minister, and Franklin D. Roosevelt, the US President, which, in the wrong hands, could change the course of the war.

One of the detectives tries the door. It is bolted shut from the inside, so he knocks.

'Don't come in,' a man calls out.

The detective knocks again.

'Don't come in!' The voice is more indignant this time. M can hear traces of a whispered conversation and the irregular clunk-clunk-clunk of people moving about suddenly and at speed.

One of the detectives walks away from the door, turns and prepares to charge. His name is Inspector Pearson and he is built like the side of a barn. The rest of the men clear a path to give him a clear run at the door and for a moment in that corridor, while elsewhere in London people are making their way to work, and across the English Channel German forces continue to bomb, shell and shoot their way towards Paris, all is still.

It is hard to say precisely what is running through M's mind at this point in the operation, only that very recently in his life he reached a crossroads. The outbreak of war nine months earlier forced him to confront a ghost from his past. Now as he stands in the corridor, waiting for the policeman to break down the door, he is facing a decision that will change the way he is seen for years to come. This MI5 spymaster knows that he must choose between his friends and his country, punishing one in order to protect the other, and if he does not make this decision soon, very soon, it might be made for him. M is a man who has always valued loyalty above any other human quality, yet at this point in his life, to his dismay, he must contemplate a betrayal.

Inspector Pearson jogs down the corridor. *Thud-thud-thud-thud-thud-thud. Crack.* M watches his body slam into the door. The wood gives way with an easy splintering sound, and the passage is filled with light. The men race in.

PART I

BECOMING M

I

A MAN ADRIFT

It began in 1923, when Maxwell Knight agreed to meet a man called Makgill.

Knight, or just Max, as everybody knew him, was an energetic twenty-three-year-old unhappily employed as a school games teacher. He was good-looking in an unconventional way, ears a little too big, nose more prominent than he might have liked. He wore his hair scraped back under a film of pomade. He had an easy, sporty air and the enviable ability to put people at ease. Yet on that particular day, the day that he went to meet Makgill, it is unlikely that he was feeling his usual relaxed self.

Although there is no record of where this interview took place, it was probably at the Guards Club, in central London, where Makgill had conducted meetings like this in the past. Entering the club, Max would have noticed the sudden change in atmosphere as the doors to the street cracked shut behind him. It was worlds away from the sweaty, swaying clubs of nearby Soho where he spent most of his evenings. The air tasted cleaner in here. The lighting was sharper, more refined. It was quieter, too, the silence broken only by the hushed drum of his footsteps and the distant flutters of conversation.

Indeed, most features of this venerable gentlemen's club, from its polished neo-Georgian furnishings and Palladian proportions to the enormous elevated portraits of gimlet-eyed army officers, had been chosen to impress upon visitors the calibre and standing of the men who belonged to this military tribe. Usually, it had the effect of putting newcomers on edge. Making matters worse, Max had almost no idea what he was doing there.

He had agreed to the meeting after a chance encounter at an event staged by the British Empire Union, a right-wing political group that campaigned against the spread of Communism. Max had got into conversation with John Baker White, the son of a Kentish landowner. Baker White had asked the young games teacher whether he might be interested in doing some part-time work of a patriotic nature. For reasons that will soon become clear, Max agreed immediately.

The man that Max was now set to meet was Sir George Makgill, eleventh Baronet and de jure eleventh Viscount of Oxfuird, a square-jawed industrialist who was also a Freemason, a novelist and a terrifying interviewer. Another young man who went to meet Makgill in similar circumstances would confess that 'except for an uncomfortable twenty-four hours I spent with the *Troisième Bureau* [part of the French Security Service] some time later, I have never experienced such searching cross-questioning'. Max had just walked into the job interview from hell, for a position that had not yet been described to him.

Makgill's aim in the cross-examination that followed was simple. This no-nonsense, gruff industrialist wanted to get the measure of Maxwell Knight, to find out what this twenty-three-year-old stood for, the type of man he was and, most importantly, whether he could be trusted.

All of us are guilty in job interviews of projecting a version of ourselves, or at least trying to do so. Max would have gone out of his way to present himself to Makgill as an upright ex-naval officer from a good family, a young man who was patriotic, tough and utterly trustworthy. In some ways, he was all these things. During the last two years of the First World War, Max had been an officer in the Royal Naval Reserve, having volunteered for active service at the age of seventeen. He had served on destroyers and converted trawlers, and although he did not see enemy action, he was thought to have done well and was promoted to Hydrophone Officer, first class, finishing the war with the rank of Midshipman. Even though Max was forced to take shore leave on one occasion as a result of seasickness, he was judged to be 'a promising young officer'.

Before that Max had spent several years as a cadet on HMS *Worcester,* a doggedly strict naval training vessel. So, no one could quibble with his describing himself as tough. As for his family background, Max could draw faithfully on childhood memories of exploring the grounds of the Knight family pile in Wales, Tythegston Court, a manor house set amid glorious rolling parkland. His ancestors had been clerics, antiquarians and landowners. One of his cousins was R. D. Blackmore, author of *Lorna Doone,* the classic Victorian romance. Although they were not quite landed gentry, the Knights had been men and women of private means and admirable reputation. When asked about his politics, Max could point to his having been talent-spotted at a meeting of the British Empire Union as evidence of his hatred of Communism and his unwavering patriotism.

So far, so good. This was the version of himself that Max had arrogated and wanted the world to see. But there was another side to him, a shadow self that he would not have presented to Makgill during that interview. Max did not volunteer that he had recently been declared the black sheep of his family, cut off financially by the family patriarch and banned from future Knight family gatherings, or that he spent his evenings drinking champagne and dancing in grungy Soho cellar clubs. He probably kept to himself that he had been kicked out of the civil service after less than a year, and that the most likely reason for his decision to join the British Empire Union was neither patriotic nor political. It was to impress his girlfriend.

We all contain contradictions. Max Knight, by the age of twenty-three, cleaved to more than most. He had shown himself in the last few years to be patriotic and tough as well as rash, directionless and a source of intense frustration to his family. The job Makgill had in mind was an unforgiving test of character. It was demanding and dangerous and could last for years. To satisfy himself that Max was suitable, this middle-aged industrialist needed to get beneath the young man's veneer of clubbable charm in order to understand the person he was at his core. One way to do that was by examining his past.

Charles Henry Maxwell Knight was born on 9 July, 1900, and spent most of his childhood in the village of Mitcham, which was not yet part of London but no longer part of the surrounding countryside either. His father was a solicitor, as well as a philanderer and a spend-thrift. Max's mother, Ada, who was by then on her second marriage, was large and loud and loved to sing. She was the livewire of the Knight household. When her cheating husband ran out of money, as he frequently did, it was Ada who packed up their modest belongings and took their youngest, Max, and his two siblings, Eric and Enid, to stay with their rich uncle in Wales. The reason Max had such vivid memories of life at Tythegston Court, with its servants, its manicured formal gardens and its rambling grounds, was that his father was so often broke.

Yet the defining characteristic of Max's early years was not this financial insecurity, and the peripatetic life which followed; it concerned his relationship with wild creatures. As a child, Max was obsessed with animals. By the age of nine, he had kept lizards, mice, rats, hedgehogs, slow worms, many different species of bird, 'and, of course,' he wrote, 'the inevitable tortoises'. Rescuing animals and taking care of them was a fixation for him, and it helped to bring this otherwise shy boy out of himself. 'I was brought up never to be afraid of any animal without good reason,' he once wrote. This hobby burnished him with a lifelong love of the outdoors. It may have also given him an underlying fearlessness.

His most treasured boyhood memories were of going onto Mitcham Common to hear the churring of the nightjars and the harsh, rasping call of the corncrake, or those moments in his life when he had found an injured creature in the wild, captured it, tamed it and nursed it back to health. When asked about his favourite boyhood pet – Agatha, a white Agouti rat – he described her as 'more intelligent than any other rat I ever owned – and I had many'. More than other boys his age, Max seemed to relish the slow, sleuthing discovery of character. He treated each animal as an individual and liked to spend hours alone with his pets, studiously working out their separate personalities.

His family tolerated all this – often it amused them – yet none of them could really understand why these creatures responded to him as they did. This sometimes withdrawn boy appeared to have what naturalists call 'the gift'. Within a month of finding a female toad, for example, which, for reasons known only to Max, he had christened Ted, he had tamed her. 'I got her to feed out of my hand, and she would even take hold of an earth-worm suspended from my fingers and try to pull it out of my grasp.' Few wild-born toads will feed from a human hand. Fewer still are happy to do this after so little time in captivity.

'He handled them brilliantly,' a cousin later recalled. 'They seemed to come to him easily, trustingly.' In the way that some gardeners are green-fingered, Max had an apparently intuitive understanding of how to handle animals, a personal magnetism. They trusted him, especially female creatures, it seemed, and throughout his childhood he continued to display this rare gift.

At the age of twelve, he was paid seven shillings and sixpence for an article of his on animal welfare. In the same year he proudly sewed onto his shirt the naturalist badge that he had been awarded as a Boy Scout. His ambitions at the time were to be either a zookeeper, a vet or a taxidermist. It was clear to anyone who knew Max, or those who saw him handle pets, that his career would involve animals.

Then came 1914. In May of that year, Max's father died unexpectedly at the age of fifty-three after a short illness. Hugh Knight's death seemed to confirm an absence in his son's life rather than create one. His father had been a peripheral presence, one whose place in the family hierarchy was rapidly assumed by Hugh's brother, Robert, who was parsimonious, prudish and much less forgiving of Max. He saw his nephew as wayward. Others might have been charmed by Max's love of animals, or his growing interest in music. Not Uncle Robert. Soon after Hugh's death, Robert Knight had his nephew dispatched to HMS *Worcester,* a training vessel for those going into the merchant navy. Max's mother was by then financially dependent on her brother-in-law Robert and was either unable to intervene or unwilling to do so.

To describe the regime on board this naval training vessel as Spartan would be unkind to that ancient Greek city-state. HMS *Worcester* had it all: barbaric initiation ceremonies, arcane traditions, a rigid pecking order, rampant bullying and a rule against boys having more than one bath a week. The food was 'unfit for human consumption'. Cadets were deprived of sleep, and during the winter it was knee-shakingly cold. Yet life on board HMS *Worcester* certainly had the desired effect of hardening up its teenage cadets.

By the end of 1914, Max was living in a country that had gone to war, his elder brother was fighting in the trenches, his father had recently died, while he himself had started a harsh new life as a naval cadet. Aged fourteen, he had been fast-tracked into adulthood.

After several years on HMS *Worcester,* Max volunteered for the

Royal Naval Reserve. Although he emerged from the conflict unscathed, in the last year of the war his brother, Eric, was killed on the Western Front. This left Max, by the end of the war, bereft of the two most important men in his life. He finished his naval career in 1919 and went to live with his mother and sister in London, where he took a lowly job as a clerk at the Ministry of Shipping. With no father or brother to rein him in, he was soon sucked into a subversive new movement. While other men his age worried about the protean political shape of the world, eagerly signing up to trade unions and political parties, Max joined a different kind of party. He got into jazz.

The jazz scene in postwar London was irreverent and wild, an uncharted, exotic land where it seemed that anything went. 'You can call off imaginary figures, yell "hot dog" in the midst of some perfectly decorous dance, and make a donkey of yourself generally. That is jazz,' said Paul Whiteman, the so-called King of Jazz, adding: 'anybody can jazz'. Jazz was a musical movement as much as a youthful provocation. It was rebellious, out of control and for many people in Britain its sudden popularity signalled a breakdown in morality. The nineteen-year-old Maxwell Knight could not get enough of it.

On leaving the navy, right after the end of the war, Max set up a jazz band composed of ex-servicemen. It was, he claimed, 'London's first small, hot combination'. If they really were 'hot', then some credit for their playing should go to the man then giving Max clarinet lessons: Sidney Bechet, the legendary jazz saxophonist who was then based in London, a musician whose playing fell upon the listener, wrote Philip Larkin, 'as they say love should, / Like an enormous yes'. Max later recalled a 'sort of jam session' with Bechet in which the maestro played on a soprano saxophone 'Softly Awakes My Heart', from the opera *Samson and Delilah,* while the young civil servant 'did my best to be with him on the clarinet' – possibly the same instrument he had just bought from Bechet. Max also became friends with members of the Original Dixieland Jazz Band, including its leader, Nick LaRocca, who gave him the first pressing of their hit record *Rag Tiger*. It did not survive. 'Some ass of a friend of mine a few years later went and put his foot on it.'

In these loud and out-of-control months after leaving the Royal Naval Reserve, jazz became a governing passion in Max's life, but it did not replace the other one. Even as he threw himself into the demi-monde of London's new jazz scene, making new friends everywhere he went, alive to its possibilities, Max continued to collect animals. Like a young man who refuses to pack away his boyhood train set, and expands it instead, he now had more animals than ever before. As well as mice and a bush baby – a small furry primate with worried-looking eyes and the pointed ears of a bat – there was a parrot living in his flat and several grass snakes. On at least one occasion, his two hobbies collided when he tried to impersonate a snake charmer by playing his clarinet 'fairly close' to his pet snakes. To his lasting disappointment, the snakes did not respond.

Just as it seemed that there was no room in his life for another animal, Max acquired a new pet that he called Bessie. Yet few people remembered this animal's name. They found it hard to see past the fact that Bessie was a bear.

This particular bear, Max recalled, was 'the most attractive bundle of cunning and mischief that you could possibly imagine'. Bessie the bear caused mayhem wherever she went, knocking over furniture in Max's flat, rootling around in the kitchen and on one occasion getting her snout stuck in the flour jar. Max would put her in a harness and take her out for walks in the street. Passers-by mistook her for an exuberant and rather large Chow puppy.

Otherwise, Bessie spent her days inside Max's flat, in a mansion block in Putney, southwest London, where she seemed to get on well with the other pets, including a bulldog and a young baboon. This list of animals is revealing. Nobody else in London had a bear, a bulldog *and* a baboon. Max made sure to mention this to a gossip columnist that he had befriended, who made him and his exotic menagerie the subject of a short article. As a boy, Max had had no interest in looking after common-or-garden pets such as rabbits or guinea pigs, partly because he thought they were 'stupid' but also because nobody paid them much attention. Max was a watcher at heart, yet it seemed that he also liked to be seen.

There may have been another reason why he clung on with such tenacity to his childhood hobby. Looking after these animals must have reminded him of that more innocent age he had enjoyed before his life had been upended by war, adolescence, HMS *Worcester* and the deaths of his brother and father. Max's childhood was unfinished business. Caring for these pets was perhaps a way of getting back to it.

Given the jazz, the animals, the drinking and the dancing, his day job at the Ministry of Shipping was for him a distraction as much as anything else, and after no more than a year, he was out. It is unclear whether he resigned or was sacked. A respectable career as a civil servant had stretched out before him, and with it stability, status and security, but it had come too soon.

Having left the civil service, Max found a job selling paint. Not long after this unusual career move, his uncle decided to cut him off. Robert Knight was no longer prepared to endure the spectacle of his nephew's life unravelling like this. He announced that forthwith Max was banned from all family gatherings and would no longer receive his modest allowance.

This was a heavy, lasting blow. Max had never seen himself as a rebel. He wanted to lead a more unbuttoned life than most of his contemporaries and he enjoyed being the odd man out. 'In a world where we are all tending to get more and more alike,' he later wrote, 'a few unusual people give a little colour to life!' Until then, he had imagined that everyone was laughing along with him – but not his uncle, it seemed, who had come to think of him as a pleasure-seeking

Peter Pan more interested in jazz and pets than settling down to become a conscientious civil servant.

Max was still living in Putney with his sister and mother. Although the two women in his life did not turn on him in the wake of his family excommunication, they could hardly ignore what had happened. When Ada made a codicil to her will shortly after, to reflect the death of Max's brother, Eric, who was one of the executors, she chose to substitute Eric with a former colleague of her late husband. Clearly Max could not be trusted with this level of responsibility.

Max's new career as a paint salesman lasted only a few months, after which he found a job teaching games at the well-to-do Willington Prep School in Putney. Sometimes he filled in for a colleague by taking an English class, hoping, perhaps, that this might lead to more time spent teaching more challenging subjects. But it did not.

By 1923, Max was stuck. He even tried to become a novelist to escape his predicament, writing short stories in the style of John Buchan, his favourite author, whose amateur spy and all-action hero Richard Hannay from books such as *The Thirty-Nine Steps* he idolised, and sending these off to boys' magazines. But if any of them were published, there is no record of it. All the doors in Maxwell Knight's life appeared to have closed. He had a lot to prove and dangerously little to lose. He was also very short of money.

The only bright spot in Max's life was his girlfriend, Hazel Barr, a quiet eighteen-year-old schoolgirl he had met one morning on the upper deck of a bus. He had been going to work, she to school. There was a spark between them. They began to take the same bus each day. Max was soon invited to meet Hazel's parents, and made a winning impression on her mother. Indeed Mrs Barr began to wonder whether this nice young games teacher was going to propose marriage to her daughter. Although Hazel and Max did not have sex, which was normal for an unmarried couple at the time, they saw a lot of each other. Hazel later described herself as 'completely enamoured' of Max, adding, 'I think the feeling was mutual.' Hazel also appears to have taken her beau along to an event staged by the British Empire Union, which was probably how Max came to meet John Baker White.

Given the dead-end Max had reached in his career, when asked by Baker White in 1923 whether he was interested in part-time, paid work of a patriotic nature, his response would have been emphatic and fast.

Not long after, he went to see Sir George Makgill.

What did Makgill make of Max? He was certainly different from the other men Baker White sent to him. Usually, these were bluff ex-officers in the mould of Bulldog Drummond, the fictional soldier famous for his Hun-bashing, Bolshie-baiting approach to life. Max Knight kept mice. He was not terribly interested in politics, and he adored jazz – which for a reactionary like Makgill was a tuneless abomination. Here was a twenty-three-year-old drop-out whose great gift in life, his ability to look after animals, seemed to qualify him to do little more than work in a zoo. Yet Makgill saw qualities in this apparently feckless young man that might be useful to him.

It was a gamble – every agent recruitment is – but Makgill concluded that Maxwell Knight might be suitable for the task he had in mind. It was probably at this point in their conversation that Makgill began to explain a little more about himself and his organisation.

2

THE MAKGILL ORGANISATION

Sir George Makgill had been on the other side of the world when he heard that his father had died. The elder son of a Scottish baronet, he had taken himself off to New Zealand several years earlier, and had expected to be there for a long time, when he learned of his father's death and that he had inherited a title, land, property, money and a vast portfolio of shares and industrial holdings. Makgill's understanding of the world began to change. He returned to Britain, where his boyish patriotism hardened into a more prickly nationalism. During the First World War, he campaigned for a boycott of all German goods. He funded the Anti-German Union and lobbied hard for the expulsion from the Privy Council, which advised the monarch, of two of the country's leading Jewish politicians, Sir Ernest Cassel and Sir Edgar Speyer, arguing that they were not sufficiently British. But it was only towards the end of the war that Sir George Makgill found what he believed to be his calling in life.

'The whole of Europe is filled with the spirit of revolution,' warned the Prime Minister David Lloyd George in 1919. By then, Russia had fallen to Communism. Germany looked set to follow. The Austro-Hungarian Empire had collapsed. The Ottoman Empire was on the brink, and Bavaria and Hungary had just become Soviet Republics. The Communist threat to Britain in the immediate aftermath of the First World War was real and it was different. In 1920, the Foreign Secretary Lord Curzon complained that the Soviet Union 'makes no secret of its intention to overthrow our institutions everywhere and to destroy our prestige and authority'. In the past, Britain's enemies had endangered particular trade routes or far-flung colonial territories. Yet Communism and the Soviet Union imperilled the British ruling class, capitalism as an economic system and the entire British Empire. Although the British government tried to suffocate the Bolshevik experiment at birth, supplying arms and assistance to White Russian rebels in the years after the establishment of the new Communist regime in Russia, it failed. The Soviet Union emerged triumphant and was now stronger than ever. Moscow had both the resources and the will to succeed, as well as a recruiting tool of explosive potency. The Bolshevik Revolution of 1917 demonstrated beyond any argument that a speedy socialist revolution in an ageing autocracy, like Britain, was not just fantasy. It was realistic, and surprisingly easy to carry out.

Most worrying for a man like Makgill, and so many others within Britain's social, industrial and political elite, was the growing sympathy for the Soviet Union among large chunks of the newly enfranchised working class. Between 1914 and 1918, the size of the British electorate had more than doubled. For many of these new voters, the Bolsheviks had the noble appeal of the underdog. Trade union membership in Britain had rocketed. Unemployment would soon be on the rise, leaving the country hamstrung by industrial action. In 1920 alone, twenty-six million working days were lost to strikes. Even the police had gone on strike. The promise of Communism, or the threat of it, depending on your perspective, was without precedent. Sir George Makgill was one of those who became convinced that the British government had not recognised this danger for what it was. So, the baronet decided to take matters into his own hands.

With the help of fellow industrialists, landowners and politicians who belonged to the British Empire Union, of which he was Honorary Secretary, Makgill set up a private intelligence agency. It was run, according to MI5, 'somewhat on Masonic lines', and would be known by various names, including the Industrial Intelligence Bureau and Section D (possibly after 'Don', its chief agent-runner). Yet the 'Makgill Organisation' is most apt, for, like so many intelligence agencies, its activities came to reflect the fears and private obsessions of those in charge, which in this case meant Makgill himself.

Some of the principal customers for its intelligence product were factory owners and right-wing industrialists from the Coal Owners' and Ship-Owners' Associations or the Federation of British Industries. They wanted timely information on forthcoming strikes and the names of prominent Communists and trade unionists. But these were not the only people interested in its intelligence. Makgill planted agents inside the Communist Party and the more militant trade unions as well as pretty much any other group he did not like the sound of or was intrigued by: Anarchists, Irish Home Rulers, women traffickers, Occultists; everything from the Rudolf Steiner Anthroposophical Society to the Irish Republican Army (IRA). Yet there was never any hesitation or doubt in Makgill's mind that the principal threat came from the Soviet Union.

With so many groups to investigate, Makgill was almost constantly on the lookout for new agents. He used talent-spotters like Baker White to send him potential recruits, which was how he had come to be interviewing Max.

Makgill sought two qualities in his agents. The first was an almost Masonic emphasis on secrecy. 'If you talk,' Makgill had told Baker White, 'you're out.' The second was more idiosyncratic. He would only take on agents who shared his political outlook. This was the 'unique feature' of the Makgill Organisation that ensured that 'every man and woman working in it could be trusted'.

It is hard to say whether Makgill felt that Max lacked one of these qualities, but the first job he gave him was certainly unusual. Max was not asked to join a trade union or become a Communist. Instead, his instructions were to penetrate a political group that posed no apparent threat to the country, to Sir George Makgill or to any of his cronies. Max's target was an organisation that was conservative, patriotic and staunchly anti-Communist, the kind of group Makgill himself might have set up.

Max did not mind. The work sounded exciting, demanding and important, in stark contrast to his life as an impoverished games teacher. He said yes.

3

BLOODY FOOLS

Soon after being taken on by Sir George Makgill in 1923, Maxwell
Knight walked into a severe-looking building off the King's Road
in Chelsea, west London, the headquarters of a group called the
British Fascisti, where he offered his services as a volunteer. Max
had just stepped into the political fringe of postwar London. This
was a land with its own rules, and he would have to learn them all,
and fast, for Makgill provided no training. Instead, this first-time
agent had to make it up as he went along.

Max's task was to secure a lowly position inside the Intelligence
Department of the British Fascisti, or BF, as it was known, before
quietly working his way up in the years that followed. He was a
'penetration agent', but with a difference. Usually, Makgill ordered
his men to join a target organisation, gain acceptance as an ordinary
member, and then, like a young cuckoo in another bird's nest, wreak
havoc from within. Yet Max's instructions were to let the British
Fascisti carry on with its work uninterrupted. His job was simply to
keep an eye out for potential recruits to the Makgill Organisation
and otherwise to steal intelligence from the BF. Quite why Makgill
did not openly collaborate with this group, given their shared

interests and aims, is unclear. We can only assume that the wealthy industrialist had tried to do this but had been rebuffed, and in response he decided to send in an undercover agent.

In the headquarters of the British Fascisti, Max encountered a 'superfluity of voluntary workers', most of whom seemed to 'come and go as they wish and can never be depended upon'. He became one of them, taking the part-time and unpaid position of 'Research Officer'. His career as an undercover agent had begun. Now he could learn more about the organisation he had infiltrated.

The British Fascisti was the brainchild of Rotha Lintorn-Orman, a twenty-eight-year-old lesbian who had served as an ambulance driver during the war. She had been decorated for bravery but had returned to a country she frequently found hard to recognise. Many of those who came back from active duty overseas experienced a similar sense of unease and bewilderment. It was as if they spoke a different language from the civilians at home, and had acquired an alternative set of values. Lintorn-Orman was also amazed to find the country paralysed by industrial unrest. Like so many others, she blamed international Communism.

It is hard to exaggerate the impact on British society of not only five years of bloody, total war but also the collapse of the German, Austro-Hungarian, Ottoman and Russian empires and the birth of the Soviet Union, all in the space of just a few years. The effect was cataclysmic. It was as if the foundations of the established world order had been blown out, leaving an apparently endless vista of new political possibilities. Whereas some people in Britain found this inspiring, others were more fearful. Rotha Lintorn-Orman wanted to do whatever she could to prevent Britain from succumbing to Socialism, which meant protecting the country from the Soviet Union and its ideology, and in this she was not alone. One of her closest allies at this point in her political career, a woman who shared her resolve and determination, was her mother. In May 1923,

Blanche Lintorn-Orman gave her daughter Rotha the colossal sum of £50,000 (equivalent to roughly £2 million today) to defend the country from the so-called Red Menace.

At the time, Benito Mussolini was the only European leader to have successfully expunged Communism from his country's political fabric. Without really looking into the minutiae of what Mussolini stood for, or what Fascism was, Rotha Lintorn-Orman set up a group inspired by the Italian leader's example. It was run initially from the London offices of the Partito Nazionale Fascista Italiano, Mussolini's party, and was called 'The British Fascisti'.

At the time, expressing admiration for Mussolini was a lot less radical than it sounds today. *The Times*, the *Morning Post* and the *Observer* were frequently complimentary towards the Italian leader. Winston Churchill referred to him as 'the Roman genius'. Mussolini had even been employed by MI5 in 1917, when he was paid £100 a week to 'persuade' left-wing Italian protesters to stay at home. Yet the strangest feature of Rotha Lintorn-Orman's new group was not so much its name or the overt connection it had to Mussolini, but that the original programme of the British Fascisti did not contain anything that could be described as clearly *fascist*. Instead of being patriarchal, anti-Semitic and revolutionary, the British Fascisti seemed to be more interested in dressing up in uniform, organising marches and professing its love of the monarchy or its desire to defeat Communism. Rather than being entirely male, this group had been set up by a woman and its original Grand Council contained more women than men.

Lintorn-Orman's first move as leader of the BF was to set up an informal nationwide militia with branches all over the country. In the event of a socialist uprising, the idea was that these units would rise up to fight 'for King and Country' – a popular BF slogan that had also been used to recruit British soldiers during the war.

The reaction of most British people to the launch of Lintorn-

Orman's patriotic new group was one of bemusement. The group's acronym did not help. 'BF' also stood for 'Bloody Fool'. One eager member of the BF recalled those who 'decried my youthful enthusiasm and dismissed us as having Bolsheviks under our beds'. Yet there were those who took this group very seriously. Within a year of the BF's formation, tens of thousands of Britons had paid to join up, including minor aristocrats, disgruntled ex-army officers and Conservative members of Parliament such as Patrick Hannon and Colonel Sir Charles Burn, a former aide-de-camp to the King. The BF even recruited the captain of the England cricket team, Arthur Gilligan, who may have introduced Fascism to Australia during the 1924–25 Ashes tour. He probably saw this as his only accomplishment during what turned out to be a whitewash 5–0 defeat.

Apart from these headline-grabbing recruits, the rump of the BF's membership was made up of disillusioned Tories, many of whom had fought during the war and were now gravely concerned about a Communist uprising. They shared a belief that the government was not doing enough and that it was time for decent British patriots like themselves to do the job themselves. Almost everything about this new group harked back to the war. Its central message was that the country was now locked in an epoch-defining struggle against a foreign enemy. It had a hierarchy and language that appealed intrinsically to ex-servicemen, some of whom had come to miss the camaraderie and sense of purpose they had felt during the war.

Also familiar to these new recruits was a feeling that the people in charge were not doing their job as well as they might, and that applied to the country as well as the BF itself. 'The opinion of Headquarters is rather low throughout the whole organisation,' wrote Max, once he had established himself within the British Fascisti, 'and it appears not without reason.'

This was part of an early report Max delivered to his spymaster in the Makgill Organisation, a man codenamed 'Don'. His identity has never been revealed. Yet the little evidence that there is suggests that Don was Sir George Makgill's son, Donald, a Mason, like his father, and the future Viscount of Oxfuird, whose confidential account of this period in his life was 'experience of intelligence work with father'.

Sir George Makgill's son Donald was described as 'self-confident, possibly to excess, intelligent, reliable, intensely keen'. Like Max, he was learning on the job and had no training in intelligence work. Unlike him, this rookie spymaster was working for his father and could afford to make a few mistakes. What made Max's task so much harder was the toxic atmosphere he began to experience inside BF Headquarters.

The Communist Party frequently tried to infiltrate the ranks of this group, and Max's new colleagues often speculated about who in their midst might be a spy. If becoming a BF volunteer had been easy, lasting for anything more than a few months was going to take considerable skill and perhaps a little luck.

There were various ways for Max to handle himself in this suffocatingly tense, watchful environment. He could look to win over key figures or take aim at anyone who seemed suspicious of him. Instead, he did everything possible to become invisible. 'Information will come to you, it is a mistake to go out and try to find it,' Max later told an agent. 'It is so easy to feel that one would like to find out a certain point, but one often forgets that the whole of our work may be destroyed by trying to hasten.' When a new job came up in BF Headquarters, Max did not put himself forward. Instead he hung purposefully back. When a task was actually given to him, he accomplished it efficiently, in contrast to most of the other volunteers in the office.

During those first few months in the BF, Max learned the art of doing both a lot and very little, until his efforts came to the attention of Rotha Lintorn-Orman. Makgill had instructed his agent to join the British Fascisti and slowly work his way up. In one sense Max failed. His rise was meteoric. After just a few months inside this right-wing group, Sir George Makgill's operative was promoted by Lintorn-Orman to be Director of Intelligence for the entire organisation and Deputy Chief of Staff.

This was an extraordinary coup, even if it left Max with a colossal workload. When he was not teaching games to pre-pubescent boys just over the river in Putney, he now had to look after the British Fascisti's registry of 'personal files', containing information on known left-wing agitators and suspected spies, root out Communist agents inside the organisation, run Fascist cells inside the trade union movement, gather intelligence on Communist activities, supply this to local Fascist units, attend meetings as the BF deputy chief of staff and report on all this to his spymaster, Don.

Only a year before, Max had been a loser-ish jazz enthusiast who spent most of his spare time looking after pets and writing pulp fiction. That had all begun to change. Now he was a less frequent habitué of Soho, having tired of what he called the 'look of unutterable boredom which characterises the British upper classes when dancing'. Even his much-loved bear, Bessie, that emblem of his earlier life, had been removed from his flat and now lived in a zoo. This may have had more to do with Bessie's desire to mate than Max's growing maturity, but as a younger man his solution might have been to find a male bear to satisfy her needs. As he later wrote, sounding like a man who had given the idea serious thought, 'breeding bears in a private establishment is something which is not very practical'.

Instead, Max devoted himself to his two part-time careers: working for the British Fascisti and for the Makgill Organisation. The success of the latter job depended on the continuation of the former. If for any reason he was thrown out of the BF, his value to Makgill would evaporate. That was one risk. The other was more insidious: it was that he might lose sight of himself.

Leading two lives like this was both nerve-racking and psychologic-ally precarious. Max's undercover work required him to play the part of an enthusiastic young Fascist, and to do this he dutifully read BF publications, attended Fascist rallies and took abuse from Communists, Socialists and trade unionists, and he made many Fascist friends. Although he rarely spent more than a few hours in character, an evening here, a morning there, the longer he played this part, the harder it might become to maintain his inner division between the fictional personality he had constructed and his real self.

By the summer of 1924, however, he appeared to be managing it. Max's reports to Don, his 'intensely keen' spymaster, had not lost their edge. He continued to find the setup in the British Fascisti Headquarters chaotic and to describe many of his colleagues as vain or lazy. In spite of his position in the upper branches of the BF tree, Max had not become a Fascist. But, when he needed to, he could do a very good impersonation of one.

Indeed, there were times when Maxwell Knight seemed willing to go further than anyone else in BF Headquarters in the fight against international Communism. This was one of the reasons why he had come to the attention of a teenager who had recently joined the movement. This newcomer was unhappy, funny and impetuous. Max had never met — nor would he ever meet — anyone quite like him.

4

THE RAZOR'S EDGE

William Joyce was an opinionated fitness fanatic who had grown up much too fast. He was stocky, spoke with a light Irish brogue and often found it hard to say anything other than what he was thinking. There was a mischievous, Puck-like quality to him. Though born in the United States, in New York, Joyce had spent most of his life in Ireland until he and his family fled after they were threatened with execution by the IRA. This had been almost entirely Joyce's fault.

During the Anglo-Irish War, which began soon after the end of the First World War, Joyce had been a teenage informant for the Black and Tans, the British auxiliary police units dominated by soldiers who had recently served on the Western Front. They were notorious for their heavy-handed response to IRA attacks. Word of Joyce's collaboration with these government forces had spread far, and by the time the Black and Tans left he was a marked man. Joyce and his family were given just days to leave the country.

In some ways, William Joyce never really left behind that moment in his life. 'He saw battle, murder and sudden death at a very tender age,' wrote Max, and was clearly brutalised by the experience. Joyce had been compelled to see the world in terms of black and white, and now he carried within him a livid strain of British patriotism that few of the people he met were able to understand. Most of those who did, by the time he arrived in London, had joined the British Fascisti. In late 1923, so did he. Max had joined a little earlier on Makgill's instructions. It was not long before they met.

Superficially, at least, Joyce was so unlike Max as to be his opposite. At school the American had been a rebel. The Englishman had conformed. Joyce was a student; Max was a teacher. One described jazz as degenerate; the other lived for it. Joyce had been damaged by his experiences during the war; Max had come out of the conflict relatively unharmed. Yet for all these outward differences there were many traits that they shared, and this drew them powerfully towards one another. Each man was quick to see a joke, was charismatic and spoke engagingly and well. Indeed, both would later become experienced radio broadcasters speaking to audiences that numbered in the millions, although the subject of their talks could not have been more different. In this strange encounter between their two personalities there was revulsion, rivalry, admiration and friendship, enough to form the nucleus of a complex relationship, which may help to explain why, in 1924, both Max and Joyce attended a secret meeting of disgruntled British Fascists.

The men at this gathering were younger and rowdier than the majority of BF members. There were out-and-out thugs in that room as well as demobilised Black and Tans and zealous patriots like Joyce who had been too young to fight in the war but who now felt a yearning to prove themselves in battle. All had joined the British Fascisti in the hope of going toe to toe with Communist street gangs, which had become notorious in certain parts of the country for their attacks on right-wing political gatherings. Their standard tactic was to rush the stage, replace the Union Jack with a Red Flag and attack anyone who got in their way. The young Fascists had been waiting for orders to take on these Communists, but these had not come. The

BF leadership was perfectly good at issuing forthright statements about the danger of international Communism but more hesitant when it came to sending its troops into battle. Tired of waiting, the renegades at this meeting agreed to form a paramilitary wing of the British Fascisti. Though nominally part of the BF, this unit would only really answer to itself.

They called themselves 'K'. Others referred to this group as the 'K Society', the 'K Organisation' or the 'K Squad', but its original name was 'K', one that hints at the secretive and semi-mythological groups that may have inspired it, including the spiritual and utopian collective the Kindred of the Kibbo Kift, for whom the letter *K* was thought to have magical properties. 'K' might have referred to the King, in whose name they fought. There is even a chance that 'K' was a nod to the surname of a leading figure in this new unit – Maxwell Knight.

Though he was no streetfighter, Max would prove essential to K. By the end of 1924, as he told his spymaster Don, he was one of the only members of this paramilitary group to have attended every one of its meetings. His role was to gather intelligence on Communist activities, a task he carried out anyway as BF Director of Intelligence, and supply this to his comrades in K, including Joyce, who was about to emerge as the toughest and most enthusiastic member of this violent new unit.

Having recently been the leader of a jazz band, Max was now at the heart of a dangerous paramilitary gang. He had gone further as an agent than his spymaster could have predicted, and had done so in less than a year. Don was impressed, and so was his father, Sir George Makgill, who now put his mind to how he could exploit his agent's influence within K.

Earlier that year, Makgill had reacted with horror to the appointment of the first ever Labour Prime Minister, Ramsay MacDonald. Just two years earlier a Communist MP had been returned to

Parliament, something that had never happened before. For Makgill, these two events were canaries in the coal mine. He was certain that if this Labour government continued, a socialist revolution was all but inevitable. He was willing to go to almost any length to get the Conservatives back into power. Soon he devised a plan for how to use the likes of William Joyce, Maxwell Knight and the rest of K to nudge the result of the forthcoming General Election to the Right.

On 22 October, 1924, just one week before the British people went to the polls, several thousand voters made their way to a political rally at Lambeth Baths in Battersea, south London. The streets surrounding the venue were covered in messages and slogans, most of them written in chalk. Sometimes these contained nothing more than the scrawled name of a candidate and his qualifications, otherwise they were more blunt. 'Join the Fascisti' was a popular BF slogan. 'To Hell with the Communists!'

Battersea had become a key target for the Right, largely because of the incumbent Communist MP, Shapurji Saklatvala, whose 'pernicious' influence, according to *The Times,* had 'crept like duck-weed among a large section of the electors', fuelling the local 'revolutionary element'. Battersea was now a battleground, and in recent weeks most political events had been interrupted by violence. There was no reason to think that the rally that night in Lambeth Baths would be any different.

Sir George Makgill belonged to numerous right-wing groups, yet the most powerful of these was the Economic League, a newly minted coalition of trade organisations with vast financial backing. Its Chairman was Admiral Sir Reginald 'Blinker' Hall, recently the Royal Navy's Director of Naval Intelligence and now a Conservative politician. The group Admiral Hall had taken on was supremely well connected and rich, but it lacked muscle. The Economic League

needed foot soldiers to distribute its literature on the streets and to
protect Conservative, Unionist and sometimes Liberal Parliamentary
candidates when they were out on the campaign trail. Makgill had
the idea of using the K organisation.

With Max as go-between, the Economic League 'chose from
among the "K" members about 50 men to "propaganda" in the worst
Labour centres throughout the country,' explained Max. 'The men
were carefully trained and well paid' and 'did excellent work before
and during the election'.

Some of this involved simply handing out leaflets, and in the closing stages of the campaign K was responsible for distributing up to
20,000 pamphlets a week in Battersea alone. But this ragtag band of
ex-servicemen and thugs was also paid to take on local Communist
gangs and protect right-wing candidates at political events, such as
the one that was going to be held at Lambeth Baths on the night of
22 October, 1924.

The man in charge that night of an eleven-strong contingent from
K was William Joyce. He and his heavies had been instructed to police
this rally in support of the Conservative-backed candidate for
Lambeth North, a young stockbroker called Jack Lazarus. At least
one of Joyce's men turned up with a concealed weapon. Shortly
before the rally began, Max appears to have passed on to Joyce intelligence he had received from one of his informants: a Communist
gang was on its way.

By the time Lazarus got up to give his speech, the hall was packed.
He looked out over a dim-lit sea of faces. Before him were activists
as well as loyalists, fair-weather supporters, undecided voters and, it
turned out, a swarm of opponents. There was heckling from the
start. Joyce and his men removed the 'interruptors' as fast as they
could, and at one point the chairman of the meeting read the
Riot Act, but there were too many hecklers. Lazarus staggered
through to the end of his speech, yet as the opening bars of the

national anthem played, to mark the end of the rally, Joyce and his men lost control.

'Pandemonium,' reported the *Daily Mirror*. 'Scenes of great disorder,' recorded *The Times*. Men rushed the gangways. Punches flew. Fights broke out around the hall. A Red Flag was brandished. Joyce and the others from K were in the thick of it. Anyone who did not want to get hurt pushed to the exit, and in the confusion and the crush there was a brutal attack.

A band of Communists had noticed that William Joyce was for a moment unguarded. This cocky young Fascist, who had been 'untiring in his efforts' against the local Communists in the past few months, and who had 'made himself so obnoxious to the Communist Party' as to become a marked man, was now alone.

The story that Joyce later told was this: several Communists rushed over and pinned him to the ground. One produced a razor blade. He leaned into the teenager's face, placing the slip of metal in the corner of his mouth and pulled hard into the cheek. The blade sliced easily through his flesh. The man kept going until he reached Joyce's ear, then he picked himself up and ran away. A senior figure from K called Webb, a brute of a man, apparently chased after this Communist and clubbed him over the head with a twelve-inch spanner.

Joyce was left with the skin on one cheek hanging loose. There was blood everywhere. People clustered around in shock. One of them was Max. It seems that he had been close enough to witness part of this savage attack on his friend, later describing it as 'little short of attempted murder', but he had not intervened. Perhaps it had all been over too quickly, or there were too many of them.

Joyce was picked up by a policeman and carried to the Lambeth Infirmary. He lost a lot of blood and it was unclear at first just how deep the blade had gone. Yet twenty-six stitches later, William Joyce was told that he would live. For the rest of his life he bore on his cheek a mad, lilting scar that served as a permanent reminder of that bloody night. He called it his 'Lambeth honour'. Many years later he suggested that a Jewish Communist had been responsible. Yet his wife would tell a rather different story.

Almost seventy years after this attack the historian Colin Holmes managed to track down and interview Joyce's first wife, who had met her husband around the time of this attack. 'It wasn't a Jewish Communist who disfigured him,' she said. 'He was knifed by an Irish woman.'

This is not the story that Max would later tell. Yet it is easy to see how he came to believe Joyce's version of events. Every account of that night describes a sudden eruption of violence, and that for several minutes nobody really knew what was going on. There was certainly a large Irish contingent in the audience that night, and it is conceivable that Joyce's past with the Black and Tans in Galway had suddenly caught up with him, and that a woman, possibly with connections to the IRA, had recognised him and taken a blade to his face. It is also possible, given the confusion, that Joyce was able to convince his friends that his assailant had in fact been a Communist man, and was part of a gang.

We may never know. What matters is that everyone in K, including Max, believed that Joyce, their brother-in-arms, had been the victim of a vicious attack by the Reds. The next day, William Joyce woke up in the hospital as the poster boy of the British Right. People he had never met before came to visit him and commend his bravery, even if not everyone seemed to understand what had happened.

'These Fascist blackguards are damn swine to carve you up like that,' one press photographer sympathised. 'They should be shot.'

Joyce laughed so hard he nearly burst his stitches.

Less than a week later, the British people went to the polls. Although the Communist MP Saklatvala won in Lambeth North, the nationwide result was a landslide victory for the Conservative Party.

For years afterwards, even to this day, that result would reek of scandal on account of the so-called Zinoviev Letter, the name given to a fake Communist directive published in the *Daily Mail* five days before the General Election. The letter itself was hardly revelatory. It purported to show Grigori Zinoviev, a senior Soviet official, telling the British Communist Party to fire up the working class into launching an uprising against the bourgeoisie. Men from Moscow had been saying the same thing for years. Yet the political traction came from the Labour Prime Minister's response to the Zinoviev Letter, which had been to do nothing.

This was enough to remind some voters of the *idea* that a Labour government might be more sympathetic to Moscow than it cared to admit. Although the Labour vote actually grew in the 1924 General Election, there is a chance that it might have grown much more, given the collapse of the Liberal vote, had it not been for the Zinoviev Letter.

The scandal that persists even today is centred on how this forgery ended up in the public domain. There is no doubt that the document was received originally by MI6's Estonian Station and was passed on from there to MI6 Headquarters in London. Not long after, it was indirectly leaked to the press. We also know that MI6 used a report from one of Sir George Makgill's undercover agents erroneously to authenticate the Zinoviev Letter. Makgill's role in the Conservative victory of 1924 was greater than most people would ever realise.

When William Joyce heard about the result of the General Election, he was too weak to register anything more than relief. On Remembrance Sunday, almost a fortnight after polling day, he was still too frail to leave hospital. But he did so anyway. Ignoring his doctors' advice, this determined, diminutive figure made the short journey across the River Thames to the Cenotaph, where he stood alone in his trench coat, his pale face heavily bandaged, his eyes ablaze with patriotic fervour. He must have looked like a ghost from the trenches. Joyce's mind churned with thoughts of those noble Britons who had given their lives for King and Country, of their sacrifice, their courage, their commitment – when, suddenly, it became too much. He collapsed.

The first person to Joyce's aid was a girl who recognised him as a fellow undergraduate at Birkbeck College. Somehow she managed to get Joyce back to her parents' house, and in the weeks that followed she nursed him back to health. They fell in love, and although her mother did not approve, they would later get married and have children together.

This attack and the events that followed changed Joyce's life both personally and politically, yet it also had a profound effect on Max. Although he did not write about his feelings after that night at the Lambeth Baths – this was not his way – many years later he would recall the attack with telling clarity. Perhaps he felt partly responsible for what he thought had happened to Joyce, because it had been his job to warn his friend about imminent attacks. Or he may have regretted his failure to intervene. What had happened at the Lambeth Baths also changed the way Max saw his enemy. Until then he had disliked Communism in a fairly loose, possibly abstract sense. After all, he had only joined the British Fascisti on the instructions of Makgill. He was not there for ideological reasons. But now his antipathy towards those on the Left was more personal.

The razoring of William Joyce had left Max with a new desire for revenge, as well as a sense that the rules had changed. There had been many clashes in the past between Fascists and Communists, but none that had involved razor blades. From that night on, Max saw less need for gentlemanly restraint. The sight of his friend's face became proof, for him, that the enemy was playing a different and more violent game. It was time for Max to do the same.

5

REVENGE

Harry Pollitt was a boilermaker by training who would spend more than two decades at the helm of the Communist Party of Great Britain. Yet, by 1925, when he first came into Max's life, he was merely a rising star of the Left. Although capable of fantastic hatred, Pollitt was a warm and persuasive speaker. As the Labour politician Michael Foot later said, 'lots of people who were not Communists couldn't help liking him'. This was one of the reasons why, in March 1925, Harry Pollitt had been lined up to speak at a protest in Liverpool organised by the Communist Party.

After finishing work the day before his speech, Pollitt travelled to Euston Station and caught the 5.55 p.m. train to Liverpool. It was the opening move in the most unusual journey of his life. One of the train's last scheduled stops was at Edgehill, where four men approached Pollitt's carriage and, to his amazement, manhandled him out of the train. A fellow passenger, who had been sitting across from Pollitt since London, rather than intervene, actually helped these men to remove him. Evidently he was part of their gang.

'I was dragged to the barrier, struggling violently,' Pollitt recalled, in his booming Lancastrian baritone. 'The barrier is a narrow one, but on this occasion the gates were wide open and no ticket was asked for – the collector had been told that a dangerous lunatic from London might give trouble. I was hustled into a car and driven away.' One of his kidnappers remembered it differently, explaining in court, to the delight of the gallery, that he and his accomplices had removed Pollitt from the train 'gently, rather like getting hold of a man who refuses to come and have a drink, but who wants to go'.

Harry Pollitt was then driven to a nearby hotel and held overnight. The next day he was released, once there was no prospect of him making it to Liverpool in time for his speech. The young Communist was also made to endure a series of impromptu lectures from his abductors on the perils of Marxism: the men who had bundled him off the train were Fascists. They belonged to the Liverpool section of K, the paramilitary group with Max and Joyce at its heart.

Though Pollitt's kidnappers were later arrested and appeared in court, key details of his abduction remained obscure, including the identity of the fifth man involved, or how the kidnappers knew which train Pollitt had taken and the carriage he was in.

What did emerge, however, was that on the morning of the kidnap a call had come in to the organisation that had arranged for Pollitt to speak in Liverpool. The caller had asked which train Pollitt was planning to take. Given that it was Max's job to supply K with intelligence, the unidentified man on the phone was probably him. It is also possible that Max was the passenger who shared a compartment with Pollitt up from London and who had alerted the waiting Fascists to his whereabouts on the train, probably by holding something out of his window as they pulled in to Edgehill station.

Nobody in K had ever attempted a stunt like this before. It was more brazen than any earlier operation and far more aggressive. Given his new desire for revenge and his intelligence role in K, it is probable that Max was the man behind this. His involvement in the next set of K attacks on the Communists, on the other hand, is beyond any doubt.

In the early hours of 2 May, 1925, less than two months after the Pollitt kidnapping, Maxwell Knight and several other young Fascists climbed onto the roof of the local Communist Party headquarters in Glasgow. There, they smashed through the skylight and clambered into the loft. At this point one of them produced a saw and began to carve a hole in the floor. Once this had been done, the raiding party jumped down into the offices below, where they went berserk.

Max and the other men upended furniture, threw papers around and went off with all the important documents that they could find. They left the place, as the police report put it, 'in a great state of confusion'.

Less than two weeks after this first burglary, Max and his men broke in to the same Glasgow office again. This time they did not bother shattering the skylight. They forced the main door instead. As well as trashing the place, as they had done previously, the Fascists sprayed black ink over the Communists' political banners and stole as much literature as they could carry.

Nine days later, amazingly, Max and two accomplices returned to the same spot for a third time. It was late on a Friday night. Again, they wrecked the office, chucking around ink and gathering as much sensitive paperwork as they could, but just as one of the burglars left the building, at about three in the morning, he bumped into a policeman.

The man who had just stumbled out of the local Communist Party headquarters was an unemployed ex-serviceman called Joseph McCall. When asked what he was up to, McCall explained that he had been working late in the Communist office and had decided to take home one or two books. This was where his story fell apart.

McCall was carrying 20 books, 266 typewritten circulars and 76 books of lottery tickets. The offices he had just left resembled 'a scene of desolation', according to one reporter. This was after Max, McCall and one other man had spent roughly two hours in there. 'I have never seen such wreckage,' the reporter went on, 'not since the air raids, at least!' McCall was arrested. Max and his other accomplice had managed to get away.

These raids may have represented Max's first taste of burglary, yet by no means his last. Years later an MI5 colleague described him as one of the few officers who would not hesitate to burgle premises without authority. Indeed, it is striking just how many of the men and women who worked under Max acquired a similar penchant for breaking and entering. It was clearly something of a speciality for him.

The Glasgow raids were widely reported, partly because of their ferocity. Communists had been known to raid Fascist offices in the past, but not like this. The devastation carried out inside these rooms did not resemble a straightforward burglary so much as an impassioned reprisal.

Max would later describe the 'latent spark of aggression' in 'the breasts of creatures of the private inquiry world'. It seemed that another side of his character had momentarily slipped out. In the Pollitt kidnap and the Glasgow raids there was a hint of his shadow self, of Max the black sheep of the family, Max the frustrated exhibitionist, Max the young man whose brother had died on the Western Front and who had volunteered for active service but had seen none, Max the political activist who now wanted revenge for what had apparently happened to his comrade William Joyce. At the same time, not that anybody in the Makgill Organisation was concerned about this, it was becoming harder to believe that Max was merely playing the part of an enthusiastic Fascist. Instead these seemed to be the actions of a willing warrior in the war against international Communism.

These raids can also be seen as an expression of Max's growing stature within the Makgill Organisation. He had become more confident, perhaps as a result of his new role.

Having been taken on as an agent, Max was now operating as a spymaster as well. Aged just twenty-five, Maxwell Knight was running his own stable of agents. Most likely, he had begun to build up his agent network after being installed as Director of Intelligence at the British Fascisti. At first he recruited friends and acquaintances as agents, but as his self-belief grew, he had started to take on strangers. He found some recruits by placing small advertisements in newspapers. One of these appeared in the *Sussex Agricultural Express,* in late 1923, and called enigmatically for anyone 'interested in patriotic work of a definite character'.

Each of these approaches to a potential agent took imagination, subtlety and some courage. Befriending or chatting up a stranger is hard enough. Asking one to become a spy, who reports to you, is considerably more daunting. With no formal instruction Max was learning the rudiments of espionage through trial and error, and he was doing so at incredible speed. In January 1925, Max was able to tell Don, his spymaster at the Makgill Organisation, that he had recently 'secured information of some value from 52 sources'. About thirty of these, he went on, could be classed as agents of his, and ten 'deliver reports fairly regularly or are employed to investigate special cases'.

He had also managed to recruit at least one Communist student and – his greatest achievement by that point – he had taken six men from the ranks of the British Fascisti and played each of them into the Communist Party. One of these infiltrators may have been Joseph McCall, the ex-serviceman who had helped him in the most recent Glasgow raid, and who had been a Fascist before he joined the Communists. Losing the services of McCall after his arrest might have left Max blind to what was going on in Glasgow Communist circles, yet by then he seems to have had another man on the inside. This second agent was probably a BF member before Max convinced him to join the Communist Party on his behalf. Later codenamed

M/5, this second Scottish agent became a keen collector of antique weaponry and would work as a factory gun examiner. He was still reporting to Max from deep inside the Communist movement at the start of the Second World War.

Identifying, recruiting and running just one of these penetration agents required patience and finesse, as well as consistently sound judgement. To have six of them on the go suggested an unusual talent. Almost every element of Max's early career as a spymaster was remarkable. It was unheard of for a twenty-five-year-old with no training and limited resources to build up and run such a large web of informants. Agent running seemed to come naturally to him, in the way that looking after wild creatures had done. But his confidence around animals and his ability as a spymaster were not just gifts he had inherited unwittingly. These two skills informed and complemented each other, and were rooted in Max's capacity for hard work and his willingness to fail.

Other spymasters might spend months building up to their first approach to a potential agent, yet within his first year Max had made as many as fifty approaches. He was honing his tradecraft through endless repetitions, giving himself the space to fail, learn and try again. The same could be said of the way he handled animals. As a child he had spent thousands of hours with an improbable array of different creatures, sometimes getting it wrong, but almost always learning from his mistakes. Endless practice does not guarantee success, but it helps.

No less important was the way he grasped early on what would become the most important lesson of his career as a spymaster, one that emerges from the reminiscences many years later of an agent who was taken on by Max at around this time.

In early 2014, MI5 released several files that would shed light for the first time on the story of a brilliant wartime British agent known as 'Jack King'. Posing as a Gestapo officer, this man had infiltrated a number of extremist right-wing groups in Britain during the Second World War. When these MI5 files were first released, the identity of this 'genius' agent was a mystery. After much speculation, most of it wrong, it emerged that 'Jack King' was in fact Eric Roberts, a humble bank clerk who had been working at Westminster Bank when he was pulled out of his job by MI5. His manager at the time had been suitably perplexed.

'What we would like to know here is – what are the particular and especial qualifications of Mr Roberts which we have not been able to perceive – for some particular work of national importance?'

This seemed to be one of those inspiring wartime stories in which a modest English amateur is plucked from obscurity and goes on to perform heroics for his country, after which he or she returns to an ordinary life after the war. But that is not what happened.

By the outbreak of war in 1939, Eric Roberts, the self-effacing bank clerk, had in fact been an undercover agent for almost half of his adult life. It began, for him, when he was recruited to the Makgill Organisation in the early 1920s by Maxwell Knight.

Max had met Eric Roberts for the first time either in late 1923 or early 1924. Roberts was a precocious seventeen-year-old from Cornwall who had come up to London to start a new job at the Westminster Bank. Wanting to make new friends, 'Robbie', as Roberts was known, decided to join the British Fascisti, which was how he had met Max. The young spymaster recognised in Roberts the qualities that already he had come to cherish in a prospective agent, that mercurial blend of intelligence, industry, modesty, humour, patriotism and unfulfilled ambition. Just weeks after Roberts had joined the BF, Max persuaded him to resign from this group and infiltrate the Communist Party instead.

Max had unearthed a gem. Eric Roberts would go on to be one of the most successful penetration agents of his generation, infiltrating by his own account seventeen different extremist groups. He had a long and impressive career in the field, yet he never forgot his first assignment as one of Max's agents.

Roberts had been told by Max to gatecrash a Communist meeting that was due to be addressed by Maxim Litvinov, the Soviet Union's roving ambassador. Max's teenage agent arrived at the venue, strode into the room and took a seat. His heart must have been pounding uncomfortably as he began to make mental notes of who was there, the positions they appeared to hold, who was speaking to whom and what Litvinov said, before scurrying off at the end to scribble it all down 'with a leaky fountain pen'. He passed on his first report to Max. As Roberts recalled, 'M. K. was delighted.'

Why had this bright young Cornishman agreed to do this? His reasons were in some ways political. Eric Roberts had joined the BF because he saw Communism as a threat. Another lure was the familiar and intoxicating romance of being a spy, or at least the *idea* of being a spy. As a boy, Roberts had repeatedly read *Kim,* Rudyard Kipling's classic espionage novel, and it was this book, he explained, that 'set my mind working in the direction of intelligence'. Just as Max had been obsessed by the novels of John Buchan, Roberts had fallen in love at an early age with the labyrinthine possibilities of an undercover life, and this inoculated him against some of its initial hardships. The other reason he was prepared to risk being exposed as a Fascist spy and beaten up by a gang of Communists had to do with his spymaster.

In most descriptions of the way Max ran his agents there are allusions to the strange hold he appeared to have on them, his 'Pied Piper nature', which 'attracted many to become agents out of personal loyalty'. There is a hint of this in Eric Roberts's recollection. The Cornishman explained, a little gnomically, that the best way to understand his relationship with Max was by reading *Kim,* a book in which the eponymous hero becomes the disciple of a charismatic

Tibetan lama. Roberts mentioned Max's 'personal magnetism'. Another called him 'an almost mystical figure'. It was as if Max could cast a spell over some of his operatives, and that just as he had 'the gift' when handling pets he inspired a preternatural loyalty from his agents.

Yet there was no magic here. The key to Max's appeal was to do with the way he treated his operatives. Throughout his career he went to unusual lengths to discern the individual character of each and to make him or her feel special. 'Every good agent likes to think that his officer is almost exclusively concerned with him, and with him alone,' as Max once explained, 'even though the agent may know perfectly well that the officer has others with whom he deals. This is a definite and illogical kink in human nature, but it is a kink which must be fostered by any officer who is going to make a success of this work.' Here was the artifice at the heart of his craft. Max had learned early on that to be a successful spymaster he must exploit this essential weakness in the nature of his agents and build up in each an almost exaggerated sense that he was interested in them, only them and nobody else.

The need for anyone running agents to make their charges feel special, to flatter and pamper them with attention, might sound obvious today. In 1924, it was not. British spymasters did not routinely shower their informants with praise or go out of their way to make them feel unique. Government agents were more often seen as men and women of dubious morals. They were 'police spies', and for many Britons this was a contradiction. The police were there to help in a crisis and be visible, transparent and straightforward. Spies were not.

The British military men who found themselves running spies in the 1920s may not have been in the habit of doting on their agents as if they were fascinating pets. Max was different. He had what Graham Greene called 'the human factor'. 'He gave tremendous support to the agents,' one colleague observed. 'He really cared about them as people.' Even at the age of twenty-five Max understood that a recruitment is a seduction, and that the onus must always be on the spymaster to make his agent feel singular and special, not the other way around.

By the summer of 1925, Maxwell Knight was in a powerful position. He had in play a small army of devoted agents, and he had learned a lot about how to keep them productive and safe. Their intelligence was also starting to make a difference politically. Increasingly, K, the paramilitary group Max belonged to, was taking the fight to the Communists. It seemed to be getting away with it, too.

Although members of K were occasionally arrested, the punishments they received were surprisingly mild. The four men prosecuted for Pollitt's kidnap were defended brilliantly in court and found 'Not Guilty'. Max's accomplice in Glasgow, Joseph McCall, was sentenced to just seven days in prison or a £3 fine. As well as getting off lightly, some members of K had the strange belief that the authorities approved of what they were doing. McCall even told the court that the police had known about his undercover activities before his arrest. 'In the strictest confidence,' wrote one of Pollitt's kidnappers, unaware that his letter would later be published, 'I can inform you that the Police and Government and all concerned are on our side.'

These men appeared to be suffering from baroque delusions of grandeur, except that they were not. The four men behind the kidnapping of Harry Pollitt were represented in court by Sir Henry Curtis-Bennett, KC, a former MI5 officer whose military commission in the last war had been arranged by Admiral Hall, Chairman of the Economic League. One of Max's colleagues in Glasgow, a man called J. McGuirk Hughes, who also worked for the Makgill Organisation, had in the past been given money by Special Branch and the temporary command of several policemen.

K was a dangerous, right-wing paramilitary group responsible for burglary, kidnapping and violence. It was rumoured to have 'a store of arms' hidden somewhere in London. But MI5 did not class this outfit as a threat. Instead, K, by then 'one of London's most influential secret societies', was described blandly in one MI5 report as a 'well organised and efficient' organisation responsible for 'some quite good work from an intelligence point of view'.

This sounds like a chronically inept assessment. Stranger still, MI5 was more suspicious of K's parent organisation, the British Fascisti, insisting that no 'members of H. M. Forces should have any connection with the Fascisti', a society that was not 'desirable in this country', whose members 'bring discredit by their methods on all who really wish to maintain law and order'. It was as if MI5 had confused the tearaway K with the much more benign BF. But there was an explanation for all this. Right at the heart of K was a man whom they could trust.

6

THE FREELANCE SPYMASTER

Wherever he went, Desmond Morton carried around the bullet that had almost killed him. During the war, a German machine-gun round had ripped into Morton's left lung, stopping just short of his aorta, and was so deeply embedded that any attempt to remove it might have been fatal. For the rest of his life, Desmond Morton had this metallic memento mori buried deep inside him. He was an Old Etonian and lifelong bachelor whose experiences in the trenches had turned him into a more distant and inscrutable figure, a persona that seemed to be perfectly suited to the intelligence work he began to do after the war.

In the early 1920s, Morton worked for what is today called MI6, the foreign counterpart to MI5. He ran MI6's Production section, which was responsible for gathering intelligence on overseas Soviet activities directed against Britain. Though most of this work involved running agents and informants abroad, it helped for him to have sources at home. This was why Desmond Morton had developed a professional relationship with Sir George Makgill.

The two spymasters had been introduced to each other after the war by Sir Vernon Kell, the monocled and moustachioed head of MI5, and an old friend of Makgill's. It was Kell, of MI5, who had first encouraged the opinionated Scottish industrialist to set up his own private intelligence agency and had even supplied Makgill with advice and contacts. This was partly out of friendship but also because he wanted access to the intelligence that this agency might gather.

As the British government struggled to reduce the titanic national debt incurred during five years of all-out war, MI5 was savaged by spending cuts. By 1925, it had no full-time agents and a staff of just thirty-five (today that number is closer to 4,000). MI5's scope was limited to countering espionage and subversion within the British armed forces. Kell's counterpart in MI6 had even suggested that MI5's staff be further reduced, and would later push for its outright abolition. Yet, as MI5 continued to shrink, the threat of Communism seemed to grow.

Kell was 'a shrewd old bugger', as one colleague put it. He recognised that Makgill's private agency could provide him with cheap, reliable intelligence that he could gain access to without exceeding his department's official purview. Desmond Morton, at MI6, saw the situation a little differently. Like Kell, he understood the potential of the Makgill Organisation. Yet unlike the head of MI5, Morton was not willing to receive information second-hand from Makgill or from 'Don', his 'intensely keen' son. Morton wanted direct access to Makgill's operatives for himself.

This was unusual. A basic rule of agent running is that agents should report to one spymaster. Morton wanted some of Makgill's men to work for two. Perhaps overawed by Desmond Morton's position in MI6 or wanting to help out a brother Mason – Morton appears to have been a Freemason like Makgill – the industrialist accepted. By the time of the 1924 General Election, Sir George Makgill was sharing some of his star agents with Morton over at MI6, including Jim Finney, whose report on the Zinoviev Letter was used to authenticate this forgery. Another shared source was Maxwell Knight.

The problem here was that Desmond Morton worked for MI6, and as such he was not supposed to be running agents among the British civilian population. That was the responsibility of the London Metropolitan Police Special Branch – usually known as Special Branch. This was one of the reasons Morton went to great lengths to hide his relationship with Max.

Unknown to all but a handful of people, for at least a year Max had been reporting both to Don at the Makgill Organisation and to Desmond Morton at MI6. By the end of 1924, Max was also in touch with Special Branch and had a freelance arrangement whereby if he supplied them with intelligence that led to an arrest he would get paid. Summaries of Max's reports even made their way to MI5 where they were seen by Sir Vernon Kell, who might forward them to the Director of Military Operations and Intelligence.

This would explain why MI5 was so relaxed about the paramilitary activities of K. Max, one of the men at the heart of this group, the other being Joyce, was now well known among highly placed individuals in what was for him the holy trinity of British Intelligence: MI5, MI6 and Special Branch. Max's high standing among them was partly a reflection of the size and reach of his agent network, and the quality of its product. It was also testament to the way he presented himself. Max produced his reports quickly, and they were thorough and detailed. As far as anyone could tell, he did not brag about his work, invent information, disobey instructions or get carried away by the excitement of being involved in espionage. He 'makes an excellent impression,' wrote Desmond Morton, being 'very discreet, and at need prepared to do anything, but is at the same time not wild.'

This last point was crucial. Max seemed to be learning to rein himself in when it mattered. He was also described by his new MI6 spymaster as 'clearly perfectly honest'. But this was not honesty as most people recognised it. Max was truthful in his dealings with

Morton, yet when out in the field he could lie, as they say in the navy, like a hairy egg.

By the time Max returned from Glasgow in the summer of 1925, after those three wild raids on the local Communist Party headquarters, his career as a spymaster was flourishing. In the shadowy world of private investigation, he was becoming well known and for the first time in his life he had tasted success.

Max's standing within the British Fascisti was no less impressive, even if he had just been knocked off his perch within the BF Intelligence Department. Towards the end of 1924, Brigadier Sir Ormonde Winter, a formidable figure who had recently stepped down as the British government's Director of Intelligence in Ireland, had succeeded in taking Max's job as the BF Director of Intelligence. Yet before this retired army officer could take up his position, he was outmanoeuvred by another elderly Fascist, one Lieutenant-Colonel Bramley, who began to run the BF Intelligence Department instead.

Rather than remove Max entirely, Bramley agreed to take him on as his deputy. Max was given the title Chief Intelligence Officer for the BF. Technically, this was a demotion, but he had survived. He was also starting to be paid for the first time by the British Fascisti, and this meant that he could give up his job as a prep-school games teacher, which he did almost at once.

Aged twenty-five, Max was now making a decent living from his intelligence work. He was also finding time to look after his growing miscellany of beloved pets. There was at least one dog in his collection, various reptiles and rodents, and a parrot. Following the loss of Bessie the bear, his collection had a new star turn. This was Rikkitikki, his Indian mongoose, 'one of the most affectionate, playful and amusing pets I have ever had'. He was also very fond of his bush baby, Pookie, who looked like a misshapen teddy bear and was famous among his friends for the occasion when it knocked over a glass of sherry, got drunk and bounced around the flat like a kanga-roo before curling up in a ball and falling fast asleep.

Although Max was doing well, there was always a chance that the demand for his intelligence work might suddenly evaporate, casting him adrift. Most of the young men like him who had thrown them-selves into the world of private investigation hankered after a secure and permanent job at MI5, MI6 or Special Branch. The pros-pect of being an intelligence officer for the government, with greater powers, more funding, better pay and a pension, was obviously attractive. MI6 was Max's most likely destination, given his close relationship with Morton. So he may have been surprised when he received an invitation, at around this time, from the head of MI5, Sir Vernon Kell, to a gathering of his exclusive 'Intelligent People' dining club.

Several years earlier another of Makgill's agents, Con Boddington, had made the move from private to public sector when he left the Makgill Organisation and joined MI5. Now Max looked set to do the same. This would mark an almost unbelievable turnaround. Four years earlier he had been a jazz-obsessed family outcast with dreams of not much more than writing cheap novels. Now he looked set to embark on a career in a glamorously secretive government depart-ment. Even his curmudgeonly Uncle Robert would have approved.

Little is known about the dinner itself, only that it took place at the Hyde Park Hotel, there were no women present and the food was 'the best to be had in London'. Kell made a short speech, as was his custom, and at one point he spoke to Max, whereupon he made him an offer.

It was not the one that Max wanted.

Kell merely asked his guest whether he was interested in joining a reserve of intelligence officers who could be called upon during a national emergency. Kell did not offer Max a job in MI5, nor did he plan to. Maxwell Knight remained on the periphery of British intelligence.

7

THE DAY

In the months that followed this meal, Max made an offer of his own. He proposed marriage, but not to Hazel Barr, his first love, the girl he had met on a bus. She was by then in a relationship with another man: William Joyce.

By the unlikeliest coincidence, it was Hazel who had seen Joyce collapse in front of the Cenotaph on Remembrance Sunday 1924, and had brought him back to her parents' house to recover. When Hazel told her mother that she was engaged to be married, Mrs Barr nearly fainted, only because her heart was still set on Hazel marrying Max.

We may never know whether Hazel was still together with Max when William Joyce crashed into her life, but at the very least they had recently been in love. Similarly, it is hard to trace the effect of all this on Max other than through the faintest inferences in the record of his life. One of these can be found in the transcript of an interrogation led by Max some fifteen years later. He was questioning a man who was an acquaintance of Joyce. At one point in their conversation, Max asked whether he knew the whereabouts of Joyce's first wife, Hazel.

The prisoner did not.

'I knew her before she was Mrs Joyce,' Max volunteered. 'When she was a Miss Barr. Hazel Barr.'

It is not much, but the use of a full stop between 'Miss Barr' and 'Hazel Barr' rather than a comma or a semicolon suggests a pause, a moment of reflection, a stumble perhaps, as Max was caught out by the unexpected memory of his feelings for Hazel. It is hard to imagine Max forgetting his first love, especially after she went on to marry and have children with a close comrade of his, a man for whom he felt both affection and a lingering dislike. But what had happened with Hazel did not prevent him from moving on to find someone else.

On a sharp, clear morning in December 1925, several days after Christmas, Max arrived at Sherborne Abbey, in Dorset, to get married. His bride was Gwladys Poole, a lively and gregarious redhead from nearby Somerset who was later described 'as one of the county's finest riders to hounds'. Gwladys was also a keen cricketer, she drove a bull-nosed Morris with a souped-up engine and she was one of the most senior women in the British Fascists, as it was now called. The *i* had been changed to an *s* to guard against the charge that this organisation was merely peddling a foreign ideology, a particularly awkward accusation given that the BF opposed Communism on the grounds that it was a foreign ideology.

Gwladys found Max good-looking and charming. He was a 'character', in the best sense of the word. Perhaps he resembled her father, an ex-officer and a sporty, county type. It was too early to tell, for they had only known each other for a few months. Their romance had been such a whirlwind that Max had almost certainly not found time to tell his bride-to-be that he had joined her beloved Fascist movement as a spy. There are secrets at the start of most relationships, but this was a particularly potent one.

The bride arrived at the abbey that day wearing a crêpe de Chine dress and a coffee-coloured lace gown. The groom was in a morning suit. The congregation sang 'O, Perfect Love', and Gwladys gave Max a gold and tortoiseshell cigarette holder. The wedding was well attended and went without a hitch, but it was a far more sombre occasion than the newlyweds would have liked.

Just three days before the wedding, Max's mother, Ada, had died. His sister, Enid, was furious with her brother for going ahead with the wedding. Instead of deferring the ceremony, he had cancelled the reception after the service. Perhaps Max's experience with Hazel had made him wary of any romantic postponement.

After a short honeymoon in Sussex, the new Mr and Mrs Knight moved into a flat in Chelsea, and so did Max's platoon of pets. At the time this included a parrot, a toad, several grass snakes, Rikkitikki the Indian mongoose and a wheezing bulldog called Fatty. Gwladys knew about her husband's obsession with keeping animals, and had grown up around pets herself. The thought of sharing her home with so many different creatures was not in itself unsettling, but the reality of life in that flat must have brought her up short. Gwladys was now living in what was essentially a zoo. Gauze covered every window. The air was thick with the gamey smell of pet food, animal hair and soiled bedding. In each room a different combination of pets held sway, all of which had to be fed, watered and generally fussed over. Her young husband monitored the air temperature along with the state of each animal's daily droppings. It was loveably eccentric, yes, but perhaps not all that romantic.

Any doubts Gwladys may have had about her new life would have to wait. Beyond the zoo-like confines of the Knights' home, the nation was edging towards a political crisis that would involve them both. A dispute over miners' wages had escalated to the point that there was even talk of a nationwide general strike in which workers from other key industries might down tools in solidarity with the miners.

This was unheard of. For those on the Right, 'The Day' was surely coming. Among the British Fascists, The Day was shorthand for a national emergency engineered by the Communists that might be used as a pretext for a socialist revolution. The man leading the Miners' Federation, Arthur Cook, was a devout Leninist and had once belonged to the Communist Party. From a BF perspective, it was obvious that Moscow had orchestrated the threatened nationwide strike. The British Fascists saw themselves as the last line of defence against Socialism. For anyone remotely connected with the BF, let alone such prominent figures like Max and Gwladys, a nationwide strike was Judgement Day and the Apocalypse rolled into one.

On 3 May, 1926, at a minute to midnight, the Trades Union Congress called a General Strike. The following day some 1.7 million workers, among them dockers, printers, builders, railwaymen and steel workers, came out in support of the miners. Volunteers and strikebreakers tried to fill the gaps by doing the jobs of the striking workers. A visiting American recalled the sight of 'gentlemen with Eton ties acting as porters in Waterloo Station'. But there were too few of them for the task at hand, and much of the national infrastructure soon ceased to work. Parts of the country ground to a halt. The son of two cotton weavers remembered his family sitting 'in silence in our kitchen', early in the strike, 'holding their breath, waiting for the revolution to begin'.

Max had never been so busy. Although he was probably in touch with MI5 during the General Strike, he does not appear to have joined the reserve of officers mentioned by Kell. This was presumably because he was flat out gathering intelligence from his agents in Glasgow, London and elsewhere in the country. The printing and distribution of newspapers had been badly affected by the strike and this gave his agents' information even more value. Nobody in the British government could say precisely where the strike was heading, or how long it would be before order collapsed and the nation descended into bare-fisted barbarism. Detailed contingency plans were made. Civil war seemed to be just around the corner, when, suddenly, it was over.

The General Strike was called off less than a fortnight after it had begun. The government had won.

For Max and many others in the British Fascists, this should have been a moment of elation, and to begin with it was, before the implications began to sink in. The failure of the General Strike undermined the premise on which the British Fascists had been founded. Like any extreme political movement, the BF depended on the spectre of impending disaster, and its success had been fuelled by fear. The Day had come and there had been no revolution.

In the months that followed, the threat of a socialist revolution in Britain seemed to fade away, and at an equivalent rate the size of the British Fascists' membership shrank. The BF leadership responded by cobbling together a political programme. Until then the British Fascists had positioned itself as a group dedicated to nothing more than the defeat of Communism and had even refused to call itself a political party. That was set to change as it devised a manifesto to be published the following year. It called for strikes to be made illegal, the voting age to be raised from twenty-one to twenty-five and Parliamentary candidates to be British-born and of 'British race'. The BF also warned that it would oppose, with violence if necessary, 'any attempt by the Socialist Party, the Communist Party, or any other disloyal section of the community, to abolish the Monarchy or disrupt the Empire; even if such a policy is supported by a majority of the electorate.'

In other words, in the wake of the General Strike, the British Fascists became more recognisably fascist – to the dismay of many members. This only deepened its internal divisions and accelerated the loss of members. Some went to join less extreme organisations like the British Loyalists or weird splinter groups such as the Imperial

Fascist League and the National Fascisti. Others, like William Joyce, attached themselves to the Conservative Party. Presumably after long discussions with his spymasters, Max stayed within the original BF.

Just five months after the collapse of the General Strike, Max received yet more bad news. At the age of fifty-eight, Sir George Makgill had died. Makgill had been for Max a gatekeeper to the secret world and in some ways a mentor figure. His death must have felt like a break with the past for Max, just as it cast a shadow over his future. The Makgill Organisation had lost its driving force at the very moment that the demand for intelligence on socialist activities was drying up. Until then Max's success had depended on the demand from Makgill's customers for intelligence on left-wing activities, and his own seniority within a thriving Fascist movement. In the space of a few months, both had been eviscerated. Max's days as a spymaster seemed to be drawing to a close.

In just under three years, he had successfully built up a vast network of informants and agents and had begun to master the art of recruiting and running them. But he was a freelancer in what was now a depressed market. He had little choice but to scale back his operation.

'I regret very much that circumstances are compelling me to leave London for some time,' he wrote the following year, in a letter to the *British Lion,* the official BF journal. 'I have *not* resigned from the movement, but – I *am* going where I can still keep an eye (or even two) on any undesirables, inside or outside the movement who may seek to make trouble for us.' He finished this cryptic message by wishing the Fascist movement 'continued success' and signing off 'yours loyally'.

Loyally. For anyone connected to the British Fascist movement 'loyal' was a dog-whistle term used to describe themselves and their political kin. Max had never been much of a political animal. Throughout his life he would be mistrustful of intellectuals and elaborate political creeds; indeed, there were times when he seemed to believe in little more than his country, as he had known it in the years before the birth of the Soviet Union, in its history, its people and its landscape. His patriotism often appears to have been rooted in his love of the British countryside and the wildlife that inhabited it. Yet by 1927, although he did not believe in everything that the British Fascists stood for, he felt a powerful tug of loyalty towards this movement and, crucially, to the people who belonged to it. Pitting oneself against Communism in the postwar world seemed to him to be the decent and patriotic thing to do. It was what his brother and father would have done. Max felt a binding solidarity with these men and women, one of whom he had married, and had slowly come to agree with many parts of their political programme. Having been put into this movement as a spy, he appeared to have almost gone native.

This did not make Max what we would call today a 'Fascist' – even after the publication of its manifesto, the outlook of the BF in the 1920s was merely 'Conservatism with knobs on', as one former member put it, and its members would struggle to recognise the more toxic, aggressive and outwardly anti-Semitic version of Fascism espoused by Mussolini and Hitler during the 1930s, as distinct from what they had called for during the 1920s – yet by 1927, the year in which Max left London, he felt a lasting connection to his fellow members of the BF and, in particular, his street-fighting comrades in K. It was among these men that he had experienced the rugged sense of belonging, fraternal camaraderie and purpose that comes from being under attack, going into battle together and feeling yourselves to be above the law. It was a baptismal experience, one that would stay with him for the rest of his life. The bond he felt towards these people by the time he left London, in 1927, was reminiscent of his earlier experiences with the Boy Scouts or as a junior naval officer, only far more intense. It was not one that he thought would ever break.

EXILE

The story that Max and Gwladys told their friends, when asked why they were leaving London to run a pub in the heart of Exmoor, a wild and windswept moorland deep in the West Country, was that they wanted a fresh start away from the city. Gwladys also liked the idea of being closer to her family and her childhood friends, many of whom lived nearby. Max was excited as well by the thought of so much fishing and having more space for his beloved pets, such as Bimbo, his baboon and a Great Dane called Lorna. His fondest childhood memories were of scouring the fields around Mitcham and Tythegston Court looking for injured animals to rescue; his teenage years had largely been spent on the deck of a ship; and even in London he had worked as a games teacher, which usually involved being outside. Max was at his happiest outdoors. Moving to the country was a release.

The pub that Gwladys had bought, the Royal Oak Inn, in the remote village of Withypool, also had personal significance for Max. It was here that his second cousin twice removed, R. D. Blackmore, had written parts of the famous Victorian romance *Lorna Doone* (this may also explain why Lorna the Great Dane was so named). Yet there was another reason for their move, one which the Knights kept to themselves, understandably. What few people guessed was that leaving London was part of an attempt to save their marriage.

Take one Saturday afternoon soon after their arrival on Exmoor. Gwladys had bought not only a pub but an eight-mile stretch of the River Barle, which her husband enthusiastically began to fish. Max was, by his own account, 'a madly keen fisherman'. On this particular Saturday, he had gone to the river while Gwladys rode out as usual with the local hunt, the Devon and Somerset Staghounds. The trout were rising well. As Max waded down the river, casting over the most likely spots, he could hear off in the distance the plaintive blast of the huntsman's horn. Perhaps he was imagining his wife and her friends on horseback when he heard an enormous splash. He turned around. The stag that they were hunting had leapt into the shallow water behind him.

This magnificent beast sniffed the air. Its head moved this way and that. It seemed tired yet alert. Max was downwind from it and hidden from view. The stag concluded that there was no danger and began to relax, ambling about in the river before moving towards the opposite bank.

Nearby Gwladys and the rest of the hunt tore along in the hope of finding this creature and killing it. Had she been in her husband's position, she would have done everything in her power to drive the stag towards the dogs and alert the hunt to its presence. But Gwladys was not Max. She was a hunter. He was a watcher. Max kept very still and observed the creature as it crossed the river and moved off to safety, after which he quietly returned to his fishing.

The problem here was not so much that Max and Gwladys had different attitudes towards animals and hunting, though this did not help. It was that Max did not fully recognise this in himself. His reaction to being parachuted into Gwladys's world was to try to reinvent himself as a male version of his wife. In the past he had played the young naval officer, junior civil servant, prep-school games teacher, jazz musician and enthusiastic Fascist. Now he was hoping to pass himself off as a young country gent. It was a demanding role, and even more so given he was surrounded by so many examples of the real thing.

Gwladys's friends picked up on this. Her husband came across as a charming newcomer who seemed to be playing a part. In an attempt to win over his wife's more hesitant friends, he confided in some that back in London he had been working informally for MI5 and Special Branch. This was a major breach of security. Of course Max had been working for the government at one remove, effectively as a freelancer, and perhaps it is unfair to expect a level of discretion otherwise associated with a full-time, professional agent. Yet at the very least, this suggests that anonymity did not come naturally to Max. Perhaps it was for the best that his espionage career appeared to be more or less behind him.

By sharing this information with some of Gwladys's friends, Max had hoped to go up in their estimation and earn their trust. The problem was that nobody believed him. Now he was seen as both an outsider and a fantasist.

Some locals took this further, spreading the rumour that Max went out at night to fish from land that belonged to others. Others went further still, claiming that he was a werewolf.

It was hardly surprising that Max spent so many hours fishing by himself. But neither his lack of friends nor his dislike of hunting accounted in full for the tension in his marriage. Gwladys was uncertain about her future with her husband because after two years together their relationship had not yet been consummated.

How can we be sure? The sex life of a married couple rarely leaves a paper trail. The absence of a child confirms nothing. Yet the recollections of Gwladys's friends, when interviewed many years later, were consistent on this one point. Max would later confirm, under oath, that around this time his wife became estranged from her mother, and according to Gwladys's friends this was because Mrs Poole had found out about her daughter's non-existent sex life. She had urged Gwladys to leave Max and to have the marriage dissolved, but her daughter had refused.

In his letter to the *British Lion*, Max mentioned that he would be leaving London for 'reasons of health'. It is possible that he had seen a doctor about his problem, whatever it may have been, and that he had been told a move to the country might help.

Another possibility is that Max was secretly gay, as one ex-lover suggested in an angry memoir that came out after his death. That book was published in the 1980s, amid the climate of renewed homophobia that accompanied the AIDS epidemic. This take on Max's sexuality would then be repeated so many times in the following years that it soon took on the hallowed status of fact. But the evidence to support it was almost non-existent. This claim about Max's private life left his family and friends both bemused and baffled. Throughout his life there were references to him flirting with women, being attracted to women and to their being attracted to him. There are also suggestions that he had affairs with various women. One of his superiors at MI5 complained that Max, as a married man, was known 'to have lived with one of his [female] secretaries and now to be living with another'. No man ever claimed to have been Max's lover; equally the notion that he married Gwladys to hide his sexuality is tenuous. Both of Max's parents had died by the time of his marriage and it is difficult to imagine either of his spymasters, one of whom was a confirmed bachelor, being remotely concerned about his marital status.

For all this, after two years of marriage, Max and Gwladys had not consummated their relationship. There was a problem in bed, and this added to the strain on their relationship. It might have been a purely physical issue, or a more psychological one, but it seems that those long fishing trips, when Max often stayed out late into the night, were a series of escapes. He was running away from Gwladys, from his failure to consummate and in some ways he was running away from himself.

By 1929, Max was stuck. The course of his life seemed to have run into an eddy. Having so recently been a young, high-flying spymaster with contacts throughout British intelligence, he was now a pub-running fisherman thought by the locals to be either a fantasist or a werewolf. Possibly both. When working for the Makgill Organisation, he had displayed a rare aptitude for recruiting and running agents; indeed, this was the only job in which he had ever flourished. Although Max loved his wife and there were times when he enjoyed living on Exmoor, after two years of this he was desperate to find a way out.

9

MORTON'S PLAN

At last, Desmond Morton had found a solution. The MI6 officer with a machine-gun bullet lodged in his chest had been tussling with a familiar problem, namely, how to root out Soviet espionage in Britain. Technically, this was not his problem to solve. Morton continued to run the Production section in MI6, as well as Section VI, which gathered intelligence on economic preparations for war inside countries like Germany and Russia. His official area of interest was overseas, yet his attention was always being drawn back to the home front in the undeclared intelligence war between Britain and the USSR, one that Moscow was now winning.

Two years earlier, in 1927, Morton had taken part in the notoriously shambolic raid on the London headquarters of the All-Russian Co-Operative Society (ARCOS), the Soviet body responsible for Anglo-Russian trade. The British suspected ARCOS of being a front for various illegal activities. A herd of policemen, accompanied by Morton and several MI5 officers, had piled into the ARCOS building on Moorgate in the hope of finding a photocopied Signals Training manual that they believed to have come from a British military base in Aldershot. But they did not find the manual, or anything else to fully justify the search.

The ARCOS raid led to an immediate cessation of diplomatic relations between Britain and the USSR. It also ended the Anglo-Soviet Trade Agreement. Worse, when pressed in Parliament about this raid, the Foreign Secretary, Austen Chamberlain, the Home Secretary, William Joynson-Hicks, and even the Prime Minister, Stanley Baldwin, revealed that the government had access to encrypted diplomatic traffic between Moscow and the Soviet embassy in London. This was an epic blunder. The Soviets responded by changing their encryption, introducing a 'One-Time Pad' system that was theoretically unbreakable, and which ended the government's unfettered access to Soviet diplomatic traffic.

The year after this disastrous ARCOS raid, Desmond Morton helped to coordinate the arrest of two Soviet spies who were operating on British soil, Wilfred Macartney and Georg Hansen. Several months later, Morton's colleagues interviewed the first major defector from the Soviet Union, whose information only confirmed the MI6 man's fears about the extent of Soviet espionage in Britain. But the worst was still to come.

In April 1929, after five years of intricate, clever investigation by Morton and others at MI6 and MI5, Inspector Van Ginhoven and Sergeant Jane of Special Branch, as well as Walter Dale, a former policeman, were all arrested and charged with being paid Soviet agents in a spy ring dominated by former and serving British policemen. Only now did Morton appreciate how bad the domestic situation had become. The existence of Soviet spies deep within Special Branch, of all places, marked a new low. As one MI5 officer explained, for 'ten years, any information regarding subversive organisations and individuals supplied to Scotland Yard by MI6 or MI5, which had become the subject of Special Branch police enquiry, would have to be regarded as having been betrayed'.

Soon after these arrests, the Labour Party won the 1929 General Election. The new Prime Minister, Ramsay MacDonald, restored diplomatic relations with Moscow and instructed Special Branch to scale back its operations against the Communist Party.

Desmond Morton once said that he had just one enemy in life. It was not the German soldier who had fired a bullet into his chest, but 'International Leninism'. Similar to the late Sir George Makgill, Morton wanted to protect his country from the Soviet Union and its ideology, which was why, in 1929, shortly after the Labour victory, he made the decision to bypass Special Branch and set up his own secret agent network on British soil. It would target Communism in Britain and Soviet espionage.

This was risky. Morton knew that if the existence of his new operation became known beyond MI6 there would be major and lasting repercussions for him and his agency. So, the man he chose to run this network had to be unfailingly discreet.

Morton had kept in touch with Max during his exile on Exmoor and had even asked him to carry out several low-key jobs using the handful of agents that he still had in play. Usually, the work involved verifying reports received by MI6. Morton referred to Max and his men as 'Casuals'. Certainly, their work in the years after the General Strike had more in common with a casual amateur hobby than a full-time profession. Yet that was about to change.

In late 1929, Morton asked Max to renew and enlarge his agent network and to start working for him as an MI6 agent. This well-tailored yet sometimes charmless MI6 officer was essentially offering Max his previous life back, only with regular pay and more power. Max did not need to think long before saying yes.

All Morton needed was clearance from his boss, Sir Hugh Sinclair, the head of MI6 known as 'C'. Morton may have been a 'typical old-fashioned bachelor' who could come across as lacking any sensitivity, but he had the common sense to realise that his plan had one major flaw, and that was Max's past.

So he covered it up.

'I have just heard of a man, Mr Maxwell Knight, now Proprietor of the Royal Oak Hotel, Withypool,' Morton explained to C. He had known Max for at least five years. 'This man holds in his hand the threads of a small amateur detective or secret service in London, consisting of about a hundred individuals in all walks of life, many of whom speak foreign languages. I could see Maxwell Knight without disclosing my name or identity,' he went on, 'only saying that I am in some way connected with non-political circles.' The implication that Max would have no idea that Morton was an MI6 officer was absurd, yet Morton's desire to obscure their relationship was understandable. He did not want his chief to find out that over the last five years, as an MI6 officer, he had been informally running a senior British Fascist.

Over lunch with Max at the United Services Club on 27 November, 1929, Morton explained that C had agreed to his being given a three-month trial. Of course, he must not breathe a word of this to anyone, least of all to those with the slightest connection to Special Branch. Max's pay would be modest, just £35 a month, plus expenses (equivalent today to roughly £15,000 per year). As a signing-on bonus he would get £60. That initial payment was made in used pound notes that were out of series, a suitably cloak-and-dagger start to his official career as an MI6 agent.

Max began his new job while many others in the world were losing theirs. In the wake of the 1929 Wall Street Crash, unemployment soared and with it the threat of Communism. Max's work felt relevant again. He was back in London doing a job that he believed in. The patriotism of his teenage years, the frustration he had once felt after seeing no active service and his experiences in K, had all coalesced into a zealous hostility towards Communism. Now he was being paid by the government to do work he might have done for free – if only he could afford to. The memory of his two years living on Exmoor, amid a bleak expanse of rugged moorland,

and those long fishing trips alone, must have felt like an unhappy fugue.

In his new guise as an MI6 agent running a network of subagents, Max reported directly to Desmond Morton. Usually they met for clandestine debriefs in St James's Park Underground Station, which may not have been the cleverest place to convene, given its proximity to MI6 Headquarters.

Morton was encouraged by Max's early reports. 'With every passing month,' he wrote, Max 'got his agents nearer to the target area', which was the centre of the British Communist Party.

Most of these agents were individuals Max had taken on while he was working for Makgill. The shelf life of an average undercover agent is short. He or she might be exposed or find the stress of the work too much, or the quality of the agent's intelligence may drop off. Agents might also fall out with their spymaster. Max was unusual in this sense. He managed to keep his agents going for many years. Indeed, one of his sources around this time – a gay, penniless poet who would go on to become Chairman of the Labour Party and sit in the House of Lords – was still reporting to Max, and only Max, more than thirty years after they had begun to work together.

Once Max had breathed life into his old network, he began to look around for more 'little ships', as he liked to call them, to launch at the Communist Party. One of these was set to be an old comrade from K – William Joyce.

Two years earlier, Joyce had graduated from Birkbeck with a First in English Literature, one of just two first-class honours degrees awarded that year. He had since applied to join the Foreign Office. Although he was ultimately turned down, the man who had married Max's first love was now becoming a more respectable figure. He was a familiar face in his local branch of the Conservative Party, where there was talk of his one day standing for Parliament. Only the long, curving scar across his cheek hinted at a wilder and more violent past.

Max had always preferred to take on friends of his as agents, a habit he had inherited from Makgill. He also believed that every recruit should share his political outlook. Joyce was certainly a committed enemy of Communism, but this did not make him trustworthy, as Max discovered.

Very soon after approaching William Joyce about the possibility of his becoming an agent, it seems Max found out that Joyce was cheating on his wife, Hazel, then pregnant with Joyce's child. You might think that Joyce's ability to hide a relationship from his wife, or at least his willingness to do so, would make him ideal for intelligence fieldwork. Not for Max, who saw cheating on your wife as equivalent to betraying your spymaster or, indeed, your country. The fact that Joyce's wife was someone Max had cared for himself, and probably still did, only reinforced the point.

In MI6 today, trainee intelligence officers are taught to consider potential agents in terms of their suitability, their access and their motivation. Max could have persuaded Joyce to join the Communist Party, which would have given him the access. He was certainly motivated. Yet, by cheating on Hazel, he had shown himself to be unsuitable.

Max decided not to take on Joyce. Already he had learned to be wary of any man or woman who seemed to enjoy deceit for its own sake, or who lied for their own pleasure. He needed those 'whose personal honesty and motives were above reproach,' he wrote, individuals who found the distortion of the truth to be a burden, but one that they would carry for the sake of their country. Max had misjudged Joyce, and not for the last time.

'I CAN MAKE THINGS BLOODY
UNPLEASANT FOR YOU'

Every agent has a blind spot, as Desmond Morton was about to be reminded. Max had assured his boss that in his new job for MI6 he would avoid Special Branch 'like the plague'. By using Max, Morton was not only trespassing on his rival organisation's territory but also flouting the government's ban on undercover operations against the Communist Party. But if Morton's agent was trying to avoid Special Branch 'like the plague', he had a very unusual way of going about it.

Soon after being taken on by MI6, Maxwell Knight began to have regular lunches with an old friend. This was Lieutenant-Colonel John Carter, a man who was by that stage of his career Deputy Assistant Commissioner of the Metropolitan Police, and as such the nominal head of Special Branch. On 23 July, 1930, Max went to have another lunch with Colonel Carter of Special Branch. They met at their usual spot: Hatchett's, on Piccadilly. Max settled down for what he presumed was going to be another convivial meal.

It was not.

'Was Major Morton going to close down the whole of this business,' demanded Carter, 'or was he not?'

The man from Special Branch had found out about Max's network. He was apoplectic with rage, and understandably so. It seems that during one of Max and Carter's earlier meals the young MI6 agent had made a remark that piqued Carter's curiosity. It is unlikely that Max told the Special Branch man outright that he was working for Morton. More likely he was unable to resist the temptation to hint that he was up to something, that his exile on Exmoor was over and that he was back in the intelligence game.

Carter's response was to send a detective down to Exmoor to investigate. Other Special Branch detectives began to shadow Max around London. Although Max later claimed to have been aware of this, assuring Morton that he was more than capable of shaking off a Special Branch tail, it is hard to think why he would have allowed these detectives to see him meeting Morton. Most likely this observation happened at St James's Park Tube station, just a stone's throw from MI6 Headquarters.

By modern standards the idea of an MI6 agent meeting his spymaster here, of all places, sounds hopelessly amateur. But this level of tradecraft was not unusual at that time. There are many elements of MI5 and MI6 intelligence-gathering between the wars that come across as shockingly unprofessional when compared to what goes on today. Much of this was down to a lack of training, limited resources and tiny salaries. Men like Max and Morton were drawn to their profession out of a boyish love of intelligence and often found themselves making it up as they went along. But this does not fully explain Max's decision to have a series of lunches with the head of Special Branch. Like a poacher who asks to meet the gamekeeper from whom he is stealing, this may have been about brinkmanship as well, and the bravado of being in on a secret which the other person is not.

All that had now come to an end. A spluttering Colonel Carter told Max that Desmond Morton was 'a worm', and that before he was finished he wanted to see the MI6 man 'go on his knees to him on the carpet at Scotland Yard'.

'I can make things bloody unpleasant for you,' Carter told Max. 'How would it be if I gave the whole thing away to the Communist Party?'

By 'the whole thing' he meant Max's agent network. Only months after it had been revived, Carter was threatening to snuff out Max's espionage career.

'This is going to be a fight,' Carter went on. 'I am going to fight until the last ditch.' The head of Special Branch then delivered his ultimatum. If Max continued to work for MI6, Carter would 'make his life and that of his agents a misery'.

'We have a government in power now whose policy is against this sort of work,' said Carter. 'I have to carry out their policy.' His anger had as much to do with Morton trespassing on Special Branch territory as the MI6 man's disregard for the Prime Minister's instructions. Carter was right. He and Morton were Crown servants with a constitutional duty to carry out the wishes of the elected government. Yet Max did not see it like this. He interpreted Carter's anger as evidence of a left-wing bias.

By this stage of his career Max had only ever worked for men who saw Communism as an existential threat to both the country they loved and to their own class. He did not see it as a legitimate political concern within a tolerant, liberal democracy. Whether it was through force of habit or his own political conviction, the idea of soft-pedalling against the Communists, or being impartial, was anathema to him.

Desmond Morton did not go on his knees to Colonel Carter. That was not in his nature. Instead, the row between MI6 and Special Branch was allowed to grow until it became, in the words of the historian Gill Bennett, 'outright warfare'. MI5 was dragged into the fray and at one point even received information about Max from John

Baker White, the man who had talent-spotted him all those years ago. Relations between MI6 and Special Branch reached an all-time low, until it was decided, in an attempt to resolve the situation, to convene the all-powerful Secret Service Committee.

In January 1931, the head of MI6 was summoned before this august committee. He was asked to explain why his organisation had agreed to take on Max. One of the charges against C's 'intermediary', that is, Max, was that this young MI6 agent had used a British civil servant as one of his informants. Another accusation was that Max had been, and might still be, a senior figure within the British Fascists.

This was why Desmond Morton had covered up his agent's past. There was nothing exceptional about Max's anti-Communist views, and they were consistent with those held by most MI6 officers. Yet his involvement with the British Fascists was different. Although he could say that he had joined this organisation under instructions from Sir George Makgill, there was, of course, the possibility that deep down he had come to sympathise with this group's core beliefs. Over the last few years the popular perception of Fascism had changed. In Germany, Hitler's Fascist party now represented the second largest political grouping and might soon form a government. Mussolini was moving towards a new conception of Fascism as a 'universal phenomenon', one that might match international Communism in its reach and power. European Fascism was a far more dangerous prospect than it had been five years earlier, and now had the potential to threaten British interests.

Maxwell Knight was a spymaster of obvious ability, he was trustworthy, industrious and showed rare skill as an agent-runner, but he was handicapped both by his Fascist past as well as his occasional desire to show off, which was what had got him into this mess in the first place. The whole debacle might have been avoided, or at least postponed, had Max been able to resist the temptation to see Carter for lunch and drop hints about his work for MI6.

The Permanent Secretary at the Home Office, Sir John Anderson, was Chairman of the Secret Service Committee. He told C that the idea of MI6 employing a senior Fascist, such as Max, was intolerable. The possibility that this man had also recruited as an agent a British civil servant was one that he 'could not possibly countenance'. Anderson stressed 'the danger of a Government organisation such as MI6 being in any way associated with such undertakings', before adding that the situation was 'a source of grave embarrassment'.

C could have hung Max out to dry. Instead, as MI6 employees generally do when one of their own is under attack, he went on the offensive. He assured the committee that Max's network contained just four agents. As for his man being a Fascist, C claimed to have documentary proof to show that Max had severed his link with the BF. He also dismissed the idea that Max had been using a British civil servant as an agent.

Almost all these claims were untrue. Whether or not Anderson believed C, he concluded that the best solution was wholesale structural reform, an opinion shared by his colleagues on the committee, Sir Warren Fisher and Sir Maurice Hankey, two of the most powerful British civil servants of the interwar years. After three further meetings, the Secret Service Committee reached a radical decision.

The 'Treaty of Westminster', as it became known, fundamentally changed the relationship among Special Branch, MI5 and MI6, and the scope of their respective powers. Desmond Morton lost the services of Max and his network of agents, as well as the Special Branch section SS1 (which had become MI6's de facto domestic wing). Morton and his MI6 colleagues were also forbidden from running agents within three miles of British territory. MI5 came out of it all rather differently.

The committee ruled that in future Sir Vernon Kell's department would deal with *all* Communist subversion in Britain, whether civilian or military. It would be detached from the War Office and renamed the Security Service (a title that took many years to catch on in Whitehall). It was also given the services of SS1 and the man at the eye of this particular storm: Maxwell Knight.

Max's ill-advised lunches with Colonel Carter had been the catalyst to one of the greatest shake-ups in the history of British intelligence. It was also the turning point of his career. For months this MI6 agent had been living under a Damoclean sword as he waited to discover the fate of his network and, ultimately, his espionage career. He had been staring at a defeat that was rooted in his inability to make himself invisible and the extent of his Fascist past. Now he was on the verge of a new life as an MI5 officer. He would be offered his own desk, his own staff, more funding than ever before and his own MI5 section with which to carry out the task he saw as his calling in life: defending the realm from Communism. Although he would no longer be working for Desmond Morton, he would stay in close contact with his former spymaster, and this relationship would one day prove to be vital.

Yet there may have been more to Max's sudden change of fortune. Towards the end of his life, Max's most treasured possession was a gold cigarette case. It bore the royal cipher of King George V and the following inscription: 'Maxwell Knight, 1931'.

The King was not in the habit of handing out gifts like this for trivial or unremarkable acts. The few people that Max entrusted with the story of why he had been given this cigarette case died without divulging the details, saying only that it was the greatest secret of his career. At the very least, we know that in 1931 he performed some act or service for which the Royal Family, and in particular the King, was extremely grateful. Precisely what he did and for whom may never come to light. It is possible that it involved a case of blackmail and one of the King's sons, but that is speculation. What is absolutely clear is that the task he carried out for the King coincided with the start of his new life as an MI5 officer.

Before taking up his post in MI5, Max considered the question of what to call himself and his new section. He knew that the head of MI6 signed himself off as 'C', the head of MI5 sometimes went by 'K' and Somerset Maugham's agent, Ashenden, reported to 'R'. Max decided that his MI5 section should be known as 'M Section' and that he would be called 'M'. Some took this to be nothing more than an abbreviation of his first name, but there was more to it than that, as we shall see.

Incidentally, M was the moniker that had been used long ago by William Melville, a founding father of MI5. As a newcomer to Britain's counterespionage agency, Max could have been accused of claiming a slice of its history for himself. His decision to reinvent himself as M was bold and full of chutzpah. It was a sign of the confidence he had in his ability as a spymaster and the new approach he was hoping to adopt. For, by the time Maxwell Knight joined MI5, he had a plan for how to find out what was really going on inside the Communist Party and how to reach the fabled 'centre of affairs'. To do this he would use a very different kind of undercover agent.

PART II

THE RED MENACE

OLGA

Although Mrs Gray liked having her twenty-four-year-old daughter living with her, in her modest house on the outskirts of Birmingham, by 1931 she had begun to wonder when or whether her eldest was going to find herself a husband. Her daughter's name was Olga. She was a typist. Mrs Gray, the young woman's widowed mother, ran a local youth club and volunteered for the Conservative Party. Through this connection she had come to know the wife of her local member of Parliament, Neville Chamberlain, the future Prime Minister, and it was probably through Mrs Chamberlain that, in 1931, Mrs Gray was invited to a summer garden party in the home of the local Conservative Party electoral agent. Rather than attend by herself, she decided to bring her daughter.

Olga Gray was one of the younger guests at No. 21 Clarendon Road that day, as well as being the most striking. With her peroxide bob and hourglass figure, she was hard to miss. She was also quick, curious and strong-minded. Yet beneath her confident façade was an altogether different person, one who was captive to her past.

More than a decade earlier, Olga's father, Charles Gray, had been killed during the war at the Battle of Passchendaele. The news of his death had hit the Grays hard, yet it had not sent Olga spiralling off into paroxysms of grief. Instead, she confessed many years later to feeling a small sense of relief.

The turning point in her childhood, she later realised, had come several years before the start of the war when her older brother died in a tragic accident. Olga had been just five. Her father never really recovered from this loss. Overwhelmed by grief, he began to lash out at Olga. He wanted her to take his dead son's place, but he was not sure how. He told Olga to be more like him. Harder. More boyish. Olga started to morph into a tomboy, yet by the time her transformation was complete, her two younger sisters had blossomed into blonde-haired, blue-eyed girls – dainty and pretty and the epitome of everything that Olga was not. Now, her father urged her to be more like them.

He bullied Olga about her looks, telling her that she was either too feminine or not girly enough. She fought back, and a vicious antagonism developed between father and daughter, fuelled, in many ways, by the similarities between them. Charles Gray recognised parts of himself in Olga – the stubbornness, the pride, the primal certainty – and it spurred him on. When his job as Northern Night Editor of the *Daily Mail* became stressful he would take it out on Olga. He was violent towards her, but never in front of her siblings or her mother, so that when she told them about what had happened, after he had died, they did not believe her.

Fourteen years after her father's death, Olga Gray was still coming to terms with her childhood and its effect on the way she saw herself. Beneath her frank and sometimes combative demeanour was a person who despaired of her looks and found it hard to make lasting relationships with the opposite sex. She was convinced that nobody would ever find her attractive.

It is unlikely that any of this bubbled up to the surface during the sunny chit-chat at the Conservative garden party in Birmingham, one bright day in the summer of 1931. It certainly did not suit the mood of the occasion. Although the political situation elsewhere in the country was dire, with unemployment close to three million and the new coalition or 'National' Government committed to a programme of economic austerity, the mood in the local Conservative Party was upbeat. The venue for that gathering was the home of Robert Edwards, the local Conservative agent, who was confident of success for his candidates in Birmingham at the forthcoming General Election. Amid the happy hubbub of conversation that afternoon there was also the occasional happy yelp from guests playing games on the lawn. One of these activities was clock golf, in which players took turns putting at a flag while moving around the hours of a clock face. At one point that afternoon, Olga agreed to play a round of clock golf with a woman she had got to know at work: an impressive, upright individual called Dolly Pyle.

Though Olga Gray had been a disruptive presence at most of her schools, and had been asked to leave at least one, she had always done well at games. At St Dunstan's, Plymouth, she had impressed the nuns in charge by becoming captain of the school hockey team. So, she would have been good at clock golf. Who knows, she might have been winning when Dolly Pyle asked a question that would stay fresh in her mind for the rest of her life:

'I say, old thing, have you ever thought of working for the Secret Service?'

Had Olga ever thought of this? In all likelihood, yes, but only in a fantastic and essentially abstract sense.

By 1931, espionage novels were fashionable and popular, as they had been for several decades in Britain, yet this was also the dawn of the golden age of spy films. Fritz Lang's breath-taking *Spione*, in 1927, had been the harbinger, followed by the first 'talkie' from Alfred Hitchcock, *Blackmail*, and another classic spy caper, *The W Plan*, directed by Victor Saville. The popularity of spy films and spy novels was such that Olga and many others her age had almost certainly daydreamed at some point about what it would be like to be a spy. But she had never imagined that for someone like her, with her background, her qualifications and her lack of social connections, this might ever become a reality. Spies seemed to operate on some higher plane; they were grander and more debonair than anyone she had ever met. She knew nothing to suggest otherwise. Olga's understanding of 'the Secret Service' was based entirely on fictional representations of espionage. At the time even the name MI5 was classified. To be asked to work for the Secret Service in 1931 was like being invited to star in a film. It felt mysterious, exotic and stupendously unreal – which was why Olga thought Dolly Pyle was pulling her leg.

'Gosh, Doll,' she replied, playing along, 'that sounds jolly exciting. I'd love to.'

Only then did she realise that 'Doll' was being serious.

In the moments that followed, Olga had to make a life-changing decision. It is possible that she put down her putter.

Though she did not yet know what the work might involve, it would surely mean leaving home – it was hard to imagine there being many state secrets for a spy to guard or steal in the outskirts of Birmingham. In that case, accepting this offer would mean leaving her mother. This might also involve considerable risks to herself and her reputation.

The fictional female spies that Olga had encountered on-screen or read about in books were cast in the mould of the legendary female spy Mata Hari: they were beautiful harlots who used sex as a weapon. 'Any woman who values her virginity would be well advised to keep away from the spy-business,' warned one former intelligence officer. There was no such thing as a spy novel in which the female agent had a successful espionage career before going on to get married, have children and otherwise lead a happy and fulfilled life. Things did not end well for female spies. By agreeing to Dolly Pyle's proposal, Olga might be risking her reputation and her prospects; and, at the same time, this dilemma brought her up against her old enemy, her crippling lack of self-esteem. How could she ever play the part of a Mata Hari if men did not find her attractive?

Ultimately, Olga's curiosity overcame her fear.

She said yes.

The next step, Dolly Pyle explained, was for Olga to meet a man from MI5, who would introduce himself as Captain King.

THE M ORGANISATION

'The incident,' as it came to be known, happened shortly before Maxwell Knight joined MI5 in late 1931. It took place in Invergordon, a port in the Scottish Highlands, after word spread among the naval ratings that, as part of the government's sweeping austerity drive, their salaries were about to be cut. On the morning of 15 September, 1931, the crews of several warships refused orders. Others followed suit, and by midday there were mobs of sailors gathered on the forecastles of several ships giving boisterous speeches, singing songs and otherwise enjoying themselves. On board one ship a piano was hauled up on deck. Several crews refused to put out to sea for routine exercises.

This was the Invergordon Mutiny. Nobody was hurt. It lasted less than two days, and the rebellious sailors carried out all their essential duties. Yet for the British public the idea of a mutiny in the Royal Navy was truly shocking. News of 'the incident' sent the London Stock Exchange into meltdown. Markets plummeted. There was a run on the pound. Sterling lost a quarter of its value, and several days later the government made the momentous decision to leave the gold standard.

The reaction in MI5 was no less dramatic, largely because one of the songs that was sung by the mutinous sailors had been 'The Red Flag' – the Communist anthem.

In Russia, the Bolshevik uprising of 1917 had involved mutinous sailors in Kronstadt and elsewhere. The Wilhelmshaven Mutiny in Germany, the following year, had been another naval uprising inspired by socialist ideals. Eisenstein's film *Battleship Potemkin,* which came out several years later, was a riff on the same theme. For many people, and not just those in MI5, the Invergordon Mutiny was a near miss and a reminder that the possibility of a Communist uprising in Britain was real.

This was an age in which *dictatorship* was not yet a dirty word. Universal suffrage was still a recent innovation, and during the war Britain had been effectively run as a totalitarian state. By 1931, a growing number of people across Europe saw dictatorship as a viable and sensible solution to the worsening economic recession. With the Soviet Union apparently thriving, a significant chunk of the British population was at least open to the idea of a strong socialist government, and with it a reduction in democracy.

Under its new charter, MI5 was responsible for investigating Communism throughout the United Kingdom and the British Empire. Its task was to infiltrate the many tentacles of the British Communist movement, to find out what was being planned and to identify channels of communication between British revolutionaries and their controllers in Moscow, all of whom were working towards the same basic goal: a socialist revolution in Britain. The task that had been given to MI5 was about much more than keeping the peace or guarding secrets. At stake was nothing less than democracy in Britain and the future of the British Empire.

To meet this new challenge, MI5 had been given more resources and greater powers. For the first time it would have a specialised agent-running section. Yet the man chosen to run this new wing of MI5, on which so much depended, was not one of the service's established senior officers. Instead, he was a thirty-one-year-old outsider whose indiscretions at MI6 had triggered the Treaty of Westminster. He had also asked, rather unusually, that his new colleagues refer to him as 'M.'

Maxwell Knight's first visit as a member of staff to MI5 Headquarters, or 'the Office', as it was known, came towards the end of 1931. MI5 was then based just south of Hyde Park on Cromwell Road, a short walk from one of M's favourite buildings in London, the Natural History Museum, famous then, as it is today, for its collection of fossils. The scene inside MI5 was not so very different. M was introduced to a galère of ageing former soldiers, ex-Indian policemen, washed-up colonial administrators and civil servants, most of whom had reached the twilight of their career. They were older than average, poorly paid and, with the exception of just one officer, none had gone to university. There were also surprisingly few of them, as had been the case for most of the last decade. Two years earlier, MI5 had had just thirteen officers distributed between A Division, which dealt with administration, and B Division, responsible for counterespionage and countersubversion. All were sworn to secrecy. M was told that MI5 'should never be referred to in conversation with civilians'.

Most of his new colleagues had been drawn into the world of intelligence by their romantic sense of patriotism, or this had rubbed off on them over the years. They were bound together by a shared affinity for intrigue, a dwindling sense of ambition and the feeling that working for MI5 was less a job than a vocation. Although many of those in the Office were hard-working and competent, for years they had been held back by MI5's limited resources and its relatively low standing within Whitehall.

The atmosphere inside the Office was said to resemble that of a school staff room or a small family business, while the canteen looked like a café for debutantes on account of all the glamorous women from 'good' families who carried out MI5's clerical duties. One officer who joined the Office soon after the Second World War described that canteen as 'a showpiece for some of the best-looking women you ever saw, and they were all the prettier because we men were so dowdy by comparison'.

M was told that a relationship between an officer like him and one of these dazzling women was forbidden, unless, it seemed, the man in question was Eric Holt-Wilson, Deputy Director of MI5, and the female member of staff was the beautiful Aubrey Stirling, thirty-five years his junior, who joined the Office at the same time as M. Two months later she married the man fondly known in MI5 as 'Holy Willy', who got away with this largely because of his close friendship with the only officer who outranked him in MI5, the central point within this miniature merry-go-round, Sir Vernon Kell.

Kell was the person M most needed to win over, and on the face of it this should have been easy. Both M and Kell were dedicated fishermen who kept parrots at home and were known for their occasional eccentricities. M often had a lizard or mouse in his jacket pocket. Kell insisted on being chauffeured to work each day in a car with a flag on the bonnet depicting a tortoise, an unusual mode of transport for anyone, but truly peculiar for a spy chief whose job was so secret that it did not officially exist. Kell and M were both polite and principled. Their values were Edwardian, their politics were diehard Conservative. Yet Kell lacked M's charisma. Although he had natural authority and a manner that was both reassuring and equable, Kell was often slow to come round to new ideas, including the radical one that M proposed for infiltrating the Communist Party.

By the time M had joined MI5, 'the amount of information in the possession of the Department regarding secret and illegal activities' of the Communist Party was, he wrote, 'strictly limited'. This was something of an understatement. Most of the intelligence that came into MI5 fell into one of two categories. There was 'human intelligence', or HUMINT as it is sometimes known today, that mostly came from agents, informants and defectors; and there was 'signals intelligence', SIGINT, that was generated mainly by telephone checks or 'Home Office warrants' (HOWs), which allowed MI5 to intercept letters sent to a named individual at a given address. The difficulty was that each HOW had to be individually authorised by the Home Office, making these cumbersome and slow to operate. Telephone checks were easier to set up, yet with no reliable recording equipment the listening was done in real time by telephone switchboard operators who might not always understand the nuances of the conversation that they were listening in to, or indeed the language.

Meanwhile, the human intelligence trickling in to MI5 when M arrived generally came from the police, ex-Communists, Soviet defectors or from John Baker White, the former member of the British Fascisti who had once brought Max to Makgill's attention. Baker White was now a senior figure at the right-wing Economic League, where he ran his own intelligence network and supplied information to the police and MI5. Codenamed 'B. W.' or 'B/W,' he liked to provide his material over a pint in the pub to his old friend Con Boddington, another ex-Makgill man who had gone on to join MI5. After 'a little leg-pulling' between the two, Baker White passed on scraps of gossip from his sources inside or close to 'the Party', as Communists called their organisation. The quality of human intelligence coming in to MI5 was fine, but there was rarely enough and it was not always reliable, especially if Boddington and Baker White had spent too long in the pub.

Already M had several agents inside the Party. One was a young bookseller who had married a Communist; another was a Glaswegian gun examiner. M also had a well-known gossip columnist at the *Daily Express* on his books, and a young writer whose comedy sketches were being performed on the BBC. The intelligence they supplied was good, sometimes excellent, yet none of these agents had tapped the fountainhead. No matter how hard they tried, and they could never appear to be trying *too* hard, M's agents had been unable so far to break into the senior ranks of the Communist movement. Rather than wait years for one of these men to secure a top position, M's new idea was to find a female secretary and engineer a situation in which she might be given a job working for an important Party figure.

An efficient and reliable secretary is a valuable asset in any organisation, yet by 1931 good secretaries in the Communist movement were in particularly short supply. If M could find a suitable candidate, 'she might stand a very good chance of obtaining a secretarial position in a Party organisation'. It sounded like an excellent, low-risk plan. But M's new boss did not agree.

'Women do not make good secret service agents,' wrote Kell, unambiguously.

He was not the only MI5 officer to be against the use of female agents on principle. Some of M's new colleagues believed that women lacked the staying power of men. Others worried that they were more prone to falling in love with their targets than men.

M felt otherwise. 'It is frequently alleged that women are less discreet than men,' he wrote, 'that they are ruled by their emotions, and not by their brains: that they rely on intuition rather than on reason; and that Sex will play an unsettling and dangerous role in their work.' And yet, 'it is curious that in the history of espionage and counter-espionage a very high percentage of the greatest coups have been brought off by women'. He went on, 'this – if it proves anything – proves that the spymasters of the world' – in other words, Kell – 'are inclined to lay down hard and fast rules, which they subsequently find it impossible to keep to, and it is in their interests to break'.

Recruiting a female agent at the start of his career as an MI5 officer was a risk, and it would put him up against his new chief. So it was vital to M, or 'Captain King', as he had introduced himself, that Olga Gray was up to the task.

WATCHERS

There were various qualities that M hoped to find in Olga Gray. First, he had to be sure that her outlook was unimpeachably anti-Communist. Olga had been spotted at a Conservative garden party and came from a family with a diligently patriotic and right-wing outlook, so there seemed to be no problem there. It was also important that Olga was an experienced secretary. As she explained during their interview, she had spent more than five years as a commercial typist.

Next came the question of trust. Could M trust Olga, and might she trust him back? 'The agent must trust the officer as much as – if not more than – the officer trusts the agent,' he wrote. Much like a meeting between a potential bride and groom before an arranged marriage, he had to decide right away whether they were compatible. During their first interview, he asked about her 'home surroundings' as well as her 'family, hobbies, personal likes and dislikes'.

They seemed to be a good match. She could also see a joke, which helped. 'A vivid imagination and a schoolboyish sense of humour' were, wrote Eric Roberts, vital attributes in any undercover agent.

Another question in M's mind as he got to know Olga Gray was whether this young woman was, at heart, a watcher.

David Cornwell, better known as the author John Le Carré, worked for several years under M and would use him as the model for Jack Brotherhood in *A Perfect Spy*. Le Carré also drew a series of cartoons to illustrate two of M's books (*Talking Birds* and *Animals and Ourselves*), which is to say that he knew M pretty well. In Le Carré's *Tinker Tailor Soldier Spy*, there is a memorable exchange between the spy-turned-schoolmaster Jim Prideaux and his podgy, picked-upon pupil Bill Roach, in which Prideaux calls Roach the 'best watcher in the unit'.

Le Carré's erstwhile spymaster was always on the lookout for the best watcher in the unit. Indeed, Prideaux and M were both officer-ish prep-school games teachers at one point in their careers, and it is possible that this remark belonged originally to the MI5 man. Either way, M was good at spotting a watcher – the diffident outsider who had never really excelled at games and who was used to sitting it out on the sidelines, waiting and watching, because this is what *espionage* boils down to: patient observation. The word itself comes from the French *espionner,* meaning to watch or observe, and before that *specere,* to look out for. Ian Fleming, author of the James Bond books, James Schlesinger, at one time the head of the Central Intelligence Agency, and Andrew Parker, who became MI5 Director General in 2013, all described themselves as keen bird-watchers. Indeed, Fleming named his most famous literary creation after a little-known American ornithologist called James Bond. The real Bond, the circumspect birder, was undoubtedly closer to M's ideal of an agent than his fictional namesake. Strip away the mythology, the tradecraft, the gadgets and the romance, and spying is watching.

During the course of their interview, M decided that Olga might well be a watcher. She may have had another quality that drew him in. M prided himself on being able to chart the contours of anyone's personality during a long conversation like this one, and although it is unlikely that Olga opened up at this early stage about her childhood abuse at the hands of her father, M would have noticed that when she spoke about her family, and in particular her father, something was not right. For a different type of spymaster this might have set alarm bells ringing; for M it probably had the opposite effect.

This MI5 officer would later write twenty-nine books about natural history and looking after animals, and though a lot of this material is dry and factual, there are occasional glimpses of his past, or material which sheds light on the way he recruited and ran his agents, his 'tradecraft', to use Le Carré's well-judged term. From the hundreds of thousands of words written by M about pets it becomes clear that he had a preference for taking on a particular type of animal.

'There are few more pleasant experiences,' he once wrote, 'than the successful rearing of some young wild creature – particularly if it has come into one's possession through being orphaned, or through being the victim of an accident.' 'I have hand-reared many British birds,' he explained elsewhere, 'but all of these were birds which had been found exhausted, wounded or deserted, or have been birds that I rescued from some predator.' Other places he described an interest in rearing 'deserted or stray young birds', 'fledglings fallen from their homes, or found slightly injured'. In another book, he wrote, 'I have reared many injured and deserted birds by hand.' In an identical sense, when recruiting new agents M was always drawn to people like Olga who were in some way injured by their past. Perhaps he thought they would attract less suspicion, or that they were more biddable. It is also possible that deep down, in ways that he may not have understood about himself, he wanted to fix them.

What did Olga make of M? She found this MI5 spymaster 'charming' and endearingly unconventional. One secretary remembered him 'crawling on hands and knees in pursuit of some unlikely insect or animal', or grabbing a pair of drumsticks mid-conversation, with a jazz record playing in the background, and 'beating out a tune on the marble mantelpiece'. He was attractively tall and athletic-looking. There was nothing slight about him. He was big without being large – long nose, flappy ears and chunky shoulders – and although he was not classically good-looking, M had presence. Olga called him 'avuncular', a word which jars, given he was only six years older than her, yet already there was a powerful certainty to this man, one that was set off nicely by a hint of lawlessness. There was also his voice.

Much of M's charisma, and the impact he had on people, can be traced back to the way he spoke. As a boy, he had been fascinated by the effect of his voice on animals. He learned that a gentle, firm and reassuring tone could put almost any creature at ease. He encouraged pet owners to utter 'soothing words' to their animals while feeding them, and that 'the tone of the human voice influences animals to a considerable extent'. One woman described M's delivery as 'hypnotic'. M claimed to be able to make a parrot 'dance, whistle and shout just by stimulating it with my voice; I can also quieten it and make it responsive in an affectionate manner by speaking to it softly.' His speech had an irresistibly rich and mellifluous timbre, and he knew it. But if Olga had fallen for M and the way he spoke, she did not admit to this.

'I didn't have any sexual feeling for him,' she protested, 'largely because I didn't see how he could possibly be attracted to me. It just seemed impossible because at the time I felt totally unfeminine.'

Of course that might change as they got to know each other, as they now would. M decided either during or after that first interview that he wanted to recruit Olga as an MI5 agent.

He made her an offer, which she accepted. Olga Gray was then told to make her way to London for training.

CUCKOO EGGS

It is hard to say precisely what Olga expected to find as she walked into M's flat in Knightsbridge, west London, only that it was entirely different from what she saw. In most of the spy films she had watched, the fittings and furnishings of a spymaster's quarters had the male gravitas of a presiding judge. The walls tended to be clad in panelled wood, brass-tacked leather chairs were dotted around like icebergs and in the middle of it all was a monolithic desk, larger than it needed to be, behind which you would see the spymaster himself. What Olga observed as she ventured into M's flat was, she later said, 'like the den of some amiable scientist rather than a spy'.

Fish tanks bubbled away against one wall, there were cages for M's animals as well as boxes for his insects, Petri dishes for larvae, bags containing different feeds for his animals and bowls of food littering the floor. Among the various pets running or flying around the flat as Olga walked in there was a small dog and a magnificent blue-fronted Amazon parrot, also a talented mimic. 'It would make the squeak of the corkscrew, the pop when the cork comes out and the gurgling noise of the contents being poured.' There were harvest mice in there, at least one tortoise and probably a snake and a bush baby. Elsewhere Olga would have seen M's vast collection of jazz records as well as his roommate, an orthopaedic surgeon known as Val, who may have been wandering about in the background as she entered. Olga could have been forgiven for wondering to herself whether 'Captain King' was really the MI5 spymaster he claimed to be.

M had only recently moved into this maisonette flat at No. 38 Sloane Street, which had previously been rented by his sister, Enid. She appears to have moved out just after her brother was given his job at MI5. He might have preferred a larger setup, yet that was impossible given his tiny salary. Unlike most of his new colleagues, M was unable to fall back on a private income. But even if he had been paid more, or his allowance had not been cut off by his uncle ten years earlier, he probably would have spent most of it on records and pets. Throughout M's life, whenever he had more money than he needed, his instinct was to spend it, just like his father before him.

Olga may have imagined that a car would come to take them from M's chaotic home to the calm of MI5 Headquarters or to an imposing country house where she and the other trainee spies could begin their lessons. Instead, her instruction, such as it was, lasted little more than a weekend and it took place at M Section Headquarters, that is, her spymaster's flat.

M refused to run his section from the Office, where the rest of MI5 was based. Although his new agent-running unit was formally under the aegis of MI5, it remained, as far as he was concerned, the child of the Makgill Organisation, a more maverick and independent outfit than MI5 would ever be. It was under Makgill that M had learned his craft and had recruited most of his agents, a number of whom had come over with him to MI5. Even 'M Organisation', the name he liked to use to refer to his wing of MI5, was a reference to the Makgill Organisation. Dick Thistlethwaite, a senior MI5 officer, later referred to the Makgill Organisation as 'the real

"M" organisation', adding that in 1931 it 'technically joined up with us', meaning MI5, 'but was careful to keep its separate identity'. Not only did M see his new section as a continuation of the Makgill Organisation. It is also likely that the moniker he chose for himself – 'M' – was a reference to his own Christian name as much as to Makgill, the man who had first brought him into the world of intelligence.

Perhaps M explained some of this to Olga. 'I state unhesitatingly that I think it is not only desirable, but essential that an agent should know exactly what his position is,' he later wrote. 'I am against any complicated system of cut-outs; and equally against employing an agent who thinks he is working for, let us say, a news-agency. If this sort of subterfuge is practised, there inevitably comes a day when the agent has to be told what his real position is, and I think this has a very bad effect on the agent himself: he feels that he has been led up the garden, and made a fool of; and worst of all, that he has not been trusted.' He told Olga that she was working for M Section, part of 'the British Intelligence Department', and that her task was to penetrate the Communist movement.

It was hard to guess how far she might get, but for M the holy grail was finding proof of a link between Moscow and the Communist Party of Great Britain. Along the way she should look for evidence of illegal activities, the names of 'closed' Party members, communications between undercover comrades and any other details about left-wing underground networks. She might also need to answer specific questions from M's new colleagues. In M's reports, Olga would be referred to as 'M/12'. Her pay was to be £2.50 a week, approximately £150 in today's money. So she was not doing this to get rich. Yet it was vital that she received a regular salary. From his own experience, M understood the effect of being paid by results and how this could militate towards exaggeration and unnecessary risks. It would also undermine the basic lesson he preached to Olga repeatedly during that weekend, until she was probably sick of hearing it: be patient.

'The great thing is not be in too much of a hurry,' he told another agent. 'We shall not mind if you do not show any very tremendous results for a month or two. You have to be very patient in this game.'

This applied to Olga as much as to M. It was vital that he did not rush her.

M then gave her a crash course in what to report, the paramount importance of accuracy and objectivity and the need to keep her mind supple with memory exercises.

That was it, more or less.

'The very best training,' M always argued, 'is for an agent to be put into contact at the earliest possible moment with the organisation to be investigated.' This young spymaster had learned not to overload his agents with instructions and warnings. Like a film director obsessed with realism, he wanted his recruits to give untutored and naturalistic performances.

Olga was now ready to begin her mission to reach the heart of the Communist movement, which would be further than any of M's existing agents had got. Yet by the time her training had finished, in 1931, there was one other M operative who might arrive there at about the same time.

M had given this other agent the codename 'M/1,' possibly because this person had been one of the first people to be taken on by him. Having worked for M over the last few years, M/1 had recently secured a job at the new Communist newspaper, the *Daily Worker,* and was now providing M with a stream of valuable intelligence about who was employed at the paper, the stories its editors planned to publish, editorial policy, authorship of anonymous articles and other valuable scraps picked up inside this Communist propaganda machine. M/1 seemed to be just one or two promotions away from the upper reaches of the Party. M's operative was talented, courageous and resourceful, and until now this agent's identity has remained a carefully guarded secret.

MI5 does not publicly name its agents. The basic contract of trust between spymaster and informant is rooted in the understanding that the former will never give away the latter, even after death. Yet sometimes MI5 releases enough material about a particular agent to make an identification possible, but only if you are prepared to do a bit of digging.

In the National Archives in Kew, in southwest London, there are thousands of declassified MI5 files. Some include fragments of reports written by M/1. By trawling through enough of these documents it is possible to build up a rough picture of who M/1 was, where this agent worked and the names of the Communists that this agent reported on. Most of these people were employed at the *Daily Worker*. Four were not.

M usually asked that intelligence relating to any one of these four 'should be disseminated with very great care', a clear sign that this information came from personal conversations between one of these targets and M/1. If that intelligence was acted on by the police, it would be easy for the person arrested to guess who had tipped off the authorities. These four people were Elsie McMeakin, Edith Martin, Arthur Glyn Evans and his wife, Peggy Evans. They had various things in common, yet one stands out: they all lived in the same building.

Indeed, M/1 was something of an expert on the comings and goings at No. 22 Adelaide Road, a large house in Camden, north London, where these four people lived at different times. In one report, M/1 described a letter arriving at this address late in the day before it was taken by hand to Communist Party Headquarters early the next morning. In itself this indicates that M/1 probably spent the night at that house. Yet reading between the lines of this and many other reports, it seems pretty clear that M/1 either was sleeping with someone who lived at No. 22 Adelaide Road or was living there, too.

According to the annual electoral registers, during the years that M/1 was active, nine individuals were based in this property at one time or another. Five of the nine were reported as being in conversation with M/1 or were under suspicion by MI5, which means they cannot have been M/1 themselves. This leaves just four people registered as living there who might have been M/1.

Here are some other details about this MI5 agent: he or she was employed by the *Daily Worker*; belonged to the St Pancras branch of the Communist Party in London; and frequently attended meetings of the Workers Press Commission. This allows us to cross off several names from the list, leaving just two people.

The strangest thing about these last two is their relationship to each other: they were husband and wife. Their names are Kathleen Beauchamp and Graham Pollard. Both professed to be devout Communists. One of them appears to have been an MI5 agent.

There is another clue about M/1's identity, but it is confusing. In one report, M appears to refer to M/1 as 'H. G.' Usually a detail like this is redacted before a file is released to the public, but this one slipped through the net. The initials 'H. G.' seem to rule out both Beauchamp and Pollard, who were, of course, K. B. and G. P.

Perhaps M/1 did not live at No. 22 Adelaide Road after all? Or was 'H. G.' a codename?

The 'H. G.' clue appears to blow us off course but for one thing. 'Graham' was not Pollard's first name. It was his middle name. He was 'H. G. Pollard', and, just as H. G. Wells was sometimes known to friends as 'H. G.', so was H. G. Pollard.

Not only did Graham Pollard live at No. 22 Adelaide Road during this period, he belonged to the St Pancras Local at the same time as M/1, he attended meetings of the Workers Press Commission when

M/1 did and, crucially, he was on the staff at the *Daily Worker* at the same time as M/1. So, too, was his wife, Kathleen, a director of the newspaper's controlling press. As a result of her position, she was found in contempt of court when her newspaper printed an article protesting against the conviction of a leading Communist, and in January 1933 she was arrested and jailed. Shortly after her imprisonment M received a report from M/1, which appears to rule out Kathleen Beauchamp as an MI5 agent.

Graham Pollard was hailed after his death in 1976 as one of the most distinguished bibliographers of his generation. He was a learned, twinkly-eyed civil servant whose birthday, towards the end of his life, was noted each year in *The Times*. Pollard had an extraordinarily catholic range of interests including bookbinding, type design, the history of medieval Oxford and the newspapers, nineteenth-century literary forgeries and the book trade. He was admired for his remarkable 'facility in mastering a new subject and his convincing manner when talking on almost any topic'. Now it seems that we can add to his long and varied career a stint as an MI5 agent deep inside the Communist Party.

It is even possible to pinpoint the period when Pollard was recruited. In 1921, when M began to teach at the prep school in Putney, southwest London, a seventeen-year-old Graham Pollard happened to be living just a few hundred yards away, and he had good reason to visit the school: he had recently been a pupil there himself.

The year after these two presumably met, Pollard won the top history scholarship to Jesus College, Oxford, where his father, the great Tudor historian A. F. Pollard, had once been. Roughly a year later, M began to insert penetration agents into the Communist Party. One of the first appears to have been Graham Pollard, a teenager, who told his Oxford friends at exactly this time that he had suddenly become a Communist.

'Pollard did not often proclaim his faith,' noted Peter Quennell, critic and author, with evident suspicion. Indeed, the only time that Communism seemed to enter Graham Pollard's life was 'when a railway-strike happened to coincide with an important London book-sale; and he was much exercised as to whether he should miss the sale, or run the risk of travelling on a train behind a black-leg engine-driver'. Pollard was far better known at Oxford for his love of rare books, for being a member of the aesthetes' den the Hypocrites Club, for having a room that looked 'like a bookseller's shop', and for the occasion when he beat Evelyn Waugh in the 'half-blue' at spitting (at a distance of ten feet). Hardly the portrait of a devout Communist.

Yet on leaving Oxford, Pollard married Kathleen Beauchamp, a young Communist and a former pupil of his father's. M's young agent became increasingly accepted in Party circles after coming down from Oxford and involved himself in the production of various Communist publications. He also began to run part of the famous Birrell and Garnett bookshop in Soho, central London, having bought a share of the business from the Bloomsbury luminary David 'Bunny' Garnett.

Pollard's life was now a heady mix of books, extreme politics and espionage. He started each day with lunch at Chez Victor, one of the most fashionable restaurants in town, before drifting into his bookshop for an afternoon of work. Then he might head off to a Party meeting, file a report for M and go home to his Communist wife. His life as a bohemian, a political activist, a bookseller and an undercover agent was exciting and exacting, and it required him to play many parts. By the end of 1931, as Olga was about to launch herself at the Communist movement, it seemed that Graham Pollard might just reach the heart of the Party before she did.

All the same, M had so much riding on his experiment with female secretaries, and was so determined to see it succeed, that he recruited another one. 'A cuckoo is not content to lay one egg only,' he once wrote, 'but only one egg is normally laid in one nest.' Rather than enlist just one undercover secretary, M took on two and launched them at different parts of the Communist movement. As well as Olga, codenamed M/12, he began to run another female typist referred to as 'M/2'. Like Olga, she came from a respectable, middle-class family from outside London and she had strong connections to her local Conservative Party.

There was no way of telling which of these two women would flourish as an intelligence agent, or whether he had given them enough training. Rather like a cuckoo hen in the hours after depositing her eggs, all that M could do now was wait.

TRAILING ONE'S COAT

Every agent remembers the first job. M had instructed Olga Gray to attend a meeting of the Friends of the Soviet Union (FSU). This was a bland, left-of-centre organisation with branches all over the world. It raised money for impoverished Russians or else campaigned against the negative media portrayal of the Soviet Union. The FSU attracted political progressives and milk-and-water liberals, all of whom sympathised with the plight of the Russian people and subscribed to some of the basic tenets of Marxism, but few of them went so far as to call themselves Communists.

Unknown to most of these people, the FSU was a Communist 'front' organisation secretly under Soviet control. The many branches of the FSU, including the one Olga was about to visit, were referred to as 'Innocents' Clubs' by Willi Munzenberg, a senior figure in the Soviet body quietly pulling the strings in the FSU, as well as many other front organisations. Munzenberg worked for the Communist International, better known as the Comintern. Based in Moscow, the Comintern had been set up by Lenin in 1919 to coordinate the overthrow of global capitalism. Since then its agents had been midwives at the birth of almost every national Communist Party, supplying instructions, expertise and money, before staying on as governesses while each national Party agitated for a worker-led revolution. By 1931, the Comintern was a vast centralised network unparalleled in scale and ambition. Each day a flood of messages, propaganda and money pulsed out of its nerve centre deep in the Soviet Union, while in the opposite direction came intelligence, fresh recruits and a growing sense that momentum was on their side and capitalism would soon crumble. One of the ways the Comintern broadcast its message was through the activities of front organisations such as the FSU. 'These people have the belief they are actually doing this themselves,' wrote Munzenberg, of those who joined the FSU, and 'this belief must be preserved at any price'. Olga's task was to become one of them.

M had instructed her to play the wide-eyed innocent and to present herself at an FSU meeting as 'an ordinary, interested and sympathetic enquirer' who wanted to know more about the Soviet Union. She was going to 'trail her coat', in spy parlance, in the hope that a Party official might befriend her and take her on as his secretary.

Playing the part of a willing ingénue might sound easy. For Olga it was not. She had been brought up to see Communism as a political aberration. Now she had to pretend the opposite, to twist her mind inside out and convince a part of herself that what she had once believed to be wrong was instead right.

It worked, as far as Olga could tell. During the meeting, she got into conversation with various attendees. Nobody accused her of being anything other than what she claimed to be, and by the end of that session she had made several acquaintances. But that was it. She went home empty-handed.

This was Olga's first taste of life as an MI5 agent. She might have to endure hundreds of meetings like this, forever playing the political naïf, seizing upon ideas and phrases she found absurd as if they were full of genuine possibility, and even then there was no guarantee that she would be taken on.

Yet at a subsequent FSU meeting, 'very shortly after' the first, Olga was approached by the Assistant Secretary of the FSU. 'He may have had,' reported M, an 'interest' in Olga, seeing her 'as a personable young woman'. This was one way of saying he took a fancy to her. He listened carefully to her cover story about the job she had as a secretary for an author with unpredictable hours. This was wish fulfilment on M's part, as he had always wanted to be a professional writer. It was also designed to be tempting bait. The supposedly 'unpredictable' nature of his hours implied gaps in Olga's schedule that she needed to fill. The FSU man asked whether 'she had any free time which she could devote to doing voluntary work for the FSU'. She replied that she did.

Very soon after, Olga Gray began to work as a part-time and unpaid secretary at the FSU office. M's first cuckoo egg looked set to hatch.

Her new surroundings turned out to be shambolic, yet this allowed her to demonstrate her considerable abilities as a secretary. She 'speedily reduced the existing chaos to some semblance of order'. Her new colleagues were impressed.

'Form the habit of taking notes of what you see and hear as soon as possible after an incident or observation,' wrote M. 'We may have good memories, but they play us false every now and then.' Olga soon got used to writing down or memorising key details about anything unusual that she observed. She would then produce a written report and post it to M, or else she held the information in her head and either gave him a call or passed it on in person. They might meet in the lobby of a shabby hotel, in the cinema or in one of their homes. M preferred his agents to get their intelligence down on paper right away, but, as he soon discovered, Olga had a phenomenal memory and this was not always necessary for her.

During those first few months of working for the FSU, Olga Gray supplied her spymaster with 'a considerable amount of information'. The main problem, for M, was that none of it had any great intelligence value. The other issue was that Olga's chances of being offered a more senior position inside the Communist Party had plummeted, for reasons that were out of her control.

'Efforts are being made to send spies into the Party,' revealed the Communist-run *Daily Worker* on 29 March, 1932, very soon after Olga had begun to work at the FSU. The wife of a Party member had been approached by a Special Branch detective who had tried to recruit her as an informant. Instead, she had reported him to her comrades.

'Revolutionary vigilance against spies and provocateurs is an essential part of the working-class fight against war,' thundered the newspaper where Graham Pollard worked. There had never been a good time to be a government agent inside the British Communist movement, but the weeks after this exposé were especially tough.

M was livid. This botched Special Branch recruitment had caused 'an acute attack of spy mania, and I have already heard from two sources that instructions are being given to [Communist Party] Locals to tighten up considerably, so as to make it very difficult for any unauthorised persons to obtain details of Party procedure etc. Recruits are to be examined more carefully, and the closest investigation is to be made into the reliability of persons offering themselves as members of the CP. It will be readily understood that this sort of thing increases the difficulties of our work most enormously, for it always has the inevitable results of making leading comrades extremely reticent, even to those whom they believe to be quite trustworthy.'

Olga could only bide her time. She continued to pass on to M any titbits she picked up at the FSU, yet by the summer of 1932, after half a year as an MI5 agent, she had not been offered a job as a secretary by a senior Party member. Instead, Olga had reached the point when, as M put it, 'an agent becomes a piece of the furniture, so to speak: that is, when persons visiting an office do not consciously notice whether the agent is there or not'. The only danger was that she had blended in too well and had been all but forgotten.

M/2, M's other female secretary, was not doing any better. On 9 February, 1932, she made what appears to have been her first report, telling M that Reg Bishop, a prominent Communist, would soon be 'coming into local activity in S. E. London'. This was quickly followed by M/2's second report, several days later: 'Bishop is not now going into the S. E. Local.'

M's experiment with female agents was not working. Both women were being outperformed by his more experienced male agents, such as Graham Pollard. In June 1932, Pollard reported to M that the same Reg Bishop had set sail for the USSR. Pollard also supplied the date of Bishop's departure and noted the presence on board this ship of workers from the Government Experimental Aircraft Works at Aldershot. This was precisely the kind of valuable, timely intelligence that neither Olga nor M/2 had been able to provide. As M pointed out, these government employees travelling to the Soviet Union 'might be pumped for very valuable information while in Russia'. He was right. As a result of that trip, two of these men, Fredcrick Meredith and Wilfred Vernon, who would later become a member of Parliament, were recruited to a Soviet spy ring.

Meanwhile, M's agent in Liverpool, M/4, continued to send in useful, if unspectacular, details from the Merseyside Local. The Glaswegian gun examiner, M/5, was also getting closer to the action. Although some of his reports revealed little more than the peccadilloes of senior Party figures, in the summer of 1932, to M's delight, this agent was asked to take part in illegal Party work. Back in London, the *Daily Express* columnist, M/8, was still feeding his spymaster crumbs from the edges of the Communist movement.

The only drawback to using him was his refusal to meet in the lobbies of grungy hotels or in any other out-of-the-way place. M/8 was a more flamboyant character and insisted on expensive lunches at the Overseas Club, the Grosvenor Hotel or Hatchett's, the scene of M's ill-advised lunches with Colonel Carter of Special Branch. Although most of M/8's intelligence was gossipy and low-grade, this agent was important to M. He may not have been a penetration agent like Graham Pollard or Olga Gray, for he had been recruited long ago as a Communist student, but he was an 'access agent' whose material from lower down the Communist food chain often made sense of the higher-grade information coming in to M.

These four agents were valuable to the new MI5 spymaster, yet by the summer of 1932 there was another source who was becoming one of the most prized assets in his stable of agents. This was a barrister who belonged to the Middle Temple, one of the four Inns of Court. He was referred to in all MI5 reports as 'M/7'. He gave free legal advice to *Labour Monthly* and the *Daily Worker,* two well-known left-wing publications, which involved checking copy for libellous material and giving advice about future legal actions against the Communist Party. This gave him access to sensitive details about how the Party was being run. M/7's intelligence was remarkable in terms of how much of it there was, its value and, ultimately, the fact that it was being delivered at all. Arguably M/7's greatest achievement as an MI5 agent was that he was able to persuade the people he worked for that he was a genuine Communist, given his personal background.

Although the identity of M/7 has remained a secret for many years, it can now be revealed. Later on in his career, as we shall see, M instructed M/7 to have lunch with a political extremist who had come to the attention of MI5. The meal was not a success. M/7 found his target to be 'very deaf' and 'almost childish in what he says'. Yet the feeling was mutual, for the man he was spying on later described M/7 as 'rather an odd fish'. We know this because his target kept a diary, which was deposited with the National Maritime Museum long after his death. Elsewhere in this same diary entry M/7 is referred to as 'Nunn – a barrister'.

M/7 was Vivian Hancock-Nunn. He may not have been a well-known or particularly successful barrister, but he was a superb MI5 agent. This was largely because of his canny ability to play a part, which M had correctly identified. Hancock-Nunn's father had been the president of the local Conservative Party Association, which may explain how he first came to M's attention; his wife, Eileen Hewitt, was also a staunch Conservative and the daughter of Edgar Hewitt, KC, a prominent 'Die-hard' Conservative. Indeed, everything about Vivian Hancock-Nunn screamed dyed-in-the-wool Conservative. He had grown up in a large country house, Lealands, in Sussex, and was fond of hunting, shooting and fishing. His ancestor was Thomas Hancock, famous for the discovery of vulcanisation, and his family had made a fortune in the rubber industry. He was a cricket-playing, privately educated, straight-down-the-line younger son of a landed country squire. Yet M had felt that Hancock-Nunn might be able to pass himself off to suspicious Communists in the offices of the *Daily Worker* and *Labour Monthly* as an ardent Socialist, as he successfully did.

Like his spymaster, Vivian Hancock-Nunn saw Moscow as the greatest threat to the future of his country, and the British Communist Party as the enemy within the gates. Although Hancock-Nunn found some of the people he spied on 'quite agreeable to talk to, for a short time', most left him cold. In a novel he later wrote under a pseudonym, some years after leaving MI5, Hancock-Nunn railed against the 'haughty disdain' of Marxists very similar to the ones he had been reporting on for M, men and women for whom economics was 'a subject which they seemed to regard as peculiarly their own and on which nobody was so well informed as themselves'. Yet Hancock-Nunn kept at it, diligently passing on to his spymaster every pertinent detail, while doing valuable legal work for people he did not much like.

Just a few miles from the offices of the *Daily Worker,* where both Hancock-Nunn and Pollard worked part-time, Olga Gray had started to flourish among the well-meaning progressives of the Friends of the Soviet Union. 'The increased efficiency of the administration of the FSU began to be noised abroad in Communist circles,' wrote M, until 'officials in other Communist organisations began to be a little jealous of the "find" of the FSU'.

One of those Communists who heard about Olga's secretarial prowess was Isobel Brown, a tiny political activist from Newcastle-upon-Tyne who had been jailed previously for making an inflammatory speech to a group of British soldiers. More recently, the Home Office had described her as an important Communist 'engaged in some particular form of revolutionary activity'. MI5 thought she was involved in 'anti-militarist work' and suspected her of having recently gone to the Soviet Union for 'a special course of instruction'. But they had no further details. In August 1932, that looked set to change after Isobel Brown offered Olga Gray a part-time position at the two organisations where she herself worked. Both were Communist fronts with a more direct connection to Moscow than the FSU.

M was thrilled, about Olga's new position as much as the manner in which she had acquired it. Rather than volunteer her services, Olga had waited for the approach to be made to her. 'It is an immense safeguard if an agent can be actually invited by some member of an organisation to join up', for if the agent's bona fides were ever questioned, it would always be remembered 'that the agent did not in any way thrust himself forward'. It had taken almost a year, but M's experiment with female secretaries was at last starting to pay off.

AN AUTHOR WITH
UNPREDICTABLE HOURS

M liked his agents' cover stories to contain an element of truth, and, as we know, Olga had been told to pretend that she was working for an author with 'unpredictable hours'. But this does not really explain why her spymaster now began to write a book.

Many years earlier M had written short detective stories, and although he had made it into print on several occasions around this time, it had not been for his fiction. In 1923, M had had several articles published in the magazine *Animal Ailments*. These were well-informed pieces about how to treat eczema and mange in pets or the dangers of inbreeding, all surprisingly lively, in spite of the subject matter. Now ten years later, he began work on what he hoped would be his first full-length book.

It had nothing to do with animals. Rather than take on a subject he could write about with insight, passion and encyclopaedic knowledge, he chose instead to describe the cartoonish exploits of an imaginary gang of American drug smugglers as they tried to hijack a cruise ship.

Everyone in M's book plays to type. His English toffs say things like 'my hat!' The Italians are emotional. The naval officers are sturdy.

At one point the French maid exclaims 'oh là là!' M gave the American gangsters names including 'Lobo the Killer', 'Eddie the Swede', 'Fingers Reilly' and 'Duke Lyman', the last of whom he describes rather confusingly, in a phrase that speaks for the whole novel, as a man who was 'about as reliable as a tame rattlesnake'.

As M himself acknowledged, his story was full of characters and scenes reminiscent of 'a hundred similar ones in stage comedy-dramas'. Although the plot becomes darker towards the end, with one character ending up in a vat of acid, M's book was intended to be what Graham Greene would call 'an entertainment'. 'They amused me,' said M of this book and another one. 'I don't know whether they amused anybody else.' What they did, instead, was reveal a lot about their author.

M emerges from these books as a diehard devotee of American gangster films, and a writer who owed a lot to Damon Runyon, whose stories inspired the musical *Guys and Dolls*. He also comes across as being suspicious of foreigners or anyone who was Jewish. A similar charge could be levelled at most British novelists writing in this genre during the 1930s. Given that one of M's most trusted agents in later years was the German Jewish actor Ferdy Mayne, and that possibly his only Jewish colleague in MI5, Victor Rothschild, was a man he admired and greatly liked, there is not too much to read into this. It is evidence of the passive anti-Semitism of 1930s Middle England, one that usually melted away when challenged by reality.

These books also reveal something about the man that M aspired to be. An M hero tends to observe a situation before stepping in at the last moment. He is courageous, tough and endlessly patient. He can throw a good punch, but does so only in self-defence. He is not above taking the law into his own hands to protect the people he cares about. He has a dry sense of humour and is an excellent judge of character. Above all, he is loyal – loyal to his country and loyal to his friends.

Another feature of M's first book is that the plot does not feature any happily married couples. While the MI5 spymaster slogged away at his first novel, his wife continued to run a pub out on Exmoor. M tried to see her on weekends, but the pressure of work, the distance between them and his desire to finish his thriller made these visits infrequent. Gwladys still saw a lot of her childhood friends, and the pub was loud and jolly, but around this time she began to feel increasingly lonely.

When Gwladys read M's manuscript, perhaps she felt a pang of recognition at the scene in which the hero and heroine are about to consummate their relationship before both pull back. 'You are not my style,' she tells him, 'nor I yours.' Instead, they agree to remain close friends. In a similar sense, M's marriage to Gwladys had become an act of distant companionship. They were two friends who got on well and could make each other laugh, but who seem to have accepted that nothing was going to happen between them sexually, and that for now they were unable to live together.

Gwladys may have been curious about the inspiration for the main character in her husband's first novel. M described his protagonist as a young man who had spent several years on HMS *Worcester* before leaving to become a junior naval officer, just as M had done himself. Yet his physical characteristics are not M's. Instead, he was 'a decent, well-built young chap, little more than a boy, with a rather florid face and bright brown eyes'. Then there is the character's name, which is the giveaway.

The hero in M's first book was called 'Joycey', and he was, very simply, a hybrid of William Joyce and M. The MI5 spymaster could have chosen anyone, yet he decided to splice his own character to that of Joyce, a man he would soon describe as having a 'very violent temper', a 'tendency towards theatricality' and a 'marked conspiratorial complex', the kind of person who would never 'be swayed by arguments where his inherent instincts are touched'. But Joyce's considerable flaws were balanced out, M believed, by his 'boundless physical and moral courage; considerable brain power; tremendous energy and application'. He was 'well-read politically and historically', 'patriotic' and, the ultimate accolade, he had 'a sense of humour'. M was also impressed by the fact that William Joyce had pulled himself up by his own bootstraps. 'It has been alleged that he is a pompous, conceited little creature,' he went on, 'but a tendency to agree with this should be weighed up against the fact that he has made his way in his own small world entirely by his own efforts and in the face of very considerable difficulties.' He was also 'very loyal to his friends'.

M had a strange and abiding fascination with this man. Although he resented Joyce's cheating on his wife, Hazel, the woman M had once loved, his marriage to her only drew the two men closer together, and M was a frequent visitor to the Joyce household. While there were elements of Joyce's character that M obviously disliked, he was drawn to the others in spite of himself – Joyce's unpredictability, his virility, his learning and his wicked, lively intelligence. They were also bound forever by their experiences together at the heart of K, and that fateful meeting at the Lambeth Baths when Joyce had been attacked. Perhaps the MI5 spymaster still experienced flickers of guilt about this, feeling that he should have done more to warn Joyce of what was coming that night, which distorted the way he saw his old comrade.

Unaware that he was being used to inspire a character in M's novel, William Joyce had taken a job by then as a teacher at the Victoria Tutorial College in London, and now had a young family to support. He had also enrolled recently for a PhD in philosophy and psychology at King's College London, and his future seemed to lie in academia.

Although Joyce may have reminisced occasionally about his days with the British Fascists, like most former members of K he recognised that this organisation was in its death throes. Fascism in continental Europe seemed to have an irresistible momentum behind it. In Britain it was going nowhere. Yet unknown to either Joyce or M, by 1932, one Englishman was mapping out a very different future for the movement.

Sir Oswald Mosley, a colourful former MP for the Labour Party, had recently gone to meet Mussolini in Rome. On the same trip he had visited Nazi Germany, and was so impressed by what he saw that on his return he decided to start a new Fascist party in Britain.

Mosley contacted the extant Fascist groups to propose a fresh alliance with a visionary new leader at its head – him. The men he approached at the British Fascists were two of M's former comrades: Neil Francis-Hawkins, a doctor's son who had once been touted as a future leader of the movement; and Geoff Roe, a schoolmaster from Lewisham who asked to be known as E. G. Mandeville-Roe. Both men recognised that the BF was close to collapse and there was little to lose by joining Mosley's alliance. They also felt that it was time to embrace a more European version of Fascism, including its pronounced anti-Semitism.

Francis-Hawkins and Mandeville-Roe formally proposed to the leadership of the British Fascists that they join Mosley. Rotha Lintorn-Orman wanted nothing to do with this, and she voted against the proposal. So too did every representative of the BF Women's Units. The motion was rejected. Rather than accept this, Francis-Hawkins and Mandeville-Roe joined Mosley's new venture anyway, taking with them several senior BF figures and the all-important membership list.

In the subsequent issue of *British Fascism*, the BF's paper, both Francis-Hawkins and Mandeville-Roe were named as disgraced former members who were now to be deprived of the 'Order of the Fasces'. Curiously, on the same list of prominent members who had recently jumped ship, there was the name 'Mr Knight'.

Although C, the head of MI6, had assured the Secret Service Committee several years earlier that M had left the British Fascists in 1927, it seems that he did not formally part company with them until 1932, almost a year after joining MI5. Of course, if he was questioned about this by his colleagues in the Office, he could always say that he was merely keeping tabs on this group. Yet given the feeble state of British Fascism at that time it is doubtful that any of his colleagues were particularly interested, at that point, in M's Fascist past.

Several months later, Sir Oswald Mosley launched his new political party. His previous venture had been the New Party. This one was to be called the British Union of Fascists (BUF). Among Mosley's earliest recruits were Francis-Hawkins, Mandeville-Roe and another of M's old friends, William Joyce, who had decided to get back into politics.

HEART AND SOUL

One of the senior figures in the office where Olga Gray had begun to work was called Percy Glading. He had full lips, lank hair and wore large round glasses that made him look like an overgrown schoolboy. Glading was quick-witted and likeable. He was also thought to be one of the most dangerous Communists in Britain.

For years MI5, MI6 and Special Branch had been trying to uncover Glading's connection to Moscow. Now M had an agent inside this man's office. It was up to him to exploit the situation, and to do that he needed Olga to become one of Glading's closest confidantes.

It was no secret to those who knew Percy Glading well where and when his political radicalisation had taken place. Although he later described his childhood in the East End of London as full of 'the usual joys experienced by hundreds of poor proletarian families', it was not this in itself that had turned him into a dedicated Communist. The eldest of five children, Glading had left school at twelve to provide his family with another income. His first job was delivering milk, which he claimed to have done 'from 6 a.m. to 1 a.m. each morning including Sundays', one way of saying he worked very hard, and at the age of fourteen he became a railway engineer, before taking a job as an engineer's turner and universal grinder at the Woolwich Arsenal, a vast military-industrial complex that supplied weapons and munitions to the Army and Royal Navy. Aged seventeen, he became an active trade unionist and a member of the Social Democratic Party. During the First World War, he refused to fight on political grounds, and after being laid off towards the end of the conflict Glading decided to join the Communist Party.

Yet the first great rupture in his political firmament took place several years later, in 1925, after the Party sent him out to India. His instructions were both simple and open-ended: he was to foment opposition to British rule. What he witnessed, many miles away from home, left an ache of injustice that would remain with him for the rest of his life. The Indian police that Glading saw were more violent than their British counterparts, and the workers were more clearly oppressed than those at home. Indeed, the conditions in India often resembled those in Britain during the mid-nineteenth century, when Marx had produced his revolutionary critique of capitalism. Glading came home full of zeal. But his political radicalisation was not yet complete.

MI5 described Glading at this time as 'a red-hot Communist'. In May 1928, Special Branch argued that he should 'be dismissed at the first opportunity'. He was subsequently hauled in by his boss at the Woolwich Arsenal, which was run by the Admiralty, and told that unless he severed all ties to the Communist Party he would lose his job.

Glading was outraged. 'I refuse to renounce my beliefs or membership of the Communist Party. I did not adopt my present political views lightly or thoughtlessly, but after deep study and considerable experience of working-class life.' More to the point, 'I was not aware that the Admiralty employed Communists, Labourists,

Liberals, and Tories, but engineers and craftsmen, and that the test was fitness for the job. Now it appears we are to have a test of technical fitness and a test of political fitness.'

He appeared to be right. From a legal standpoint the Admiralty was unable to sack an employee based on his or her democratically held opinions. Yet the government did not see Communism as a legitimate political belief. It was classed instead as a revolutionary ideology, and as such Glading was sacked.

The dismissal of Percy Glading became national news. Those on the Left fulminated against his employers at the Admiralty, yet the decision stood. Glading had joined the aristocracy of the dispossessed. Very soon after, he disappeared. The next time he popped up on MI5's radar, several years later, he was a man reborn.

Percy Glading, Mark II, was bolder, faster and more furtive. He had been radicalised, but nobody in MI5 knew quite how or by whom. Glading had a new wife, Rosa, whose parents were Russian and who had worked for various companies bankrolled by the Soviet Union. He had also been promoted to National Organiser of the Communist Party and was a paid official at a Soviet front organisation, where he was joined in late 1932 by one of MI5's only female agents, Olga Gray.

Olga's new working day began with a journey from her flat in an elegant Regency-style crescent near Holland Park, in west London, to the office that she shared with Percy Glading and others on a noisy, traffic-jammed road in Clerkenwell. Here she got on with various jobs for the two Communist front organisations, while also carrying out her duties for MI5. She typed up or copied documents, processed bills, filed away papers and otherwise kept an eye out for anything that might interest M. At the end of each day she wrote down useful intelligence or went straight to M's flat to pass it on to her spymaster, as well as the various animals, fish and insects also in attendance. M's rooms continued to resemble a miniature zoo. There was no sign of this letting up; indeed, he was now becoming known among the keepers at London Zoo as a man who would take on almost any small animal in need of a temporary home.

Olga's reports rapidly provided M, and his colleagues in MI5, with a detailed portrait of the two front organisations operating out of No. 53 Gray's Inn Road. Though both were controlled by the Comintern, they were very different in character, and represented two consecutive phases of Moscow's engagement with the West.

The older of the two was the League Against Imperialism (LAI), which had once been intended as the focal point for the global anti-imperialist movement, such as it was, and a counterpoint to the League of Nations – hence the 'League' in its title. Yet the LAI's inability to do much more than echo Stalin's thinking, including his wrong-headed 'Class Against Class' policy, which urged Communists to attack moderate left-wingers, meant that the LAI came across as little more than a clumsy Soviet tool. Which it was.

The other organisation for which Olga now worked was the Anti-War Movement (AWM), which seemed comparatively young, friendly and open-minded, like the LAI after an intense course of media training. The AWM embodied the new Comintern policy, which happened to be a complete reversal of its previous one. In 1933, on April Fool's Day, of all days, Moscow announced that Communists all over the world were now to embrace their former enemies on the Left and form a 'United Front' or 'Popular Front' against Fascism.

'We no longer referred to ourselves as "Bolsheviks",' wrote one Communist, Arthur Koestler, 'nor even as Communists – the public use of the word was now rather frowned at in the Party – we were just simple, honest, peace-loving anti-Fascists and defenders of democracy.' Olga was now a Conservative pretending to be a Communist, surrounded by Communists pretending to be Liberals.

The new line from Moscow may have been a complete U-turn,

but it seemed to work. The Party was attracting not only more recruits but also men and women from a wider range of backgrounds, a shift reflected in the type of people now being seen at No. 53 Gray's Inn Road. One of those who seemed to have fallen for the new Comintern policy was a British civil servant and former Royal Air Force pilot called Dickson. Olga often saw him in conversation with Glading.

Although Olga was now getting close to Percy Glading, M needed her closer. The main difficulty was that she only worked in the office part-time. Another problem was the presence there of so many disciplined Party members, all looking out for government agents like her. Olga could never appear to be gravitating towards Glading, the one man in that office who was clearly involved in underground work. Instead, she had to show herself succumbing slowly to the logic of Communism, until she became what she later called a 'Moscow-sympathising trendy'.

The problem was, this guise bore increasingly little resemblance to her real life. In October 1932, only weeks after she started work for the two Communist front organisations, Olga decided to join the Ealing Ladies Hockey Club. She went straight into the First XI at left back, and was even selected for one of the Middlesex County teams. Most of her new friends were well-off, privately educated girls who lived in Kensington – the very opposite of Percy Glading and everything he stood for.

The life of all undercover agents is remote. It becomes more so if, like Olga, they end up operating in a city that they do not know. Although she saw a lot of M, Olga had begun to miss female company. Joining the hockey club was a risk, but she desperately needed to take the edge off her loneliness. Olga had even considered the idea of asking her mother to move in with her.

Before that could happen, Olga Gray had a breakthrough at work. It was suggested to her 'that she should rearrange her time, in order that her secretarial work for the author should become a secondary matter', and she could start working full-time at No. 53 Gray's Inn Road.

This changed everything. 'The tempo of her work increased,' wrote M, with some relief, 'and the value of her information also.' Now his agent 'was frequently brought into touch with other prominent Communists and revolutionary figures; and on more than one occasion, she was able to assist the Department in identifying important persons who were doing underground work in one or other section of the Communist movement'.

The value of Olga's reports improved, and so did their quality. By now she knew, without needing to be reminded, that a fragment of overheard conversation meant nothing to her MI5 spymaster without a description of who had said it, to whom, where, when and, ideally, with a sense of how the person had said it. As well as reporting the names of individuals, Olga frequently provided descriptions of their appearance, complexion, eye colour, height and any distinguishing features. If she really wanted to impress M, she would also supply the person's address. When unsure about any detail, if she felt just a shiver of uncertainty, she knew to hold back.

'Detective work,' wrote M, 'means that observations must be accurate; it means having a great deal of patience and, most important of all, avoiding hasty conclusions without being able to prove them.' Or as Le Carré's Jack Brotherhood put it: 'Never make it up if you think you don't know and ought to.'

Olga was providing M with a landslide of valuable information about the two leading Comintern-controlled organisations in Britain. She was even being taken on trips to mainland Europe with delegations from the Anti-War Movement. Although no reports from these trips have been released by MI5, perhaps because M was wary of documenting agents' activities in MI6 territory, these journeys not only improved Olga's 'position and prestige, but also produced for the Department a great deal of information regarding the ramifications of the work being done by this body'. She was gathering 'a vast amount of information pertaining to Communist affairs,' wrote M, and was rapidly cementing her position as one of his most valuable agents. Indeed, things were going so well with Olga that M felt that he could pull out the other agent he had working intermittently in the same office.

In an interview Olga gave fifty years later, she referred to having seen in the office where she worked the thriller writer 'John Dickson Carr', adding that he 'was also an MI5 agent'.

This is remarkable. Although this Pennsylvania-born novelist is less well known today, John Dickson Carr was, at the time, internationally renowned as the master of the 'locked-room' murder mystery. Writers sometimes become spies, spies often become writers and, in one sense, the thought of Dickson Carr as an MI5 agent sounds about right. Yet his biographer Douglas Greene was confused, as well he might have been.

There is no hard evidence that John Dickson Carr was connected to the LAI or AWM, let alone MI5 and M. Nor did anyone else in the office remember a famous American novelist working there. Greene suggested that Olga might have been referring to a different man. He was right.

Olga did spot an author called J. Dickson, but it was not John Dickson Carr. The man she saw, codenamed M/3, was Jimmy Dickson. He was a gregarious, fast-talking Londoner who wrote novels under the name Grierson Dickson and who, by the end of the decade, had become a famous thriller writer – hence the confusion with the other best-selling J. Dickson.

Although Jimmy Dickson later became an MI5 officer, and has been identified as such, his long career beforehand as one of M's agents has never been described in print, let alone the details of how he and his spymaster met and why M was so reluctant to describe Dickson's past.

M and Dickson got to know each other after they both joined the British Fascisti. This was in 1923 (around the same time that Joyce became a member). Several articles written by Dickson make it all but certain that he too belonged to the right-wing paramilitary group K. At some point after this, M asked Dickson to infiltrate the Communist Party on his behalf. By the time M was moved to MI5, Dickson, one of his old comrades from K, was a trusted agent and one of his closest friends.

Jimmy Dickson was quick and restless. Like Olga he had a superb memory. He smoked up to a hundred cigarettes a day and could survive on very little sleep. As a boy, he had had problems with his heart and had been unable to play any sport. No doubt those hours spent on the sidelines had helped turn him into something of a watcher. After a few months as a teenager in the RAF, at the very end of the war, he had started to write in his spare time and would later claim that for many years every story he had ever submitted to a magazine ended up being published – in stark contrast to his spymaster's record. He was a womaniser, and briefly tried his hand as an actor. In 1930, as one of M's subagents inside the Communist Party, he had a comedy sketch of his performed on the BBC. Yet the strangest detail about Dickson was what he did for a living.

Throughout his career as one of M's agents, Jimmy Dickson was a civil servant at the Ministry of Labour. He had started to work there in the early 1920s, and was almost certainly the man referred to angrily by the Permanent Secretary at the Home Office, in 1931, when he grilled the head of MI6 about M's network.

The idea of using a civil servant as an MI6 informant had been shocking at the time, and had helped precipitate the Treaty of Westminster. It was even more shocking now, several years later, given that M knew what the repercussions could be. A different spymaster might have accepted that he could no longer use Jimmy Dickson. But M refused to let his old comrade go. He rated him for his memory, his energy, his ambition and his ability to compose a lucid report. Above all, he trusted Jimmy Dickson. The feeling was evidently mutual. Dickson would soon ask M to become godfather to his son. Clearly, for M, the risk of being hauled in front of the Secret Service Committee was eclipsed by the value of having inside the Communist Party an old friend from his days inside K. This may also explain why M refused to run his section from the Office, for fear that Dickson's identity might leak out to his colleagues in MI5. From the moment he joined MI5, it seems, M was trying to cover up elements of his Fascist past.

Equally valuable to M was M/5, his Scottish gun examiner, who had just been 'initiated' into the 'illegal section of the Party' and who now belonged to an underground Communist cell in Glasgow. M/5's reports were starting to sound like excerpts from a John Buchan novel. At one secret meeting he had been told about a 'specially trained comrade from Russia' who was coming over to England 'to consult with "the big cheese"'. M/5 had won the trust of his fellow Communists. Very soon, it seemed, he would be uncovering details of actual espionage.

Graham Pollard, the bookseller of Soho, was still married to a devout Communist who knew nothing of his MI5 work. Pollard continued to supply intelligence from the *Daily Worker* office, some of which overlapped with material sent in by the gentleman barrister masquerading as a diehard Communist, Vivian Hancock-Nunn, who was now producing the best intelligence of his career. This included juicy scraps about the legal standing of the Party or how the Communists were planning to defend themselves during a forthcoming trial, information that could easily have been passed on to the Crown prosecution.

By 1933, M's agents had blended seamlessly into the fabric of the British Communist movement. When a leading Party man called Jimmy Shields ran into the offices of the *Daily Worker* shouting that 'all incriminating documents' must 'be immediately burnt', because the police were coming, one of the men he yelled at was Graham Pollard. Two months later, Shields attended a celebratory dinner for the *Daily Worker* at which he was handed Tom Wintringham's menu card to sign as a memento of the evening. He made his scrawl just a few inches from a signature which read: 'Vivian Hancock-Nunn'. When Glading, a close friend of Shields, worried that there might be an undercover agent working in his office, he shared his concerns with Jimmy Dickson.

The so-called Cambridge Spies, including Kim Philby, Guy Burgess, Anthony Blunt and Donald Maclean, a group of British-born Soviet agents who successfully penetrated Whitehall during the 1930s and 1940s, are seen today as some of the most notorious traitors of the twentieth century. It is often assumed that they got away with their deception for so long because they belonged to the British 'establishment', and that this group had a peculiar inability to suspect its own. Yet the same charge can be levelled at just about any self-contained group, including the British Communist Party during the 1930s, as M's agents demonstrated.

By getting his operatives to speak in the right way, read the right books and make friends with the right people, M had assimilated his agents into the Communist movement with enormous skill. Under his direction, Olga Gray, Jimmy Dickson, Vivian Hancock-Nunn and Graham Pollard, among others, gained the trust of those that they were spying on. What made this so impressive was that, unlike the Cambridge Spies, M's agents had ventured into an alien world. Philby and Blunt were surrounded by friends from school, from university and from the clubs they belonged to. M's agents were not. One of them, Pollard, had even married into the movement he had been told to infiltrate. As well as learning a different way of speaking and being, these agents had managed to make themselves small and apparently insignificant. Pollard, Hancock-Nunn, Dickson and Gray were all lively and at times combative characters, yet to carry out their work for MI5 each one agreed to hide their personality behind a wall of incuriosity. They became, as M put it, 'grey people'. Their job was to remember everything, in the hope that nobody remembered them.

The man controlling them had a different and often more demanding task. As well as safeguarding his agents, by seeing that they did not get too close to one another, or make mistakes that might jeopardise their cover, M had to manipulate his band of informants in such a way that they could keep up a continuous flow of intelligence and be able to answer specific questions from his colleagues in MI5. This was delicate, challenging work. M was running his agents in the way that he had once led his jazz band after the war, keeping an eye on individual performances while moderating the tempo, faster there, slower here, keeping the melody in mind as much as the overall direction of the piece, and, like all the best jazz band leaders, he was always ready to improvise.

By 1933, the greatest threat to British domestic security continued to be Communism, be it the possibility of espionage, subversion or sabotage in the event of war. The intelligence produced by M's agents over the last two years had transformed MI5's understanding of the Party and was now beginning to affect government policy. For more than a decade, the Director of MI5, Sir Vernon Kell, had pressed for an Incitement to Disaffection Bill, which would make it easier to control subversion inside the Armed Forces. Only now, armed with so much intelligence on left-wing activities, much of it from M Section, was his case taken more seriously. By the end of 1934, to Kell's huge satisfaction, this bill was passed into law.

In late 1933, Kell gave M a Christmas bonus. The young spymaster was overjoyed. He wrote back to his chief, a man old enough to be his father, and one who was perhaps starting to replace Makgill as a father figure, telling him 'how very happy I am working for the show, and also how very much I appreciate the marvellous way in which my small efforts are backed up by all concerned'. He might have finished there, but M went on. 'I am heart and soul in the work (without I hope being a fanatic) and it is grand to be doing something which is really of use & which is so very pleasant at the same time.'

This last sentence is revealing. While it underlines his hatred of Communism, which we know about anyway, it also introduces the idea that within the Office he was known – jokingly, perhaps – for having a deep-seated loathing of the Left, and being an individual whose politics were further to the Right than anyone else's. It was no secret within MI5 that M had once belonged to the British Fascists, but he had always been able to say his membership had been purely operational. Yet as his colleagues got to know him better, some of them must have wondered whether his time among so many right-wing extremists had changed the way he saw the world, perhaps more than he realised.

For all the good work that M and his agents had done, they had not found incontrovertible proof of Soviet espionage. No foreign spies had been arrested. MI5 still needed evidence of links between Moscow Centre and the Communist underground in Britain, presuming these connections even existed. Nor was it true that all of M's agents were flourishing.

M's other female secretary, M/2, was struggling to produce useful intelligence. She had attended meetings of various left-leaning organisations in the hope of being picked up, 'trailing her coat' as Olga Gray had done, but nobody had taken the bait. M/2 had been active for more than a year, and it must have been tempting for M to let her go. But he chose to keep her on. Spying is watching, and spying is waiting. There might yet be time for this agent to prove her worth.

Her counterpart, Olga Gray, continued to edge closer to Percy Glading. She reported that Glading and others 'appear to be engaged on some matters of a confidential nature'. Glading had also been heard to mention Communists lying 'doggo' in the Woolwich

Maxwell Knight as an infant.

Knight as a naval cadet.

Tythegston Court, in Wales, where Knight went as a boy when his family ran out of money.

Sir George Makgill,
industrialist, Freemason,
and terrifying interviewer.

Knight as a jazz band leader. He
described his group as 'London's
first small, hot combination'.

Sidney Bechet, the legendary jazz musician who gave Knight clarinet lessons.
COURTESY OF DANIEL BECHET.

Sir Desmond Morton, of MI6, who ran Knight during the 1920s.

The Royal Oak, Withypool, scene of Knight's exile from London.

Olga Gray, or 'Miss X', the secretary who brought down a Soviet spy ring.
COURTESY OF VALERIE LIPPAY.

Eric Roberts, recruited by M as a teenager, who infiltrated as many as seventeen subversive organisations.
COURTESY OF CRISTA MCDONALD.

Jimmy Dickson,
best-selling novelist, civil
servant, and MI5 agent.

The country squire
who masqueraded as
an ardent socialist:
Vivian Hancock-Nunn
seen here with his wife
outside Lealands, his
family home.

Kathleen Tesch, one of M's most unlikely agents, once found herself almost alone in a room with Hitler.

M posing for his friend and agent Jimmy Dickson.

H. G. Pollard, bookseller, bon vivant, bibliographer, spy.

E. G. Mandeville-Roe, one of many former Fascists to work for M.

Knight's first wife, Gwladys, who died in 1936 of an overdose of painkillers.

© The British Library Board (NATDE014).

Knight on his 1944 wedding day with his new mother-in-law (centre) and his third wife, Susi (right), who survived him. Courtesy of Harry Smith.

Arsenal, waiting to carry out 'jobs', and a secret rendezvous with a man suspected by MI5 of being a Soviet agent. But that was it. There was never anything more detailed. Percy Glading had a knack for remaining just out of reach.

In the offices where Olga worked there was an outer area, for general purposes, and an inner one, where Glading met his trusted comrades. Olga had not yet been allowed into this private sanctum. The same could be said of all M's agents: they had penetrated the outer office of the Communist movement, and they had done this well, but they had not been given access to the safe room. M needed his agents to delve deeper, to take themselves further into this foreign land, but for Olga this was going to be hard.

Just as she needed to come across as an increasingly devout Communist, Olga's mother had moved in with her. Mrs Gray's presence must have reminded her of her past, her childhood, her father and all the niggling insecurities that had once barnacled themselves onto the keel of her personality. Meanwhile, Mrs Gray wondered to herself, and no doubt out loud to Olga, when her twenty-eight-year-old daughter was going to find herself a husband. What surprised Mrs Gray most about Olga – for she did not know that her daughter was working for MI5 – was that she chose to spend so much time with Communists. If it was radical politics she was after, perhaps it would make more sense, given her right-wing background, to join the other new political movement that was starting to take shape.

BLACKSHIRTS

The rise of William Joyce in the British Union of Fascists was fast, but for Joyce himself it was not fast enough. He was one of thousands of men and women who joined this new party soon after its launch. Most were drawn to the commanding presence of its leader, Sir Oswald Mosley, who painted himself as being cosmopolitan, dashing and decisive, a man of destiny who was also wealthy, aristocratic and something of a maverick. He was unusual. Indeed, there was no one else quite like him in British politics at that time. As one shrewd civil servant wrote: Mosley was 'a "hero" in an "heroic" age'.

Unemployment was up. Public spending was down. There were frequent predictions of national bankruptcy. Hardly a week went by without news of another protest, strike or demonstration, including the 'Hunger Marches', in which thousands of unemployed workers tramped down to London to petition the government for jobs. Britain was in need of strong, dynamic leadership. Instead, it was saddled with Stanley Baldwin and Ramsay MacDonald, two able and sensible politicians who came across at that point in their careers as tired and short of ideas.

Mosley was different. For all his pomposity and his vaulting ambition, he was full of plans. Joyce described him as 'the greatest Englishman I have ever known'. It is unlikely that Mosley returned the compliment, partly because the greatest Englishman he had ever known was the one who greeted him each morning in the mirror, yet the Leader, as he asked to be addressed, seemed to admire certain qualities in William Joyce, in particular his ability to fight.

Mosley asked Joyce, once a hardened streetfighter for K, to lead the paramilitary wing of the British Union of Fascists, which was known as the 'I Squad', or just 'I'. This made Joyce a busy man, as most BUF meetings ended in violence. Occasionally, it was started by Communist gangs; otherwise, it was staged or provoked by Joyce's men.

Mosley understood the political value of violence at his rallies. It lent his cause a sense of victimhood and this pulled in new recruits, many of them young men looking for danger and adventure. The toughest were dragooned into Joyce's I Squad, where they received courses in self-defence before turning out at BUF rallies dressed up like European Fascists. The Nazis had only recently come to power, with Hitler installed as the German chancellor, and for many people in Britain it was still possible to feel a certain admiration for this strong new leader, the order he had imposed on his country and the way he had defeated Communism. Mosley was at pains to make the visual connection to Hitler, and made sure that new recruits to the BUF were given military-style haircuts, similar to Joyce's, and wore jackboots, peaked caps, leather belts as wide as cummerbunds and black shirts modelled on Mosley's old fencing tunic.

Joyce was in his element. Just as he enjoyed the dressing up, the militarism and the ferocious anti-Communism, he relished the sense that he was part of a political movement with real momentum behind it, one that seemed to be part of a broader European shift to the Right. It was also the first time that he had ever belonged to a party that was so well funded, even if it was not yet clear where the BUF's money came from.

Above all, the young American liked the feeling that he was being listened to. Soon after being put in charge of the I Squad, Joyce began to speak at BUF events. As an experienced teacher, he was comfortable on stage. He could quote at length from Dryden, Shakespeare and Virgil, and, when he needed to, he could be very funny. 'You would not believe anybody with such mannerisms could be such a mimic,' wrote M. But the key to Joyce's stage appeal was his extraordinary anger, underscored by a hint of vulnerability, which made his performances strangely compelling.

By the summer of 1933, William Joyce was doing so well in the British Union of Fascists that he was asked by Mosley to accompany him as his right-hand man on a forthcoming trip to Berlin. Even though Joyce was a pronounced Germanophile who spoke German and had studied Germanic philology at university, he had never actually visited the country. So, he was understandably excited by the trip. There was one snag. He needed a passport to which he was not legally entitled.

Although Joyce had been brought up to think of himself as British to his core, and he knew that his membership in the BUF depended on his British citizenship, he was in fact an American. On 4 July, 1933, American Independence Day, no less, Joyce lied to the British passport authorities about his place of birth by claiming to be a true-born Briton. With this he secured his passport. In so doing, as he would later find out, he had sentenced himself to death.

Otherwise, his trip to Germany was a success. Mosley had pulled out of the visit shortly before their departure, leaving Joyce to lead the BUF delegation. He met various minor Nazi officials and, alongside Unity Mitford and Diana Guinness, he attended the epic 'Day of Victory' celebrations in Nuremberg, a Wagnerian spectacle involving just under a million participants which left both Mitford and Joyce mesmerised.

On his return Joyce abandoned his plans to become an academic and gave up teaching. Instead, M's old comrade took on the full-time role of Director of Propaganda at the BUF. In the space of no more than a year, William Joyce had become one of the most important figures in a resurgent British Fascist movement. M watched with interest.

Several months later, on 20 November, 1933, after Mosley had been forced by illness to pull out of making a crucial speech, Joyce was asked to take his place on stage. That night he gave an electric, lacerating performance, one that marked him out for the first time as a potential leader of the BUF. John Beckett, a former Labour MP, described this twenty-seven-year-old as 'one of the dozen finest orators in the country'. He seemed to say the unsayable, and do so with relish. Listening to him felt like a transgression. In his speeches he weaved together truisms, quotes, jokes, facts and half-formed prejudices into a coherent narrative, railing against the political establishment, Socialists, intellectuals and democracy itself, which he dismissed as 'a psychopathic expression of inferiority'. He also attacked Jews, claiming that his assailant outside the Lambeth Baths had been not only a Communist man, but a Jew as well. He never let slip that it might have been an Irish woman who disfigured him, or that the right-wing politician he had agreed to protect that night, Jack Lazarus, was himself Jewish. Like so many British Fascists who had joined the movement in the 1920s, Joyce's anti-Semitism was a recently acquired prop that was fast becoming a crutch.

Another of Joyce's new hobby horses was his admiration for Hitler and Mussolini. Although Mosley had appeared earlier that year on a balcony in Rome with the Italian dictator, and BUF delegations had visited Nazi Germany on numerous occasions, the official relationship between the BUF and the Fascist regimes in Italy and Germany remained opaque. Mosley dismissed the rumours that the BUF was being bankrolled by Hitler, Mussolini or both. Yet these allegations did not go away.

The question of Mosley's connection to foreign Fascist regimes was one of the reasons why, three days after Joyce's explosive speech, and shortly before M received a Christmas bonus for his infiltration of the Communist movement, the heads of MI5, Special Branch and the Metropolitan Police met to discuss the problem of Fascism in Britain. Sir Russell Scott, Permanent Secretary at the Home Office, began the meeting by asking 'whether the time had now come when Fascist activities in this country should be watched in the sort of way that Communist activities were watched'. The most recent conviction of a Briton under the Official Secrets Act had not involved a Communist passing intelligence to Moscow, but a Fascist, Norman Baillie-Stewart, conveying secrets to Berlin. The Metropolitan Police Commissioner, Lord Trenchard, agreed with Scott wholeheartedly, and would soon be pushing for the BUF to be outlawed. Yet the Director of MI5 was curiously reserved. Sir Vernon Kell warned that his department was unable to look into Fascism until it had received the necessary funding.

Nonetheless, it was decided that 'MI5 should undertake to look after Fascism in this country in the same way as they look after Communism'. MI5 would deliver monthly summaries to the Home Office of intelligence from the police, Special Branch and its own agents. This appeared to mark a turning point in MI5's approach to British Fascism, but really it was nothing of the sort.

The Home Office would be forced to wait more than half a year before it received a report on Fascism from MI5. By that time there were no MI5 agents inside the BUF, just three casual sources, run by M, who were merely 'quite reliable'. MI5 was even being outperformed at this stage by the Trades Union Congress, which had a spy inside Mosley's party. Kell seemed to be holding back, and it is possible to see why.

In March 1933, eight months before that meeting at the Home Office, the deputy head of MI5's B Division, Guy Liddell, went to

Nazi Germany. His aim was to gather intelligence about the German Communist Party and the Comintern-controlled League Against Imperialism, but this was not an undercover mission. Instead, Liddell spent ten days in Berlin as a guest of the German political police, or Abteilung 1A, later known as the Gestapo.

Guy Liddell was once described by Somerset Maugham as resembling 'a motor salesman, perhaps, or a retired tea planter'. Yet beneath his plump and unprepossessing exterior there lay a shrewd intellect. Liddell was a fine cellist, a skilful dancer and he was brave, too, having been awarded a Military Cross during the last war. But this Smiley-esque character had his blind spots. He frequently displayed a certain deference towards those he felt socially or intellectually inferior to, such as his wife, the Hon. Calypso Baring, who divorced him, and his future MI5 assistant Anthony Blunt, the art historian and Soviet agent, who would ruthlessly befriend and betray him. Liddell's judgement could also go awry on the subjects of German Jews and Communism.

On his return from Berlin, Guy Liddell concluded that although some of the Nazi claims about Jews were exaggerated, 'there have undoubtedly been some very serious cases of corruption in government institutions where the Jews had a firm foothold. For the last ten years it has been extremely noticeable that access to the chief of any department was only possible through the intermediary of a Jew. It was the Jew who did most of the talking and in whose hands the working out of any scheme was ultimately left.' Liddell also noted that 'there is certainly a great deal of "third degree" work going on', that is, torture, and 'a number of Jews, Communists and even Social Democrats have undoubtedly been submitted to every kind of outrage and this was still going on at the time of my departure'. Yet if he did raise any objections to his hosts, as he might have done on his last night in Berlin, over dinner with the senior Nazi official Joachim 'von' Ribbentrop, there is no record of it.

Guy Liddell was neither an anti-Semite nor an advocate of torture, yet he was willing to accept much of what he had been told by his Nazi hosts largely because he wanted to maintain the new working relationship between British and German intelligence. Rather than be critical of the Gestapo, Liddell preferred to focus on their shared enemy. 'The Comintern remained a more serious problem,' he concluded, 'than the Nazi regime.'

We may never know how long this intelligence-sharing relationship between MI5 and the Gestapo lasted, or whether it went both ways, so that material gathered by MI5 was passed to the Nazis, but this understanding helped to cement the belief within MI5 that Communism was the principal threat to British security, not Fascism. This helps to explain why Kell's response to a more thorough investigation of British Fascism was so lacklustre.

When MI5 did at last get to work on this, Kell's tone was decidedly cool. He told local police chief constables that Fascism in Britain was simply a reaction against Communism, and a movement that 'insists on the common interest of all classes in an intensified economic nationalism inspired by patriotic sentiment'. This was not quite an endorsement of BUF philosophy, but nor was it going to make any police chief sit up and take notice. Kell's defensive account of the BUF was repeated in MI5's first report on Fascism, along with a warning against hastily branding anyone opposed to Communism as a Fascist.

For more than a decade, MI5 had seen the British Fascist movement as legal and essentially constitutional. Of course, it contained some troublesome and overenthusiastic patriots, but generally these were not the kind of people to get mixed up in foreign espionage or subversive activities. That was the view held by the Director of MI5 as well as its in-house expert on Fascism – M.

By the time MI5 produced its first report on Fascism, the BUF's membership had rocketed to 50,000. The proprietor of the *Daily Mail,* Lord Rothermere, one of the country's richest men, had recently given his support to Mosley, and the BUF was now spending £3,000 a week on publicity. Sir Oswald Mosley's new party was popular, rich and on the rise. At its helm was a man described by his biographer, Stephen Dorril, as 'the last of the great platform speakers', whose rhetoric pulled in recruits from across the social spectrum, ranging from unemployed Lancastrian cotton workers to the wife of T. S. Eliot. British Fascism had been revived and reinvented under Mosley, and at BUF Headquarters in Chelsea, the 'Black House', where sentries stood guard at the door, a rumour began to circulate about some thirty Conservative MPs who were set to join the BUF. The optimism was almost unbearable.

M had acknowledged some time ago that Mosley's party was 'in distinct opposition to the original organisation', that is, the BF, and that some of the new party's more active members were 'not the type to behave particularly constitutionally should any opportunity for doing otherwise occur', a slightly muddled statement that spoke to the uncertainty M was beginning to feel. Although the BUF was in 'a very disorganised and loose state at the moment', it was, he agreed, 'well worth investigation'.

Yet he refused to believe that Mosley was receiving any money from Hitler or Mussolini. Indeed, M was adamant that 'no evidence whatsoever can be produced to support this contention' and dismissed it as 'quite untrue'.

M was certain of this mainly because none of his sources inside the movement had confirmed the rumour. These casual informants included his old friends William Joyce and E. G. Mandeville-Roe, who had recently met Hitler. Another of his sources was the BUF's Contact Officer. Amazingly, this was M's original spymaster, 'Don,' now Sir Donald Makgill. Ten years after they had been first introduced, their roles had swapped. Having once received reports on the BF from a young Maxwell Knight, 'Don' was now reporting to him from inside the BUF.

For M to have so many trusted friends inside Mosley's organisation was useful, and it kept him, and MI5, up to speed on most of the major developments inside this party. But it also weighed him down with a false sense of certainty. M was so close to the movement that he found it hard to accept any interpretation of its threat that contradicted his own analysis. Only in April 1934, after months of having dismissed the idea, did M finally admit that the BUF *might* be receiving money from overseas.

One of his BUF contacts, 'a far more reliable source' than Sir Donald Makgill, who appears to have been better suited to life as a spymaster than an agent, reported that before Mosley's visit to Rome the BUF coffers had been virtually empty. After his return, they became mysteriously full.

'It is considered,' conceded M, begrudgingly, 'that this is an example of cause and effect.'

The idea that the BUF was now on Mussolini's payroll was worrying, even if there was no hard proof, and it should have elicited a change to M's approach. Yet in the weeks that followed he did not recruit a mass of new agents and direct them at the Fascist movement. Instead, he turned his attention elsewhere. For the first time since joining MI5, M's political past appeared to be influencing his present.

19

COURIER

In May 1934, as Olga and M walked out of a cinema in Leicester Square, a black cat crossed their path. Although neither one was hugely superstitious, both began to wonder about the kind of luck coming their way. The next day Olga had what she later took to be an answer. She was approached at work by the General Secretary of the Communist Party, Harry Pollitt, the man who had once been kidnapped by K, who asked her to undertake a 'special mission'. It would involve 'carrying messages from here to other countries'. Later that day, Percy Glading took her aside to elaborate on this: they wanted her to become a courier for the Comintern.

It is easy to see why. Olga had no criminal record. She was intelligent and scrupulous and had a fantastic eye for detail. She was also a she, which made her far less likely to attract suspicion from either the police or customs officials. These were some of the same qualities that had brought her long ago to the attention of M. The characteristics that had made her an ideal recruit for MI5 looked set to get her a job working for Moscow.

Another facet of Olga's character that her spymaster had come to appreciate was her sense of when to hold back. Pollitt's proposal was the big break she had been working towards for two years. The temptation to accept immediately must have been considerable, yet she resisted it. 'With very becoming self-restraint, Miss "X",' as M later referred to Olga, 'did not appear too keen: when Glading renewed his suggestions, Miss "X" asked him where she would have to go and what she would have to do. The reply was that she would have to go some distance for a short time, to take messages, etc.'

Olga agreed to the mission, and only then did Pollitt reveal that she would be going to India. Their original idea was to send her to Mumbai (Bombay, as it then was), with no plausible cover story and during the monsoon season, 'a time of the year when normal people do not choose to travel to India,' complained M. 'They proposed that she should stay there for a matter of only a few weeks, another unusual circumstance; and the Party showed themselves so out-of-touch with general social matters, that they did not realise that an unaccompanied young Englishwoman travelling to India without some very good reason stood a risk of being turned back when she arrived in India, as a suspected prostitute.'

It was poor tradecraft, as far as M was concerned. He concluded that Glading and Pollitt had not shown 'themselves as being very clever'. Yet it was essential to him that this Comintern operation was a success, both for what it might reveal and so that his agent would be entrusted with more secret work.

To make sure that Olga was not arrested as a prostitute, M devised a more suitable cover story. She was to say that this trip had been her doctor's idea, and that she was going to visit a relative in Mumbai. M conceded that the story was 'rather thin', yet in some ways it needed to be. Olga's cover had to be good enough to get her to India, and back, but not so good that Pollitt and Glading might suspect that she had received help.

Another question for M was whether to alert the Indian authorities to Olga's presence. It would be easy for him to send a telegram to the relevant officials in Mumbai, but there was then a chance that Olga's identity as an MI5 agent might leak out. M's attitude had always been that 'a secret agent should be a secret agent'. Olga would have no protection.

Having accepted Harry Pollitt's proposal, Olga was given a large sum of money and details of an address in Paris. Once there, she would learn more about her onward journey.

As Olga packed her bags on the night before her departure, the scale of her mission must have dawned on her. Only recently she had been a humble typist from Birmingham. Now, Olga Gray was an MI5 agent who had been taken on by the *Otdel Mezhdunarodnykh Svyazey* (OMS), the branch of the Comintern, in Moscow, that supplied Communist Parties around the world with money and directives. Having mastered the art of allowing herself to 'drift along with the tide', as M put it, she would have to be more active, stronger and more assertive. After being an 'extra' over the last few years, it was as if Olga had been told to play the lead, knowing that if she fluffed her lines she could end up in jail or worse.

On 11 June, 1934, Olga Gray set out for Paris. Her spymaster could only imagine what happened next and the scene on the passenger ship as she made her way to India. But this would not have been hard. Most of the action in M's first novel, which was about to be published, was set on an ocean-going liner not dissimilar to the one his agent was about to board.

'If your last cruise was dull try this one!' was the headline on the publicity blurb for M's first book, *Crime Cargo,* published by Philip Allan just three months after Olga left London. M's hope was that his novel would do well enough to provide him with a little extra income. It was not his intention that the book's publication might jeopardise his MI5 operation.

In spite of this, several characters in M's novel were clearly based on individuals who were then under investigation by MI5. 'Kerrigan', a foul-mouthed Scottish engineer in *Crime Cargo,* was obviously modelled on Peter Kerrigan, the leading Scottish Communist who belonged to the same illegal cell as M/5. 'Baldy McGurk', the 'bald-headed pig-eyed Irishman' in the book, was indistinguishable from J. McGuirk Hughes, a former colleague of M's at the Makgill Organisation and now Director of Intelligence at the BUF. Unsurprisingly, the fictional McGurk meets a nasty end. In M's follow-up book, there would be a barrister named 'Vivian' who was identical to his agent Vivian Hancock-Nunn. There is also a Bill Allen who is not dissimilar to the real Bill Allen, then one of Mosley's closest allies.

None of this would have been a problem if M had chosen to write under a pseudonym, yet he did not. This MI5 spymaster even agreed to a series of hammy publicity shots to promote *Crime Cargo,* all taken by the celebrity photographer Howard Coster. Although M usually smoked 'long hand-made cigarettes from a little tobacconist's shop in Sloane Street', he posed in these with a pipe, in an attempt to look like a latter-day Bulldog Drummond. You might expect this from any other debut novelist, but not from MI5's only dedicated agent-runner whose ability to manage his agents depended to a large extent on his anonymity.

M's admission on Exmoor, some years ago, that he had worked occasionally for MI5 and Special Branch was perhaps forgivable, as his espionage career seemed by then to be essentially over. This was different. Choosing to write this book under his own name, given its content, was a huge risk and for little gain. So why did he do it? He appears to have been blinded for a moment by a desire to do more than sell lots of books. He also wanted to be a well-known author. This urge to be seen and known was not new in him. Indeed M's niggling inability to dissemble himself when he needed to was one that recurred throughout his life, and it appears to have had its roots in his childhood.

In M's recollections of growing up, the figure of his father is prominent, until you begin to wonder whether his mother and siblings were there at all. Hugh Knight was 'my ally', he wrote, a kind and sensible man who 'encouraged me in every possible way' and was 'a keen naturalist' with 'a good library'. If ever young Max misbehaved, his father was 'more amused than angry'. When a problem arose, Hugh Knight could be counted on for 'a sensible and rather cunning suggestion'. He was full of integrity, too, and 'never threatened anything that he did not intend to carry out. I wish to goodness that there were more parents like him today.'

It is a portrait that sounds much too good to be true, and almost certainly was. Others recalled Hugh Knight as a distant figure, who was too busy having affairs and spending money on his mistresses to dote on his youngest son. M's depiction of his father reads like a sketch of the father he longed to have. Though it is a mistake to ascribe too much of M's personality to the relationship he had with his father – Hugh Knight is not the master key that opens up M's hinterland – the distance between father and son, and the way that he later obscured this, reveals something about the man he became. One of M's cousins remembered him as a boy who 'tried almost too hard to please adults'. It seems he desperately wanted to impress his father and to get his attention, which was perhaps why he began to collect unusual pets, in the hope that they might pique his father's interest. The legacy of this was that thirty years later, as an MI5 spymaster, he seemed to have buried inside him a troubling desire to be known and recognised, even if it ran counter to the most basic requirements of his job.

What can't have made any of this easier for M, as he counted down the days to the publication of his novel, was that one of his agents had suddenly become a best-selling author himself. In July of that year, just two months before M's book was published, Graham Pollard and John Carter released their book, *An Enquiry into the Nature of Certain*

Nineteenth Century Pamphlets. Despite its unpromising title, this was a thrilling account of their investigation into a series of literary forgeries. The quality of their investigative work, wrote *The Times,* was worthy 'of Sherlock Holmes'. Ian Fleming later called this book 'a superb piece of detective work'. Pollard and Carter's work was hailed as 'perhaps the most dramatic, and certainly the most dramatically presented, piece of literary detection ever published'. Its authors were 'first notorious, then famous'.

Pollard was thrilled. M less so, mainly because of the impact on his agent's work. M/1's reports had become less frequent over the last year, and there were signs that Pollard was edging away from the Communist movement, having separated from his Communist wife. M's response was to coax Vivian Hancock-Nunn into covering more of Pollard's patch. Meanwhile, M/4 and M/5 kept up their drip-feed of information from Liverpool and Glasgow. With Olga away, Jimmy Dickson began to report from No. 53 Gray's Inn Road once again. Although M/2 was still struggling to produce useful intelligence, M judged that she was able to keep going and around this time he urged her to join a trade union. M also had an agent in Birmingham, and others elsewhere in the country.

For almost any other spymaster, this would be too many agents to run. Yet like an attentive mother hen, M was able somehow to keep abreast of his many agents and rarely seemed to lose sight of them. No doubt he was relieved, at around this time, when he heard that one of his charges had made it home.

After forty-seven days away, Olga had made it back to London. There followed a long debrief with her spymaster.

Her first challenge had been to smuggle Pollitt's money into France. Her solution was ingenious, and was not one that any of M's male agents would have come up with. She hid the cash in her sanitary towels.

This worked perfectly, and she took the money to an address in Paris. Here she found Percy Glading waiting for her. Seeing him in the French capital must have felt illicit yet familiar, like an office romance. They had known each other as colleagues for several years, but this was the first time they had been together as part of an illegal Soviet operation. Glading converted the money into US dollars and returned it to Olga, along with instructions and questions for the leadership of the Indian Communist Party. Now all she had to do was take these to an address in Mumbai.

From Paris, Olga almost certainly travelled to Marseille, where she boarded a ship bound for India, a 'vile little boat', as she called it, probably a P&O mail packet taking post and a handful of passengers to Australia. The journey was mostly uneventful, and Olga had little to do other than attempt to mark the banknotes with the invisible ink M had given her. She was also busy fending off the unwanted advances of a male admirer, who proposed marriage towards the end of the trip. Olga was not interested, and later said that the reason he had done this was that she 'was the only single girl travelling'. Still, she found it hard to think that anyone would find her attractive.

Olga negotiated the Mumbai port authorities with her customary cool and continued to the Taj Mahal Hotel, where M had told her to look up an old friend of his, a jazz band conductor. This was probably Crickett Smith, who had once played with M's former teacher, the legendary Sidney Bechet. This jazz conductor helped Olga find a boarding house, where she prepared for the next phase of her mission.

M's agent had arrived in Mumbai at a tense moment in the history of Indian industrial relations. Over the past few months, there had been strikes and worker-led protests in Kurla, Shelapur, Nagpur, Delhi and Kanpur as well as Mumbai, the epicentre of the illegal Indian Communist movement, where the police had recently opened fire on a 'riotous mob of over a thousand strikers'. The Delhi Intelligence Bureau, the Indian equivalent of MI5, understood that the Comintern wanted to 'render all the aid within their power' to the Indian Communists and that 'the channel' for this 'lies through Great Britain'. They were expecting a Comintern courier to arrive from Britain at exactly this time bearing messages and money. But they had not been tipped off about M's agent.

Olga delivered the Comintern's cash and messages without being arrested. The Indian Communists told her to return to the boarding house where she awaited further instructions.

The days that followed were gruelling. It was monsoon season, and Olga spent most of her time indoors. Each morning she looked out onto a sky that was heavy with thick, blueish cloud. The heat was muggy and close. As the rain emptied down, her mind began to play tricks on her. Olga became convinced that one of the Indian Communists had been arrested, and that he had revealed her name. She was housebound, lonely and scared, and later described those days in the boarding house as 'the first time I had been really afraid', adding, 'I realised I wasn't playing spy games any longer.'

Most of M's agents would experience at some point a similar moment of disillusion. The romantic depiction of espionage in novels and films could only take them so far, making the initial experience of life as an agent thrilling and fun. But there would almost always come a point when this wore off and either the danger of the work or just the quotidian drudgery of what they were doing finally kicked in. M's challenge as a spymaster was not just choosing and recruiting his agents but helping them through that nadir. It was Olga's bad luck that when she first experienced it M was thousands of miles away.

She stayed in the boarding house for three weeks until at last she received a message. She was to go back to London empty-handed.

On the way home, Olga had time to reflect on her situation. Over the last few years, she had carried out important work for MI5. Yet this had come at a price. There are only so many lies that any of us can tell. She was beginning to feel the nervous strain of her work, and although M may have noticed this on her return he desperately wanted her to keep going.

Although Olga's mission to India had taken its toll emotionally, in intelligence terms it had been a success. Olga had gathered valuable details about the Indian Communist Party and the inner workings of the Comintern courier system. She had also earned the trust of Harry Pollitt and Percy Glading. MI5 had been opening their post for years, it had been tapping Pollitt's telephone, searching transcripts of his political speeches for seditious content and monitoring both men's movements, but never before had it had an agent so close to either man. Her information allowed M's investigation of Glading to move into a new phase. Usually, there are three stages in a counter-espionage operation. First, identify the suspected agent. Next, find evidence of espionage. Finally, have the agent arrested. Thanks to Olga's intelligence, M had completed the first stage of his investigation into Percy Glading: he was convinced that this man was working for the Comintern.

He was right. In the months after his dismissal from the Woolwich Arsenal, Glading had secretly gone to Moscow, where, as he put it, 'I started my education again.' The re-education of Percy Glading took place at the International Lenin School, the Comintern's finishing school for revolutionaries. This institution brought together the brightest young Communists from around the world and taught them ideology, tradecraft and the importance of absolute and unyielding loyalty to the Soviet Union. Graduates of the International Lenin School, like Glading, represented a new and more terrifying breed of Communist. Stalin called them 'men of steel'. They were less forgiving than their predecessors, all reconciled to the reality that worldwide socialist revolution would not be achieved at the ballot box. Instead, they returned to their native countries and made alliances with others on the Left while secretly carrying out subversive activities and otherwise preparing for the workers' revolution. MI5 had never faced a threat quite like this. Britain was being targeted by an enemy that was ruthless and well resourced, and had working for it a small army of agents who were patient, professional and utterly dedicated. By the time Glading returned from Moscow, he had become a cipher for Stalin and was ready to give everything for the cause. Like a modern-day jihadi who has returned from an 'Islamic State' camp, his commitment and faith were incorrigible. Although M did not yet know about Glading's time in Moscow, he was certain that this man was working for the Comintern and as such he might soon be given instructions to carry out espionage in Britain. M's hope was that when that happened, if that happened, Glading would turn to his agent for help. Although Olga needed a break after her exertions in India, the MI5 spymaster urged her to keep going.

THE HONEYMOONING SPY

Less than a week before Olga Gray set out for Mumbai, on the day that fifteen thousand people went to see Sir Oswald Mosley perform at a Fascist rally in Olympia, west London, M decided to reactivate a former agent. He had let this man go soon after the General Strike, in 1926, as demand for intelligence on Communist affairs dried up. Now he had a very different mission in mind for Eric Roberts.

Roberts had kept himself busy since his first fleeting taste of espionage as a teenager, after M had pulled him out of the British Fascisti and asked him to infiltrate the Communist Party. Indeed, he seemed incapable of sitting still. By day this enterprising young Cornishman was a clerk at Westminster Bank. By night he indulged an almost Victorian appetite for self-improvement. Roberts took classes in everything from judo to stock-exchange law, and he served as a Special Constable, or volunteer policeman, for the City of London, while also teaching himself graphology, Spanish and German, among other subjects. If ever there was a bank clerk whose job left him wanting something more from life, it was this one.

Eric Roberts's forebears had specialised in 'the down to earth business of farming,' as he once put it. He had grown up in a remote village on the Lizard, in deepest Cornwall, in a house that was too small for such a large family, yet had chosen to leave all this behind. It was as if these evening classes were part of an unconscious desire on his part to distance himself from his rural working-class background, or at least to prove to himself that he had made the right decision by moving to London. One way to get ahead was by acquiring reams of knowledge. Another was to befriend establishment figures and prove himself in their eyes, which may explain why, in 1934, Eric Roberts had written several letters that led to him getting in touch again with M, after which he more or less offered his services to his former spymaster.

'In all approaches made to animals,' wrote M, 'it is a golden rule to let the animal make the first move.' The fact that Roberts had contacted him was promising. M's former agent had even proposed a specific mission. He wanted to report back from his forthcoming visit to Nazi Germany. Roberts obviously believed that he would have time to kill, in spite of this trip being his honeymoon.

'I shall be very pleased to meet you and your wife when you return from Germany,' replied M, 'and I shall also be interested in anything you may have to tell me regarding what you see there.'

There is no record of what Roberts reported from his honeymoon, but several months later M was in touch again.

'I am anxious to see you as soon as possible,' wrote M. 'I have what might be a very interesting and mildly profitable proposition to put up to you. It is one which I cannot discuss on paper, but if we can meet early in September I can give you full details.'

They met, as suggested, but M did not reveal the 'full details' of his plan, which was for Eric Roberts to become the first MI5 penetration agent inside the British Fascist movement. M had finally accepted the strategic need for this. He could no longer survive on scraps provided by his former comrades from the BF, yet he did not want to scare off Roberts by outlining what he had in mind. Instead, he gave him a simple, one-off mission as a way of easing him back into the work and hopefully whetting his appetite.

Although we do not know what this job was, Roberts accomplished it well. 'Very many thanks for your interesting report received safely,' wrote M. 'It was just exactly what I wanted and I am very grateful to you.'

Now M could make his pitch. 'Supposing that I find there is a certain amount of cash available for the enterprise, do you consider that you could spare say, two evenings a week?' M offered Roberts a salary of £1 a week for a probationary period of three months, plus travelling expenses of 10 shillings a week, the equivalent today of just over £200 a month. The payment was tiny but significant. It made the work feel like a job rather than a favour and was sufficiently small that if Roberts's motivation was financial he would lose interest.

'How would that suit you?' asked M.

Very well, it seemed, for Roberts accepted.

More than a decade later, M was able to say of his MI5 section that 'no purely mercenary agent has ever been employed'. M had recruited an old friend and a former member of the BF who was evidently patriotic, intelligent and patient. Now he could explain to him in more detail what he wanted him to do.

'We should like you to endeavour to get into touch with our friends at their head office [BUF Headquarters] and to put in some evening work there as and when it is most convenient to you and to them, but we should much appreciate at least one weekly report. It is difficult to indicate lines of enquiry so early on, but doubtless your first two or three visits will indicate some basis for future work. In general we can say nothing is too small to report, particularly with reference to the personnel and their activities, and also indications of internal dissension.'

M posted the letter and began to look forward to receiving the first report from his new agent. But his instructions had been too broad. Roberts was not yet ready.

He wrote back to his spymaster explaining that his manager at the Westminster Bank was not fond of Fascism, which would make it impossible for him to wear a blackshirt.

'It is not necessary for every member to wear a uniform,' replied M, 'and I should make it very clear from the start that owing to your position in the bank and the unsympathetic views of your manager, it would be impossible for you to do this.' Roberts also wanted more guidance. What should he do when he first arrived at BUF Headquarters? Who should he look out for? What was the best way to present himself?

'I cannot give you any particular detailed advice at this stage, but will help you in every way possible when you have started to gather in a certain amount of information,' came M's reply. 'Generally speaking, however, I should simply do whatever task is allotted to you as well as you can, and allow yourself to drift along with the tide, so to speak. If there are any special points on which you require an opinion, I will deal with them by return.'

So it was that in late 1934 a Cornish bank clerk who was also an MI5 agent, and feeling slightly unsure of himself, walked into the National Headquarters of the British Union of Fascists and offered his services as a linguist. He was directed to the Foreign Relations Department. This was promising. If Roberts could secure a position in there, he might be able to uncover more about the financial connections among Mosley, Mussolini and Hitler. But, as he reported back to M, the men in this department wanted nothing to do with him.

'Do not be disturbed about the attitude of the Foreign Department,' M assured him. 'It seems to me to be quite reasonable. I think they will obviously regard with suspicion any new recruits and wait until they have proved themselves elsewhere. I should not make any more obvious attempts to get in touch with them or find out about them for a week or two, but you might take to reading one or two suitable foreign newspapers and making cuttings of anything which you think might interest the Foreign Relations Department. These you might hand to the man at HQ who seems to be the most friendly to you and ask him to pass them on. In this way you will gradually establish confidence.'

Roberts's first report had provided nothing of any great value, yet this did not stop M from showering him with praise. 'Very many thanks' for your 'most interesting' report, which was 'exactly what I want. You cannot do better than carry on like this.' M understood the enervating insecurity of life as an informant, especially at the start. He knew this because he had experienced it himself. He appreciated that it could take months and sometimes years for an agent to produce useful intelligence. Roberts, however, appeared to have got there much sooner.

The next offering from M's new agent really was 'an excellent report; it provides us with a great deal of new information and presents several lines for further investigation'. The following week's effort was also superb. Information was now pouring in from Roberts. It was as if he had opened a tap, until there was so much of it that his spymaster became worried.

M urgently warned Roberts against appearing 'to be unduly curious'. The following week he made the same point. 'May I again emphasise that for the next few weeks you should studiously avoid the asking of questions which might in any way be deemed improper by the BUF. It is obvious from what you report that they are suffering from spy mania, and it would be a pity to spoil your excellent start by appearing too anxious for information. Don't imagine that for one moment that we are impatient. You obviously have the ability to deliver the goods, so we shall not be at all upset if we hear nothing very sensational for a month or two. It is far more important that you should become intimate with one or two persons as you have already indicated. Information will come to you. It is a mistake to go out and try to find it.'

This was essentially the same advice M had doled out to each of his agents. Just as he monitored the health of his pets every day, he scoured his agents' reports for signs that an informant was pushing too hard, or not enough. Were they making the wrong friends? Did they need more attention? Had they received the latest payment? Was the pressure of the work getting to them?

M had never been taught to do any of this. Yet these were vital parts of the vast body of knowledge, his tradecraft, which he had honed during his career. Eleven years after being thrown in at the deep end, M had reached a point where he displayed an indigenous grasp of how to penetrate subversive groups, including the importance of never asking too many questions. M was attentive to Eric Roberts partly because it had been almost a decade since this agent had last been in the field, but also because there was also a lot riding on his success. Although M had at least a dozen paid operatives by late 1934, all of them, except Roberts, were deployed inside the Communist movement. Usually M gave his agents a numbered codename, such as M/12, yet for Roberts he came up with a new nomenclature.

On 31 May, 1935, M/F, an agent who has never before been correctly identified, reported that 'the sister-in-law of Miss H. B. Tudor-Hart recently cabled £25 to a Hungarian', adding that Edith Tudor-Hart gives large subscriptions at irregular intervals to a particular school, and that when she sent this money to the Hungarian she 'seemed excited and urgent'.

This was the kind of intelligence that could only really have come from an employee at Tudor-Hart's bank, most likely the individual who handled this actual transfer. This points clearly to Roberts. So does the fact that on the same day, Rita Retallick, M's secretary at No. 38 Sloane Street, wrote to Roberts thanking him for his recent report and telling him, in response to his question, that 'the sister-in-law of Miss T-H is, I gather, the wife of Dr T-H', before asking Roberts for 'further' details about this woman. Until now it has been suggested that 'M/F' was a codename used by M to refer to his own reports. Instead, it seems that M/F was Eric Roberts.

Why did M give him the letter *F*? Presumably it stood for 'Fascism', which may have been M's way of saying he only really needed one agent to investigate Fascism. Looking out on the world just then, one could have been forgiven for thinking otherwise.

Nazi Germany had recently withdrawn from the League of Nations and had begun to rearm. Hitler would soon announce the resumption of military conscription and the existence of the Luftwaffe – both violations of the Treaty of Versailles. Mosley was strengthening his relationships with Italy and Germany and had met senior Fascists from France, Belgium, Norway, Ireland and Spain. By the end of 1934, international Fascism was a coherent political force and Mosley's British Union of Fascists was undoubtedly part of it. There was a growing need in MI5 for reliable human intelligence from the heart of the BUF. Most of its hopes rested now on a newly married bank clerk who might have just given himself away.

Very soon after M cautioned him against making too many enquiries, Roberts was befriended by a senior Fascist. This man was unusually critical of the party's leadership. He tore into Mosley, telling Roberts he was part of a dissident faction that hoped one day to oust the leader. He then asked the MI5 agent to join them.

Roberts was intrigued and uncertain. It was his first major dilemma as M/F. Should he find out more, or report this man to the BUF Intelligence Department?

M agreed that the situation was 'very tricky'. He was tempted to encourage Roberts to accept, for this was bound to produce valuable intelligence, but he worried that if this dissident was genuine then ultimately he would be exposed, leaving Roberts tarred by his association with him. There was also a chance that this was a trap.

'Up to date I think you have done admirably and have reacted in exactly the right way,' M told his agent. 'You must bear in mind the *possibility* that the whole of this business may have been staged for your benefit. It may be in the nature of a test to see whether or not you are reliable, whether you are addicted to listening to gossip etc. etc. Therefore it is of the utmost importance that your attitude should be one of scrupulous loyalty to the Movement and to the senior officers. While listening sympathetically to the criticisms of your friends, you should under no circumstances allow yourself to be drawn into criticising your seniors. Don't utter a single word or phrase that could be used against you on some future occasion. Express surprise – anything you like, but not agreement.'

All M could do now was wait. The next report from Roberts would reveal whether he had given the right advice.

It is hard to say how much this episode preyed on M, only that he would have had little time to dwell on it. 'You're always saying we should have hobbies and recreations,' his fictional counterpart is reminded in John Le Carré's *A Perfect Spy*. M was an inveterate joiner, much like Eric Roberts and Jimmy Dickson (who would become close friends). By late 1934, M belonged to the Overseas Club, the Paternoster Club, Surrey County Cricket Club and the Zoological Society of London; he would soon join the Authors Club and the Society of Civil and Public Service Writers and be elected a Fellow of the Royal Microscopical Society and the Royal Geographical Society. Later he would also belong to the Royal Societies Club, the Quekett Club, the Royal Entomological Society, the Linnean Society, the British Mycological Society, the British Herpetological Society, the Royal Institution, the Freshwater Biological Association, the Ray Society and, strangely, the Medico-Legal Society, in spite of having no medical or legal experience.

M liked to divide his world into many different compartments, and to keep each one well furnished. His spare time was dominated by this mass of clubs and societies, as well as his pets and his jazz. Each provided not only a refuge from his work but a reminder of his youth. They anchored him to an earlier, often wilder version of himself: Max the boy, obsessed with animals; Max the cadet, learning to look after himself; Max the schoolmaster, lacking direction; Max the black sheep of the family, a man adrift; and Max the aspiring writer.

It was this last version of himself that was keeping M most busy over those winter months as Eric Roberts found his way inside the BUF. M had decided to write a second novel. This was despite the reaction to the first.

His debut, *Crime Cargo,* had been described in the *Manchester Evening News* as 'a novel for that large and increasing class of reader that likes its blood red', a warning, perhaps, that it contained several gory scenes. *Truth* called it 'a real good rousing yarn'. In the *Straits Times,* of Singapore, it was hailed as 'readable'.

Crime Cargo did not sell well and mustered only a handful of reviews, the most prominent of which was easily the most partial. Soon after the book came out, M/8 wrote it up in his *Daily Express* column as a 'thriller with a contemporary theme: kidnapping racketeers on a luxury cruise . . . American slang well done'. M's agent then followed up with a lively, if selective, biography of the author.

'Knight – lean, long-beaked, knowing-eyed – has had many jobs. In the Navy . . . Ran his own dance-band, proudly claims it was "London's first small hot combination." . . . Sold paint . . . Sportsmaster at a prep school . . . Ran pub on Exmoor at which part of "Lorna Doone" was written. Lived at one time in small Chelsea flat, where envious jungle-sounds produced by a parrot, a bulldog, a bear-cub and a monkey failed to drown his clarinet accompaniment to "Beale Street Blues" on the gramophone.'

It must have been strange for M to read this. Here was a portrait of a younger version of himself, the one that Gwladys had fallen in love with almost a decade ago. Several months after the publication of *Crime Cargo,* Gwladys had sold the pub on Exmoor and moved to nearby Minehead, where she began to run Madame Miranda, a beauty salon that offered everything from hairdressing and manicures to lingerie. Gwladys was never one to dwell on her unhappiness, or any physical discomfort, yet she could no longer ignore the gloomy state of her marriage. It was not just their sexual incompatibility that she found upsetting, but the way they had drifted apart over the last decade. When she and Max had first met, they were two sporty rural types, both rising stars in the British Fascist movement, who no doubt talked about having a family. Most of this future they had imagined together had now fallen apart, but they could not bring themselves to formally end their marriage.

Shortly after Gwladys sold the pub, M discovered the truth about the dissident Fascist who had approached Eric Roberts. It *had* been a trap. His agent's lukewarm response had been reported to the BUF Intelligence Department approvingly. Roberts had passed his first real test.

Over the months that followed, M's agent settled into the routine of being a full-time bank clerk and a part-time MI5 operative. Instead of getting dressed up in the evening as a Special Constable and patrolling the streets of London – a position he had been forced to give up after joining the BUF – he pulled on his Fascist regalia.

'I rather liked myself in my blackshirt, knee boots and breeches,' wrote Roberts, many years later, 'but found it awfully embarrassing after leaving the bank to change in some public toilet. There was a frightful occasion at Sloane Square where an ex-naval type saw me enter a lavatory cubicle in office garb and emerge minutes later in jackboots, blackshirt et al. His dignity as janitor was clearly grossly offended. "You Fascist B — —. Get out of here and never show your face again or I'll do you." I followed his advice. I had no wish to be "done."'

Nor did Roberts want to lose his job at the bank, which was why he hesitated when asked to carry out a new mission for the BUF. The senior Fascist J. McGuirk Hughes had asked that he join a secret Fascist cell of bank workers.

'I am always glad to hear from you over the phone so long as it is safe, so don't be afraid to ring up,' wrote M after the conversation that followed. 'Your problem is indeed a knotty one, and until I can take advice from my boss I do not want to give you a definite opinion. The real snag is that it is entirely against our principles to ask anyone to do something which might lead to trouble for them with their employers.' M was concerned about Roberts losing his job at the bank, but not so worried that he ruled out his involvement. 'On the other hand, if you feel you can assist them to some degree without running the risk of getting yourself known in banking circles, then I feel that it might lead to greater things as you rightly suggest. Can you not interest yourself in a mild way to begin with, thus giving me time to take further advice?'

The following month MI5 sent another report on the Fascist movement to the Home Office. It included information on Fascist cells such as the one Roberts had been asked to join. Although the political threat of the BUF was in decline, some MI5 officers were now convinced that Mosley was being manipulated by a foreign power.

M was not one of them, and this was partly because of his relationship with William Joyce. Although he described his old friend as 'a rabid anti-Catholic, and a fanatical anti-Semite', a man whose 'mental balance is not equal to his intellectual capacity' and who had 'decided tendencies towards absolute monarchy, absolute government, dictatorship etc.' – a report later described by a Joyce biographer as 'one of the most insightful profiles ever written about him' – M was receiving intelligence from Joyce about the inner workings of the BUF.

'For your own private information,' M revealed to Roberts, in January 1935, 'I can tell you that Joyce has a well organised intelligence service of his own, and he is kept fully informed of what goes [on] among the various [BUF] factions.' There is little doubt that some of the fruits of Joyce's 'intelligence service' were being passed on to M.

M's job was to gather timely intelligence about subversive organisations, including the British Union of Fascists, so by using Joyce as an informant you could say he was simply doing his job, and doing it well. Yet by taking so much intelligence from Mosley's No. 2, and remaining close to him and his wife Hazel, he was in danger of being unable to see the BUF for what it really was.

Slowly, however, M's understanding of Fascism appeared to be changing. The catalyst was not so much the reports he was receiving *from* William Joyce but those *about* him. The best of these came from Eric Roberts.

In January 1935, Roberts reported that Joyce was giving 'the impression that he has an actual working agreement with the Nazis'. Several weeks later Joyce declared that 'if Fascism is to succeed, it must have an international basis' and that the BUF had much 'in common with German and Italian Fascists'. Next to an account of this speech in Joyce's MI5 file went the following comment: 'M. thought this remark very significant.'

M's sympathies were in flux. At last, it seemed, he had begun to accept that Mosley's BUF might be closer to Mussolini and Hitler than he had been prepared to admit. But still he wanted proof.

OLGA PULLOFFSKI

In July 1935, M was in the seaside town of Eastbourne, on the south coast, recuperating from a case of pneumonia, when he heard that Olga Gray had been rushed to hospital.

On her return from Mumbai the year before, Olga had resigned from her job with the Anti-War Movement and the League Against Imperialism. Although she kept in touch with the two leading Communists Percy Glading and Harry Pollitt, and she continued to pass on gossip to M, Olga no longer worked inside the two front organisations. The strain of her work had become too much, and over the months that followed she had begun to build a new life for herself, even if the old one was not yet ready to let her go.

'I was approached by Glading,' she recalled, 'and asked to take on a paid job as Secretary to Harry Pollitt at Communist Party Headquarters.' This was February 1935. M had never before had an agent working inside this office, known as the 'Kremlin', least of all one employed as secretary to the most powerful Communist in Britain. 'No official or other single individual ever has the same opportunity for obtaining information covering a wide area as does a clerk or secretary,' wrote M. 'A woman so-placed will have a much wider grasp of the day-to-day doings in a movement, than any of the officials of the movement will ever dream of. I would state categorically that if it were possible for any business magnate or government official to be able to see into the mind of his secretary, he would be astounded at the amount of knowledge concerning the general affairs of the business or department in question which lay in the secretary's brain.'

M was desperate for Olga to accept this offer. He later suggested that the 'temptation' of taking the job 'was too much both for the Department and Miss "X"', yet the 'temptation' was undeniably greater for him than it could ever have been for Olga. Ultimately, she agreed to become Harry Pollitt's secretary.

'The work was very hard,' she wrote. It was also varied. One afternoon in the so-called Kremlin, Olga was 'stitching reports into the lining of Soviet sailors' great coats to carry home'. Another, she was taking minutes at staff meetings of the *Daily Worker,* typing up Pollitt's letters, going through his correspondence or sitting in on meetings with key Communists.

The quality of Olga's new intelligence was exceptional. M must have been in a state of controlled, rolling euphoria as he went through her reports and passed on to his colleagues the 'most valuable information', including, at last, proof of 'the existence of Harry Pollitt's covert link with Moscow'. Olga also 'explained how the cipher system was based on a book'. As the historian Nigel West has shown, this key piece of intelligence enabled British government codebreakers to begin their decryption of 'MASK' wireless communications between Moscow and London, a breakthrough that transformed MI5's understanding of undercover Soviet operations inside Britain.

Olga's new job was different from her earlier work in terms of its intensity, its secrecy, the number of reports she had to write up for M. It was also unusual because her relationship to the people she was spying on had changed. Previously, she had been reporting to her spymaster on the activities of suspicious Communists. Now she was informing on people that she had occasionally come to like. What had once been espionage was starting to feel like betrayal.

Harry Pollitt was, she insisted, 'an honest Communist', a likeable individual who clearly trusted her. Percy Glading 'was a very nice man with a little daughter,' she recalled. 'I remember him being a very stimulating conversationalist and about the only person who could make an account of a film or play he'd seen absolutely riveting.'

You can only betray the people you love. During her three years inside the Communist movement, Olga had naturally grown closer to some of her targets, and there was even a rumour that around this time she started to have an affair with Percy Glading.

Joe Thomas, a Communist who claimed to have known both Glading and Olga at the time, later suggested that Olga 'had been sleeping with Glading throughout the whole adventure'. We may never know whether this was true. If it was, however, M would not have approved.

'It is important to stress that I am no believer in what may be described as Mata-Hari methods,' he wrote. 'I am convinced that more information has been obtained by women-agents, by keeping out of the arms of men, than ever was obtained by sinking too willingly into them.' His reason was simple: the man 'will very speedily lose his interest in her once his immediate object is attained'.

Yet M did not want his female agents to be too austere either. 'A clever woman who can use her personal attractions wisely has in her armoury a very formidable weapon,' he wrote. 'Closely allied to Sex in a woman, is the quality of sympathy; and nothing is easier than for a woman to gain a man's confidence by the showing and expression of a little sympathy.'

A little sympathy. It is hard to say whether, in Olga's case, this extended to sleeping with Glading or merely being fond of him. Either way, the distance between them had shrunk dramatically and this was making her job harder.

The other problem in Olga's life concerned a song. 'Olga Pulloffski, the Beautiful Spy' was a catchy number that had come out just after she began to work at King Street. The song was so popular that when this MI5 agent walked into Communist Party Headquarters her colleagues used to sing it out to her in greeting:

> She's Olga Pulloffski, the beautiful spy.
> The gay continental rapscallion,
> Some say that she's Russian,
> And some say she's French,
> But her accent is gin and Italian.
> Shame on you, shame on you,
> Oh fie fie!
> Olga Pulloffski, you beautiful spy.

You could make this kind of thing up, but nobody would believe you. An MI5 operative deep inside the Party was being serenaded by the people she was spying on with a song that made her out to be a spy. Olga became convinced that her colleagues knew her secret and were merely waiting for the right moment to punish her.

M tried to see Olga as often as possible. If he did not meet any of his agents in person, he fired off letters to them, spoke to them on the phone, reassured them, even when there was no operational need to do so. It was the same with his pets. 'Some "superior" people are inclined to sneer at the idea of fondling captive animals,' he wrote, 'but this attitude merely shows their ignorance of what a young – and often an adult animal – requires. Stroking, gentle scratching and, what for want of a better word we call fondling is not only much appreciated by many animals, it gives them security too.'

In May 1935, however, M had come down with pneumonia and for the next two months he was mostly bedridden. His duties were carried out by the only other employee in M Section, Rita Retallick, who later became an officer for MI5 and then MI6. She did her best to look after his family of agents, yet she was only a surrogate for M. The umbilical connection between Olga and her spymaster had been broken.

With M still recovering, Olga bumped into a man she had known from Birmingham, possibly a former boyfriend. Her instinct was to unburden herself about the last few years of her life, to tell him about Mumbai, Glading, Paris, M and the strange, debilitating pressure of leading two lives that had been set up, as if part of some cruel joke, in direct opposition to one another. But she did not. She could not. Instead, she held everything in.

Olga had never felt either so trapped or so alone. We are used to thinking of spies as the heroes of their stories. Now Olga had become the victim of hers. In early July 1935 she had what was later described as a nervous breakdown. She was taken to the National Hospital for Nervous Diseases in Queen Square. Soon her room was filled with flowers, presumably including those from her two sympathetic employers, MI5 and the Communist Party – a floral reminder of how she had ended up there in the first place.

Later Olga described the pressure of those weeks leading up to her breakdown, of a life spent 'looking over your shoulder, all the time. Even when sleeping, you're not at ease.' It was like being afraid of the dark as a child, she said, 'but permanently so. It did a lot of damage.'

The pressure of lying to people you know, not once or twice, but hundreds, possibly thousands of times, requires some form of release. For some people it is enough to talk it out; others may turn to drink, become depressed or experience panic attacks – perhaps the only constant is that the pressure of this work requires an outlet and that usually the spymaster is a vital part of this process. It was no coincidence that Olga's breakdown took place during one of M's few absences.

We have become used to thinking of Post-Traumatic Stress Disorder (PTSD) as a condition experienced by soldiers after an acute traumatic experience, or by victims of accidents and natural disasters. But it can also be rooted in the experience of spending years pretending to be someone you are not. In 2016, a former MI5 agent appealed against his murder conviction on the grounds that he was suffering at the time from PTSD, adding that 'he was told that his flashbacks and nightmares were not uncommon for undercover agents'. Historical diagnoses are tricky, but it seems extremely likely that by 1935, as a result of her work for MI5, Olga had begun to experience a condition very similar to what we would today call PTSD.

When she next spoke to M, presumably at the hospital, Olga was clear about her next step.

'I informed the officer of the Intelligence Department for whom I worked, that I found the work too great a strain and would prefer to drop my connection with the Communist Party and return to ordinary life.' If M had pushed her before, he did not do so now. He accepted that Olga's career as a government agent was effectively over.

'As may be readily understood,' M conceded, 'she was tired, suffering from some nervous strain; and rather disposed to feel that she had done enough.' Guy Liddell would tell Eric Roberts that 'in an agent context, no man could go on indefinitely. Sooner or later, he became tired and jaded, if not blown.' For more than three years, Olga had reported with tenacity and skill on the Communist underground movement. The intelligence she had produced had changed the government's understanding of Soviet activities in Britain and Moscow's relationship with the British Communist Party. Now her life as an MI5 agent was set to finish. Soon after being discharged from hospital, Olga was elected to be Secretary of the Ealing Ladies Hockey Club and before the end of the year she had found a job working for an advertising company.

M also knew that Graham Pollard's career was essentially over, now that he had been awarded a Leverhulme Research Fellowship to write a history of the book trade. But his link to M was not severed. If Pollard happened upon anything interesting, he would pass it on to his spymaster. And the same went for Olga; the bond between M and his agents was one that never fully broke.

'On instructions,' she wrote, of the months after her nervous breakdown, 'I continued to maintain purely friendly contact with Pollitt and Glading.' There might still be another chapter in her MI5 career.

22

MUSSOLINI'S MAN

Shortly after Olga had been elected Secretary of the Ealing Ladies Hockey Club, in 1935, Italian forces under the command of General Emilio De Bono marched into what is today Ethiopia, marking the start of the Second Italo-Abyssinian War. In the bloody engagements that followed, Italian troops armed with tanks, planes, machine guns and mustard gas attacked Ethiopian troops and civilians, many of them defending themselves with little more than antique rifles or spears. It was brutal and one-sided, at least this was how it seemed to most contemporary observers.

Amazingly, you might think, some people in Britain urged the government to look the other way while Mussolini indulged his imperial ambitions. The loudest of these pro-Italian voices came from Sir Oswald Mosley's British Union of Fascists. The BUF was soon spending more than £3,000 a month on its propaganda in support of Mussolini. It organised meetings in support of the Fascist aggression in Ethiopia and its members chalked slogans onto the streets, such as 'Mind Britain's Business' or 'Mosley Says Peace'. At first this seemed to be part of a BUF strategy to win more votes at the forthcoming General Election. But when it came, the BUF did not field any candidates.

By late 1935 Mosley appears to have accepted that his party was never going to achieve power democratically. As the image of European Fascism continued to sour, and more became known about the behaviour of paramilitary thugs in Germany, the extent of Fascist anti-Semitism or indeed its attitude towards all opposition, the British public turned against the BUF's militarism as well as Mosley himself. Most voters saw him by late 1935 as conceited, pompous and lacking in self-awareness. P. G. Wodehouse would soon caricature him as Roderick Spode, leader of the Blackshorts, so dim that he was outwitted by Bertie Wooster.

MI5 had a rather different take on this man. Kell's department had recently established that Sir Oswald Mosley was secretly being paid by Mussolini a monthly subsidy of £3,000. The first of these payments had been made as early as 1933. Since then the Italian dictator had ploughed into the BUF roughly £70,000 a year (equivalent to more than £2.5 million today). The money was brought over by couriers in a variety of currencies, before being deposited in a secret bank account at the Charing Cross branch of Westminster Bank, or it was used as cash in hand to pay off existing debts. Although there were private donors to the BUF in Britain, such as the financier Alex Scrimgeour, who gave money directly to William Joyce, most BUF income came from Benito Mussolini.

This marked a sea change in MI5's attitude towards British Fascism. From that moment, wrote M, 'the Fascist party in this country was regarded with very grave suspicion'. The political movement that M had once infiltrated, married into and helped to build up was now being talked about in the Office in the same terms used to describe the Communist Party.

Indeed, the Fascists and Communists in Britain had a surprising amount in common. Both political parties now received roughly £3,000 a month from a foreign dictator and had the potential to become instruments of theirs in the event of a war. The one consolation for MI5 was that if there was an international conflict it would only have to deal with one or the other, because the idea of the Fascists and the Communists being on the same side was absurd.

For years MI5 had seen the Soviet Union as the most likely adversary in a future war, which was why M had been told to investigate Communist underground networks. Yet by late 1935, MI5 was beginning to think about homegrown Fascists in similar terms. If the country ever went to war against Italy or Germany, it was possible that Mosley's BUF might be repurposed to help the enemy. At the heart of this new analysis was the idea that some homegrown Fascists might feel a greater sense of loyalty towards international Fascism than to their own country.

Mosley's party had appealed to the British people for democratic support, but it had been rejected. Like a spurned lover, the BUF was now becoming angrier and more insular. At a march in London on 24 May, 1936, Empire Day, observers were struck by the similarities between the new uniforms worn by Mosley's men and Hitler's SS. Later that year, at the so-called Battle of Cable Street, in the East End of London, some 100,000 protesters gathered to prevent a BUF delegation from completing its march. One eye witness recalled the look of 'grim determination' on the faces of the anti-Fascists. All over Britain people were waking up to the threat posed by Fascism, both on the Continent and on their own doorstep.

A Special Branch informant described one of Sir Oswald Mosley's speeches at this time as 'a genuine statement of intent to undermine the political stability of Britain'. William Joyce's pronouncements were becoming wilder as well, as if such a thing was possible. In one speech he slammed Churchill, then a hawkish backbench MP, as 'an imitation strategist, the Butcher in Chief to His Majesty the King'; Stanley Baldwin, the Prime Minister, was 'the steel merchant metamorphosed into a squire by casual experiments in pig breeding'; his predecessor Ramsay MacDonald was dismissed as the 'Loon from Lossiemouth'; and Lord Willingdon, the Viceroy of India, was a 'phenomenal freak whom it would be indecent to describe as Viceroy'. One man who heard Joyce speak wrote that 'never before, in any country, had I met a personality so terrifying in its dynamic force, so vituperative, so vitriolic'.

The evolution of British Fascism into an embittered, radical force was echoed precisely in Joyce's outlook. Having been part of this movement from the start, in 1923, when he was driven by an intense patriotism and a fear of Communism, Joyce had now embraced the angry, militant and more anti-Semitic message of contemporary European Fascism. Joyce had been radicalised by his encounter with Nazi Germany. He was an extremist with a grievance, one whose marriage was also falling apart. As M pointed out, 'it is not thought that he has enough stability to make him accept defeat very gracefully'. In the face of ridicule or alienation, 'anything might happen to him'.

M was the author of several detailed reports on Joyce, and the question of whether to have this person more closely monitored would be referred to him. But before he could make a decision on this, M's life was swallowed up first by personal tragedy and then by scandal.

A MYSTERIOUS AFFAIR

In the summer of 1936, Gwladys Knight went to see her doctor with a complaint of 'very acute sciatica', a condition that causes sharp prickly pain around the lower back and upper legs. Being Gwladys, she was completely 'unwilling to accept any treatment that necessitated resting in bed', complained her doctor, or 'undergo proper investigation as to the cause of her sciatica'. She was, he concluded, 'a difficult patient'. He prescribed her aspirin. Later that summer a different doctor gave her a course of barbiturates, powerful sleep-inducing drugs that are used more sparingly today because of their addictive potential.

Several months later, once she was feeling a little better, Gwladys went up to London to do her Christmas shopping. She arrived at Paddington Station late on Sunday, 26 November, 1936. On her shopping list for the following day were two evening dresses, flapjacks from Pugh, scarves from Femina, black bags from the Anglo-Persian Bag Company, cushion covers from Liberty and grey shirt studs for 'L'. Rather than go to her husband's flat for the night, Gwladys took a room several miles away at the Overseas Club, where M was a member and sometimes met his agents. Feeling tired, she decided to have an early night.

What happened next became a subject of intense speculation. Initially, M suggested that he had gone to the Overseas Club at around midnight on Sunday and had found his wife unconscious, after which he had called a doctor. But that is not what happened.

It was later established that Gwladys was discovered in bed the next morning by the maid who had come in to wake her up. Her husband was then called, followed by a doctor, who confirmed that Gwladys had gone into a coma. Stimulants were administered in the afternoon and a second doctor came by that evening. The next day, M arranged for Sir William Wollic, medical adviser to the Home Office, to see Gwladys. His prognosis was bad. Still in a comatose state, M's wife was moved to a nearby nursing home, and two days later, after a momentary improvement, several days before what would have been her thirty-seventh birthday, she died of heart failure.

In the *Daily Mail* her death was called a 'riddle'. In the *Dundee Courier* it was a 'mysterious affair'. While there was little doubt about the cause of her death – she had taken an overdose of the barbiturates that had been prescribed to her several months earlier – there was uncertainty over whether this had been a tragic accident or she had chosen to take her own life.

Gwladys's grieving mother and brother were in no doubt that this was a case of suicide, and that she had been driven to it by M. In their darker moments, they claimed that he might have somehow murdered her.

At the coroner's inquest, Gwladys's family was represented by a well-known criminal lawyer, Reginald Seaton, who told the coroner that his aim was 'to elucidate if this man' – he had pointed at M – 'was in any way responsible, not criminally, for his wife's death'. Seaton explained that Gwladys was wealthy and had neither children nor a will. As such, her husband stood to benefit financially from her death.

Although M's lawyer objected to this remark, the coroner ruled that it was admissible. Gwladys was indeed intestate and her estate, valued at £1,637, over £100,000 in today's money, did go to M. Perhaps swayed by Seaton's arguments, the coroner ruled that although it was impossible to show that Gwladys had *intended* to take her own life, he could not be certain that her death had been accidental. As a result he gave an open verdict.

Though this had little impact on the settling of her estate, and it formally ended the investigation, this ruling allowed an element of mystery to surround Gwladys's death indefinitely. Today, you can find wild allegations on the Internet to suggest that Gwladys died in a Satanic ritual gone wrong.

On the face of it, the coroner's open verdict was strange. Gwladys's aspirin pills were the same shape and size as her barbiturates, and a side effect of taking the latter was temporary amnesia. Most likely, she took the barbiturates, woke up in pain and took more of these pills by accident, either in the mistaken belief that she had not yet taken any, or because she thought they were aspirin.

There was also the note she had written to M shortly before falling into a coma:

Sweetheart, – Just arrived for a few days shopping. Will you give me a ring in the morning & see what we can fix up? Not too early as I will be having breakfast in bed, & shan't be leaving here until after 10 a.m.

Love, G.

This message should have been enough to convince the coroner that her death was an accident and she had had no intention to take her life. Yet the fact that M had given two different versions of her first night in London, and that he had failed to hand over this note from Gwladys for several days, was enough to create doubt in the coroner's mind.

M's behaviour was hard to explain. Most likely he was acting on a misguided desire to keep up appearances. He did not want the world to know that his wife slept apart from him. Those who spoke to the MI5 man about Gwladys's death described him as shaken by what had happened, and sad that he had not spent more time with her over the years. On top of the shock and the sadness, M now had to deal with intense public exposure. This was a man who liked to be in control. His secret ambition, he once said, 'was to be a prison governor'. Now the nation was able to pick over details of his private life as they read accounts in the press of the coroner's inquest. An enterprising journalist from the *Western Morning News* even tracked him down to his flat, the headquarters of M Section, and asked for an interview. M refused.

There had always been a part of him that enjoyed attention, but this was different. His newfound fame, or notoriety, threatened to compromise his work. It had also begun to change the way he was seen in the Office. The controversy surrounding Gwladys's death did not immediately turn M's colleagues against him, but it may have clouded his reputation in some parts of MI5.

M's geographical separation from his colleagues, the trashy novels he wrote, the jazz, the pets – all this allowed him to come across as endearingly and entertainingly original, when the going was good. Yet when the weather turned, as it had done in the wake of his wife's suspected suicide, M was vulnerable to being seen as something of an oddball, especially by new recruits to the Office such as Dick White, a future head of MI5, who took 'an instant dislike' to M on account of his 'enigmatic' personality, his unusual interests and the distance he kept from MI5 Headquarters. Perhaps M's personal politics also played a part in this, and the rumours of his Fascist past.

The line between loveably eccentric and dangerously weird will always be fine. In the wake of the coroner's open verdict on his wife's death, M had to re-establish in the minds of his colleagues which side of it he was really on. More so than at any other point in his MI5 career, he needed a victory.

PERCY'S PROPOSAL

When Percy Glading met his Soviet handlers in London for the first time, around the time of Gwladys's death, he was surprised to discover that neither man was actually Russian. They made a comic-looking pair. One was tall with long dark hair swept back from his forehead like Count Dracula. The other was short with mousy, curly hair and no visible neck. Their names were Theodor Maly and Arnold Deutsch, and they worked for the *Inostrannyi Otdel* (INO), the foreign intelligence department of the Soviet secret police, the notorious People's Commissariat for Internal Affairs (NKVD). Both were living in Britain as 'illegals': elite Soviet intelligence operatives deployed outside Russia without the protection of diplomatic cover. If discovered by MI5, Maly and Deutsch would not be rescued by Moscow, which was why they had no intention of getting caught.

Maly and Deutsch would later be hailed as two of the finest 'illegals' ever to be employed by Moscow Centre. Deutsch was the shorter of the two. He was an Austrian academic once famous in Vienna for his crusading belief in the importance of better orgasms. Since then he had shown himself to be a superb spymaster. In just two years in London, Arnold Deutsch had personally recruited some twenty agents for the NKVD. Kim Philby had been the first, followed by Donald Maclean, Guy Burgess, Anthony Blunt, John Cairncross and up to fifteen others, including several who have never been publicly identified.

Deutsch's boss in the London *rezidentura,* the local Soviet intelligence apparatus, was Theodor Maly, a tall, languid Hungarian with gold fillings in his front teeth and a past that had come to haunt him. An ex-seminarian, Maly had been captured during the First World War and taken to Siberia where he learned Russian, lost his faith and joined the Red Army. In the years that followed, he took part in some of the worst massacres of the Russian Civil War, the memory of which tormented him for the rest of his life and was part of the reason why he had asked to be posted abroad – anywhere, really, other than the Soviet Union. This was how Maly came to be running the NKVD *rezidentura* in London, in late 1936, at around the time that he and Deutsch recruited a former factory worker called Percy Glading.

Deutsch described Glading, their bespectacled new agent, as 'a devoted communist, courageous, daring, painstaking and industrious. He is also well-read and well-educated. He is a good organiser and writes well.' Glading's only weaknesses, believed Deutsch, were that he could be too trusting of his comrades and sometimes he lacked patience. It was a prescient judgement.

Whereas Philby and the other wide-eyed Cambridge recruits had been won over at once by Deutsch's mittel-European charm, his easy sophistication and his worldliness, Glading was more acerbic. He found Deutsch too cautious, at one point complaining that he was 'bumptious'. There was also a part of Glading that resented being told what to do by a foreigner, an incipient sense that one day he should be doing Deutsch's job himself.

For all this, Glading was flattered to have been chosen by the NKVD from among so many other Comintern agents. His instructions from Maly and Deutsch were to recruit a team of sub-agents inside the Woolwich Arsenal, the industrial complex in which he had worked before being kicked out on account of his Communist beliefs, and to have these agents ready to remove secret plans from the factory, photograph them and then have the negatives couriered to Moscow.

Finding British factory workers who were willing to betray their country was surprisingly – depressingly – easy. This says a lot about the political ferment of the time. Several months earlier, in July 1936, a group of Spanish officers had launched a rebellion against the democratically elected government of Spain, an uprising that sparked the Spanish Civil War. This appeared to be part of an ongoing conflict between the Right and the Left, and as such it would attract thousands of idealistic volunteers who were willing to give their lives in defence of one side or the other. The world had entered an age of political extremes in which antipathy towards Fascism could easily become sympathy for Communism, and vice versa, which was why Percy Glading did not have to look hard to find three Woolwich Arsenal workers who were willing to help Moscow in the belief that by doing so they might be fighting Fascism.

The other part of Glading's job was harder. He needed to find a place in which to have the stolen material photographed. He decided to set up a safe house. But who to run it? Ideally, this person would be a trusted comrade with experience of illegal work and a clean record, yet one who did not formally belong to the Communist Party.

Olga Gray was not entirely sure why Percy Glading had asked to see her, after he contacted her unexpectedly in February 1937, but she had a pretty good idea. Three days earlier she had told Harry Pollitt that she was finally leaving the Communist Party. She probably thought Glading wanted to talk her into changing her mind.

Instead, he asked her to run a safe house. Olga was to find a flat that did not belong to a block with a porter, because Glading did not want anyone keeping tabs on his movements, and to move into this place and carry out certain tasks. He would have his own set of keys. Glading planned to visit the property several times each month, and in return she could live rent-free in a fully furnished flat.

The easiest course of action for Olga, the most attractive, simplest and safest response, was to say no and to carry on with her life after MI5 as if this conversation had not happened. M would never find out. Instead, she told Glading that she would think about it. After that she made a call to her spymaster.

M must have gone into shock. Having endured the worst few months of his life, bar none, an agent he had written off had now presented him with what might be the biggest break of his career. MI5 had been investigating Glading for more than a decade. M's agents had repeatedly got themselves to within touching distance of this man, but no closer. M/5 thought that 'Percy Glading is the comrade in charge of the whole Illegal Apparatus' for the entire Communist Party and had even been told that Glading wanted to speak to him personally about weaponry he examined at work. This same agent heard that Glading was in charge of a series of illegal factory groups, including one in the Woolwich Arsenal. Jimmy Dickson, the civil servant and novelist, had been grilled by Glading about variable-pitch aircraft propellers and on how to get information from Communists inside the government. Graham Pollard's career as an agent had recently spluttered back to life when he reported that Glading had rebuked a comrade for being so naïve as to accept at face value a statement made by the Comintern.

Yet Percy Glading was meticulous. On the telephone he gave away nothing. He had guessed correctly that MI5 was reading his post and was shadowing him intermittently around London. As the MI5 watchers reported wearily, Glading 'seemed to be somewhat suspicious of being followed'.

Now the man who seemed incapable of slipping up had invited an MI5 agent to help him carry out an act of international espionage. All that remained was for M to convince Olga to accept.

'To be quite frank,' admitted M, she 'was none too keen to be drawn again into the Party activities'. It had been less than two years since Olga's nervous breakdown. This new mission would be the most challenging of her career. But it also provided a chance for her to bow out, and do so to a standing ovation. None of M's agents had ever been given an opportunity like this to catch a Soviet agent. Although it would be a waste to say no, it required nerve to say yes.

Olga Gray was later described by a Scotland Yard detective as 'the bravest girl I ever knew', one who 'had forgotten more about courage than many soldiers ever learn on the battlefield'. No doubt her spymaster helped to build up her self-belief. Another agent marvelled at 'M's ability to instil confidence' in his informants. Whatever it was that helped to persuade her, in the days after Glading made his proposal to Olga Gray she agreed to join his underground cell.

MR PETERS

Over the next few weeks, Olga Gray and M looked for a flat that met Percy Glading's requirements as well as MI5's. For Soviet purposes it could not be part of a block with a porter. For the British, its entrance had to be observable from the other side of the street (where a team of MI5 watchers would be installed). Eventually, Olga found a property on Holland Road, in west London, that M was happy with; and so, too, was Glading.

Having gone flat hunting with M, Olga went furniture shopping with Glading. Together they picked out chairs, chests of drawers and curtains on an instalment plan. He gave her £100 to cover the rent for the first year, and in early April 1937 Olga moved into her new home, the ground-floor flat in No. 82 Holland Road, a property that surely holds the distinction of being the only private residence anywhere in the world to have been chosen by MI5 and paid for by Soviet intelligence.

While Olga made herself at home, a team of MI5 watchers did likewise across the road. Their presence was essential if M was going to mount a prosecution of Glading and his cell, but it was also a potential weakness. These watchers were not quite as stealthy as they liked to think. The future MI5 officer Anthony Blunt would describe their methods as 'very unscientific'. For one of his colleagues in MI5, allowing these men and women to get involved 'was to put the whole operation in the direst straits'. One slip from the watchers would be enough to scupper M's operation.

Late on 21 April, 1937, Glading arrived at the safe house with a male guest. He was introduced to Olga as Mr Peters. This was not his real name. There followed forty-five minutes of 'polite conversation' in which Olga and Mr Peters tried to get the measure of one another, a mutual cross-examination hidden beneath a veneer of prim banalities. It must have been excruciating. Olga made a mental sketch of her visitor while he sized her up, and after less than an hour Mr Peters left.

'Aged about 45; very tall, about 6′4″; medium build, heavy enough not to look lanky,' she told M, in a typically precise report, 'very dark hair; thinning along left and right partings; rather small eyes, dark (possibly grey), rather heavy lids; straight nose but rather heavy; rather wide mouth, short upper lip, dark moustache; slightly cleft chin; typical shiny grey complexion of some Russians and Germans; teeth gold filled in front; hands with very long fingers, flat nails, strums with fingers on chair arm etc.; dressed in black suit, black shoes, dark tie. Spoke English very well, but slowly. Noticeable accent, but English correct. Has difficulty with "w"s, tries not to pronounce as "v" but not very successful.'

It was a superb description, as good as any that M had ever received, and it introduced him to Theodor Maly. This was the first time that any of his agents had encountered such a senior member of the Soviet Union's London *rezidentura,* even if Olga did not find out his real name. At the time, this *rezidentura* contained about twenty Soviet professionals, including spymasters like Maly as well as talent spotters such as Edith Tudor-Hart (who had been reported on earlier by Eric Roberts after she made an unusual bank deposit), and couriers, safe-house operators, photographers and mail drops. They passed themselves off in London as businessmen and journalists or, in one case, as an ice skater. Their job was to recruit and service a growing band of Soviet agents working undercover in Britain. M's agents, and others run by MI5, were supposed to catch them. But this was not going to be easy.

The diplomat Robert Cecil famously likened this 1930s contest between Soviet intelligence and British counterespionage to a football match between Manchester United and the Corinthian Casuals. The elite Russian professionals of the NKVD had been drawn against the poorly equipped English amateurs, embodied by M Section, with its permanent staff of just two. It was a contest in which there seemed to be just one possible victor.

M was certain from Olga's report that 'Mr Peters', or Theodor Maly, had not visited Glading's safe house to give orders or inspect stolen documents. 'The purpose of the meeting,' wrote M, 'was for the flat and Miss "X" to be "looked at".'

Maly was satisfied and sent a message to Moscow Centre to say that Glading's network was ready to be activated. Glading had a team of men inside the Woolwich Arsenal. He had a safe house with photographic equipment and an apparently reliable woman running it. Theodor Maly, one of the most accomplished agents to work for Moscow, had judged that Olga was everything she claimed to be. A Corinthian Casual had dodged a two-footed lunge from a Manchester United professional.

In response, Moscow Centre assigned a task to Glading and his men. Their mission reflected a major shift in Russian naval policy. For years, Stalin had adopted the 'Youth School' approach to naval development. This held that while the capitalist and Fascist nations could worry themselves about who had the heaviest battleship with the biggest guns, the Soviet Union would be different. The Red Navy had become a small, heterogeneous fleet dominated by lightweight destroyers and cutting-edge S-, K- and M-class submarines.

In 1935, Stalin changed his mind. He decided that size did matter. Now he wanted a fleet of fifteen titanic battleships and battlecruisers, yet there had been no shipbuilding on this scale in Russia since the Bolshevik Revolution, so it was impossible to construct this new fleet without foreign help. A tentative agreement was reached with President Roosevelt for American contractors to supply designs, armour plating and materials for the construction of these warships. However, the deal was scuppered by the US Navy, where there was little appetite for sharing any technological secrets with the Soviet Union.

In Moscow the question of how to obtain this expert naval knowledge was put before the country's different intelligence-gathering agencies, including the NKVD, which was how Stalin's quest for a larger, heavier and more impressive fleet came to involve an ex-factory worker from the East End of London named Percy and a typist from Birmingham named Olga. Moscow Centre needed Glading's new cell to steal the blueprints of the secret fourteen-inch naval guns that were under construction at the Woolwich Arsenal. There were just five copies of these plans anywhere in the world and they were well guarded. But if Glading's setup was as good as Maly thought it might be, his men could stand a chance of getting their hands on the secret documents.

M was aware of only some of this. Based on the intelligence that he had received, a slender Eastern European with gold teeth was running a Soviet network in London that was centred on Percy Glading, and they were planning to steal and photograph something. That was it.

MOSCOW MOVES

It was not long before Percy Glading was starting to feel the strain. Several months after Olga had moved into the safe house, he came by drunk one night and began to pour out his worries to her. The MI5 agent made a good listener. Glading explained that he had just seen six of his people, that is, agents, and complained that he was doing very little work these days for the British Communist Party. Instead, he was at the beck and call of 'other people', meaning his Soviet controllers, Maly and Deutsch.

Glading was starting to crack up, and so was the NKVD *rezidentura*. Shortly after this drunken encounter, one of Deutsch's other agents lost a diary. It contained a complete list of the men and women in Britain who were secretly working for Moscow. There was enough in this document to warrant shutting down the entire NKVD operation in Britain, which is what now happened. Deutsch fled the country. Maly was already overseas, either organising or carrying out the murder of a Soviet defector. The entire NKVD network in Britain ground to a halt, leaving Percy Glading, Kim Philby and the rest in limbo.

The incriminating diary had been misplaced by Edith Tudor-Hart, an Austrian photographer and NKVD agent who had once talent-spotted Philby. It is hard to say just how far Tudor-Hart might have gone in her attempts to recover this document, and what levels of coercion, bribery or violence had run through her mind. Yet three weeks after it had gone missing, the diary was found. It had fallen down the back of her sofa.

Moscow's response, however, was not to reactivate its British networks. At least, not right away. At that moment the Russian capital was in the grip of 'Stalin's Terror', a period of murderous paranoia in which almost anyone in the Soviet Union who was accused of being an enemy of 'the people' was either shot or sent to a labour camp. Although this was unrelated to the missing diary, Theodor Maly came under suspicion at around this time of being a Nazi agent and was summoned back to Moscow.

Maly was not working for the Germans. He was a loyal NKVD officer, and on being told to return to the Soviet Union to stand trial the man who had recently interviewed Olga might have tried to seek asylum in the West, or to go underground. Instead he returned to Moscow, knowing that he would probably face a firing squad. Soon after his return, Theodor Maly was executed. Some have argued that he was driven back by his crippling sense of guilt, and that this was suicide-by-show-trial. Either way, in the weeks and months that followed, the NKVD operation in Britain was leaderless and inactive.

M was a man who understood how to wait. As a naturalist, he had spent hundreds of hours camped out near nests and burrows, anticipating the emergence of a particular animal. He knew within himself the power of patience, yet by July 1937, three months after Olga had moved into the safe house, he was getting fidgety. None of the espionage once hinted at by Glading had taken place. Or perhaps it had, and M was simply unaware of it. Was there another safe house, and another Olga? Did this Mr Peters have tens of Percy Gladings dotted around the capital? Or should M be pouring his limited resources into investigation of the Fascists rather than the Communists?

Several weeks later, Glading arrived at Olga's safe house with two people who were introduced to her as Mr and Mrs Stephens. As usual, these were not their real names.

'They were clearly foreigners,' wrote Olga. 'They spoke to each other in French.'

She described Mr Stephens as 'very self-assured', with 'large hands', 'very thick short fingers' and a 'very slight but almost unnoticeable hesitation in speech'. Mr and Mrs Stephens were in fact Mikhail Borovoy and his wife, then travelling under the names Willy and Mary Brandes. They were NKVD illegals, like Maly and Deutsch, who had previously been in the United States. Moscow Centre had sent them to London to activate Glading's spy ring and use it to steal the plans of the Royal Navy's new fourteen-inch gun. The following month, the two illegals returned to Olga's flat where they ran through the details of the planned operation. A date was set for the dress rehearsal. The actual operation would take place three days later.

The practice run was a near disaster. This was mainly because the woman operating the camera had never taken a picture before. Borovoy had originally lined up an experienced female photographer from the Soviet *rezidentura,* but there had been a hitch: she was in love with Borovoy (or so Borovoy claimed). The feeling had not been mutual, he explained, and the photographer had apparently had a breakdown and been ordered back to Moscow.

In her place had come Borovoy's wife. Having no idea how to work a camera, she was, as you might imagine, in an age before autofocus and automatic exposures, 'decidedly nervous regarding her ability to use the apparatus efficiently'. Glading was also 'very jumpy' during the rehearsal. Although 'Mr Stephens' tried to remain calm, he was under immense pressure. As Glading put it to Olga, illegals like him 'live on a volcano the whole time they are over here'. It was a feeling Olga knew all too well.

At last, they finished photographing a map of the London Underground – a stand-in for the blueprints they planned to photograph during the operation itself. The negatives were developed and left to dry overnight, and the next day Olga took them to Victoria Station and handed them to Glading.

He told Olga that he was annoyed by the stand-in photographer's performance the night before. As he had predicted, the first roll of film was a failure. But the second was legible. Everything was now in place for 'the job' to go ahead.

The forthcoming operation 'is obviously regarded as important', Olga told M, and it would involve photographing blueprints. It was up to M to decide when and where the arrests should take place.

At last the day of the actual operation arrived. At seven o'clock in the evening, the team of MI5 watchers observed Mrs Stephens enter the safe house carrying 'a large oblong parcel'. Inside the flat, Olga watched her unfold this package. Inside was a series of plans. She laid them out on a broad refectory table, where a state-of-the-art Leica camera had been set up on a tripod. Olga tried to see what the plans were, but Mrs Stephens shooed her out of the room, telling her to make some tea. The MI5 agent reappeared a few minutes later and after handing round the mugs she tried to get a look at the plans, but was told to go to her bedroom.

Olga sat in her room for the next three hours while Mrs Stephens finished her photography. Having wrapped up the original plans, she left the flat at about ten thirty. Olga emerged from her room and found forty-two negatives drying in the bathroom.

Meanwhile, as Mrs Stephens left the building one of the MI5 watchers began to follow her. She hopped into a taxi, as did her tail, and the two cars drove to Hyde Park Corner, in west London, where

Mrs Stephens got out. One of the MI5 watchers did the same. She was then observed meeting Mr Stephens as well as another man. This would turn out to be a middle-aged councillor from Bexley, in south-east London, George Whomack, who had worked at the Woolwich Arsenal since the war and had once been described by MI5 as an 'active and dangerous Communist'. Now he was part of Glading's NKVD cell. Whomack took the blueprints from Mrs Stephens and left.

Back in the safe house, Olga stood on tip-toes in the empty bath, squinting up at the drying negatives. Amazingly, given how small they were, she was able to make out the serial numbers of the plans. She called up M to report what she had seen. He made enquiries, and established that these plans were for the Royal Navy's new fourteen-inch gun. Now he had grounds to order the arrest.

Yet Mr and Mrs Stephens were not apprehended by the police. Instead, they were kept under observation the following day and were shadowed onto a train that took them to Dover. From there they left the country.

The Soviet plan had worked to perfection. The two illegals made it safely out of Britain and copies of the secret blueprints were soon received in Moscow. Percy Glading's first NKVD mission had been an unqualified success. Olga must have been completely baffled.

Knowing precisely when to call in the police and make an arrest is often the hardest part of an intelligence operation. Just as there are risks attached to coming in too late, by striking too soon you might destroy the possibility of uncovering more valuable information. After the arrest of the Soviet spies Wilfred Macartney and Georg Hansen almost a decade earlier, there had been a feeling among some MI5 officers that they may have jumped in too early, and that, in future, in a similar situation, it would be wise to delay the arrest in the hope of gathering more intelligence. Perhaps this was in the back of M's mind when he chose not to order the prompt arrest of Mr and Mrs

Stephens. Or had he developed a sentimental attachment to Olga? Calling in the police would have effectively ended her undercover career, and he may not have been ready for that. It is also possible that in the glare of the moment, when faced with a momentous, career-defining decision, the MI5 spymaster had frozen.

By then M had mastered the art of running agents. His infiltration of the Communist Party on a shoestring budget had been an extraordinary feat. He possessed an unparalleled ability to turn unqualified men and women – bankers, secretaries, barristers, booksellers – into reliable and consistently productive agents, and to keep them going for many years. But knowing exactly when to call in the police in the course of an investigation was a very different skill, and one that M had not yet acquired.

OLD FRIENDS, NEW AGENTS

As if to compensate for what had happened, in the weeks that followed M oversaw a surge of activity from his other agents. Two years earlier, he had had just one agent inside the Fascist movement: Eric Roberts. Now he had four, including one codenamed 'M/R', whose identity has never been revealed.

M/R was evidently not a newcomer to the Fascist movement. Within a few months of being taken on by M in 1936, this new agent had access to senior BUF figures as well as high-ranking Italian Fascists. One of M/R's first reports recounted a long meeting with Gino Gario, a prominent journalist on the official Italian newspaper in Britain, *L'Italia Nostra,* in which Gario comes across as desperate to impress M/R. He even gave the new MI5 agent a guided tour of Casa Littoria, the headquarters of the Italian Fasci in Britain. This allowed M/R to make a sketch of the floorplan. Although M's new agent apologised to his spymaster 'for his deficiencies as an architect', this plan was good enough to be used by the police several years later in a raid on this building.

So, who was M/R? Other details in newly released MI5 files show that this agent was a male journalist with good connections to Italian

Fascists. From this limited description there is one candidate who stands out: a journalist then employed at the London International Press who was also a respected figure in the Fascist movement. Even the initials of his surname – M.-R. – point to the codename M/R. But we need proof.

When the journalist with the surname M.-R. wrote his will, he did so by hand. Equally, the agent M/R's sketch of the Casa Littoria floorplan was hand-drawn and contains examples of its author's handwriting. Although one document was written several decades after the other, it is possible to make a forensic comparison of M/R's handwriting and that of the journalist M.-R.

Ellen Radley of the Radley Forensic Document Laboratory, one of Britain's longest-running private forensic laboratories, has concluded 'there is strong evidence' that the handwritten plan of the Casa Littoria was made by the same person who wrote the will. The circumstantial evidence only confirms the link. It seems that M/R was almost certainly one of M's old associates from the British Fascists, E. G. Mandeville-Roe – known to his friends as Geoff.

M appears to have recruited yet another old comrade from the BF, and one of some standing. Mandeville-Roe was a founding figure of the British Fascist movement. He had composed the 'Fascist Song', the Right's answer to 'The Red Flag', and had been Editor of *British Fascism* and author of a book on the corporate state, which played a vital role in shaping early BUF policy. More recently, Mandeville-Roe had met Mussolini and Hitler and had even been announced as a possible BUF Parliamentary candidate. Now he was spying on the movement he had once helped to build up.

For M to persuade this renowned Fascist to work for MI5 was a coup. It would have taken many years for a newcomer to achieve anything like the same level of seniority. M's history inside the Fascist movement had made him initially reluctant to direct agents against it. But now that same intimacy provided him with a range of contacts that he could either blackmail or charm into working for him. M's underlying weakness might yet become his strength.

As well as Roberts and Mandeville-Roe, M asked another of his old friends from the BF to infiltrate the Right. This required a more substantial transformation. The role of every agent may change over time, moving from tactical to strategic and back again, but this was altogether different. Having spent most of his adult life as one of M's key agents inside the Communist movement, in 1937 Jimmy Dickson was asked by his spymaster to reinvent himself as a Fascist.

This was like telling an agent deep inside a violent animal-rights group to infiltrate a jihadi cell. Dickson, by then an established novelist, would have to learn a different way of speaking, a new manner and invent a fresh bodyguard of lies with which to protect his identity.

M insisted. Ultimately, Dickson agreed.

Although M may have hesitated at first, by 1937 he had clearly recognised the threat of Fascism both at home and abroad. Now he was in a rush to deploy new agents against right-wing targets. As well as Roberts, Mandeville-Roe and Dickson, M also took on at around this time 'M/S', an agent recently identified by the historian Richard Dove as Claud Sykes, the great-great-nephew of the Duke of Wellington. Sykes was an actor, author and translator whose main claim to fame was that he had once set up a theatre company with James Joyce. Like so many of M's recruits, Sykes was a prolific writer with a romantic attachment to the idea of being a spy. In one of his many books, Sykes describes what he imagined to be the thrill of life as a 'spy who goes alone into the enemy camp, where the mispronunciation of a word or ignorance of some trivial custom may betray him', insisting that this agent 'deserves as well of his country as the soldier who serves in the field'. His ambition was about to be realised.

Claud Sykes's main qualification was that he spoke excellent German. His first task as one of M's new agents was to befriend Dr Gottfried Roesel, the London correspondent for *National Zeitung,* who was soon gulled into revealing that he was, in fact, the London Group leader of the Nazi Party.

Intelligence provided by Sykes, Dickson, Roberts, Mandeville-Roe and others was starting to affect the way MI5 and the British government saw homegrown Fascism. This new 1930s version of British Fascism posed a different threat to its 1920s predecessor. As one MI5 report of 1937 explained, 'a very reliable informant inside the movement [probably Eric Roberts] has formed the opinion that there are a certain number of young people – possibly only a few hundred – who have been so hypnotised by Fascist propaganda that in the event of war against either Italy or Germany their sympathies would lie with the enemy'.

This was a stunning assertion. It implied that a homegrown Fascist might present the same kind of danger as an enemy agent. What made this so worrying for M, and his colleagues in MI5, was just how many of these right-wing extremists there were in Britain, and how much harder it would be in wartime to have them taken off the streets, given that they were British. In light of this, MI5 pushed for a bold new amendment to the War Book, the compendium of regulations and measures to be introduced when the country went to war. In 1937, MI5 demanded the wartime power to order the internment without trial of any British citizen who seemed to pose a threat to public safety or national security. This amounted to a denial of habeas corpus and the possibility of hundreds, maybe thousands, of innocent Britons being locked up as a result of nothing more than their membership of a right-wing group such as the BUF. It seemed to be a rejection of a basic tenet of the British legal tradition. Yet the intelligence from M Section was persuasive, and in July 1937 this controversial amendment was quietly approved by the Committee of Imperial Defence and added to the War Book.

Several weeks later, in an ancient tumbledown church in the New Forest, near the south coast, M got married for the second time. His bride was Lois Coplestone. They had met recently in a pub and, rather than go for a series of romantic meals, they had gone fishing together. Over the months that followed they fell in love.

Lois was attractive, self-contained and was ten years younger than her new husband. Like Gwladys, she came from a respectably upper-middle-class, Conservative-voting family, she was reasonably well-off and had grown up outside London. 'I was immediately attracted to him,' she recalled, describing M as 'a deeply charming person'. Another woman remembered 'the charm this smiling man possessed – charm of a rare and formidable order', adding that he was 'enigmatic and debonair, qualities I found irresistible'.

Aged thirty-seven, Maxwell Knight had grown into himself. He was sturdier and broader than the man Gwladys had married, his face was that little bit craggier, his nose beakier. He still wore his hair brushed back over his head, yet it was thicker than before and there was less need for all that pomade. M had for many years had a commanding presence, yet by the time he met Lois he possessed a more imposing physicality. His speech was military with undertones of the country. He exuded an air of quiet certainty. 'Be confident and unafraid in your approach,' he once wrote, one of several lines that could apply just as well to approaching an animal, recruiting an agent or meeting one's future wife, 'for your confidence, or lack of it, will communicate itself almost at once.'

M was assured and persuasive, but there was also a hint of vulnerability to him. Early on in their relationship, he told Lois about how he blamed himself for Gwladys's loneliness towards the end of her life. Lois described him as 'shattered' by her death. M was determined not to make the same mistake in his new marriage, and after their wedding in Boldre, a village close to where Lois had grown up, he arranged for his wife to move in with him on Sloane Street.

Before long it became clear that there was not enough room in the flat for Lois, M, M's jazz collection, M's pets and of course M Section. Something would have to give. This might have been the moment to move his agent-running operation into the Office, which was now just down the road from Parliament at Thames House (where it is again today), but M refused. There may have been practical reasons for this – he did not want his colleagues to know that he was still running the civil servant Jimmy Dickson – but deep down this was about identity. M was a spymaster forged in the Makgill smithy. The origins of his section lay beyond MI5, and his unit would always be more right-wing, more daring and more maverick than any other MI5 section. The man at its helm wanted to keep it that way for as long as possible.

Rather than move his operation into the Office, M decided to start running it from a flat owned by Lois's brother in Dolphin Square, an ultra-luxurious, new housing development that overlooked the River Thames. According to Dolphin Square promotional literature, this complex was for a new generation that 'thinks differently and will live differently'. That was certainly true of M and his long-suffering secretary.

Back on Sloane Street, Lois was learning to live with a man who was not yet accustomed to sharing his home with his wife. Part of the problem was his unusually large collection of pets, which was forever being added to as friends or acquaintances gave him injured or unwanted creatures. M found it hard to say no. He always relished the challenge of taking on a new animal, even if he found it hard to bear when an animal died in his care. 'I have myself felt tears welling up when I once failed to bring a monkey through pneumonia and it died in my arms,' wrote M, some years later. 'I do not think that this was pure sentiment' – he loathed the idea of being oversentimental – 'it was a combination of real grief at the loss of a pet, and compassion for the monkey whose sufferings I was unable to do much to alleviate.'

Keeping his pets alive and healthy was a major undertaking, and over the years M had developed certain rigid habits. He was a stickler for cleanliness and eliminating draughts, for instance. 'Bottles, teats, tubes and mixing dishes must be washed after each meal,' he warned. 'Failure to do this will mean sickness and possibly death.' The temperature and lighting in the flat were to mirror the outside world as much as possible, so when night fell the lights were not always turned on, unless, that was, the newlyweds were entertaining.

Although Lois got on well with her new sister-in-law Enid, who was a frequent visitor to the flat, she was not so keen on her husband's colleagues from work, including Sir Vernon Kell, who would often come by for dinner. Another regular guest was the best-selling novelist Dennis Wheatley. M greatly admired Wheatley and had recently dedicated his last book to him. The writer was no less intrigued by this MI5 spymaster. The two men were also bound together by their experiences at a séance held by the notorious spiritualist Aleister Crowley, who liked to be known as 'the Beast'. They had gone along out of curiosity, both professional and private, and were probably expecting it to be something of a joke.

'It was extremely unnerving,' M later told his nephew, adding that he and Wheatley had been 'very, very shaken'. For M, this experience appears to have confirmed or, more likely, sparked his interest in spiritualism. Although this was a little eccentric at the time, it was certainly not unusual. The number of spiritualist societies active in Britain by the mid-1930s had trebled since 1914. Thousands of séance circles met in people's homes across the country during the interwar years, usually in the hope of speaking to a father or son who had 'crossed over' during the last war. M did not hold regular séances himself, but for the rest of his life this MI5 spymaster remained open to the possibility of a non-religious life after death.

Lois did not share her husband's spiritualist bent. Like so many parts of his interior world, this one seemed to be cordoned off from her. Sadly, the same was already true of his sexuality. After several months of marriage, their relationship remained unconsummated, even if this time M may have tried to address the problem.

Lois's future sister-in-law, Rosamund Selsey, recalled bumping into M late one night in his flat, and in the surprisingly frank conversation that followed the MI5 officer described to her the pain of losing Gwladys and revealed that he was seeing a doctor about his problem in bed. It was rare for him to let anyone in like this. Perhaps the legacy of Gwladys's death would be a growing self-awareness, and a different type of relationship with his past.

What had not changed, however, was the distance M liked to keep from his colleagues in the Office. He still preferred to conceal the identity of his agents, including the latest addition to his stable, an informant he codenamed 'M/J'.

'Joyce, to my mind, is one of the most fascinating character studies in the movement,' wrote Eric Roberts in early 1937, describing him as a man who 'knows what he wants in life, and is out to get it. I feel somehow, despite the fact I dislike the man intensely, that in him there is someone who might one day make history. With all his faults he remains in my mind one of the most compelling personalities of the whole movement.'

Roberts had also predicted that Joyce and Mosley would soon fall out, based on what he had seen of their relationship. Several months later, he was proved right. Having been forced out of the BUF by Mosley, Joyce retaliated by setting up a pro-Nazi splinter group, the British National Socialist League. M's response might have been to ask for Joyce to be put under close observation. Instead, he appears to have taken him on as an agent.

We know that less than a month after Joyce was removed from the BUF the American supplied M with at least one scrap of intelligence. Several months later M began to receive intelligence from a new agent codenamed 'M/J'. This source was particularly well informed on conversations among the BUF leadership that had taken place several years earlier – the kind of high-level discussions to which Joyce had been privy at that time. Otherwise, M/J received new material 'from an informant of his in the BUF'. Again, this points to Joyce. Several years earlier M had told Roberts that 'Joyce has a well organised intelligence service of his own, and he is kept fully informed of what goes [on] among the various [BUF] factions'. Even the internal codename 'M/J' is suggestive. More than half of the agents to whom M gave alphabetical codenames were assigned letters that corresponded to their actual names. Joyce's family also claimed some years later that he had become one of M's agents at around this time.

Perhaps the only other man who could have been M/J was J. McGuirk Hughes, the BUF Director of Intelligence and a former Makgill man. He too had his own network of informants, his name fits and he moved in similar circles to Joyce. Although it is not possible to make a definite identification of M/J, there is no doubt that in 1937, in his desperation to find out more about the Fascist movement, and as a result of being 'seriously handicapped by lack of adequate finance', M recruited another friend from his Fascist past as an MI5 agent. It was probably Joyce.

Although Eric Roberts reported around this time that William Joyce 'was growing morose, savage, unstable and more unreliable than ever', M felt that he knew him better than that. 'I should not think that anything could occur to shake his basic patriotism,' M had once written. In so many ways, M's opinion of Joyce reflected his relationship with the homegrown Fascist movement in Britain more broadly. While a growing body of evidence suggested that radicalised British Fascists could pose a threat to national security in the event of a war, and increasingly M accepted this, he was not yet ready to write off everyone connected to the movement. He continued to see his old comrade 'Joycey' as a man who might say outrageous things when he was up on stage but who was, at the same time, at his core, incapable of betraying his country.

28

REPRIEVE

On 12 January, 1938, M received a call from Olga Gray. Percy Glading had just told her that there was going to be another job, and it was taking place that weekend. Moscow Centre was getting greedy, he must have thought. It would have come as a surprise to M to learn that the NKVD knew even less about this operation than he did.

Glading had always wanted to prove the world wrong. In the past he had taken orders from his Soviet superiors – Borovoy, Maly and Deutsch – yet his abiding 'aim and ambition', he once told Olga, was to take over the 'executive side of the work' being done by the NKVD in Britain. To prove that he was up to the job, Glading had decided to carry out an espionage operation without first informing Moscow Centre. As before, he wanted Olga to be part of it.

M's response was to step up surveillance on Glading's home in Harrow, north London. Three days later this Soviet agent was seen leaving his house early in the afternoon, before he was lost by the MI5 watchers. He returned three hours later carrying a folded newspaper. It appeared to conceal a small book. The watchers could not be sure. The best way to find out was by making an arrest, yet this might be just another rehearsal using an ordinary book of no consequence, in which case an arrest would be a mistake. Glading was also alone, whereas Olga had said that a Moscow operative would be involved. It did not feel right. M decided to hold back.

The following morning Percy Glading left his house with the same carefully folded newspaper lodged under his arm. The MI5 watchers began their pursuit. This time they managed to follow him to Charing Cross Station, in central London, where he was seen heading towards the main public lavatory. He descended the steps, and at the bottom met a young man carrying an attaché case.

With one of the MI5 watchers just a few yards away, Glading handed over the newspaper and its contents to the man with the attaché case. This second individual was followed by the watchers to a residential address in Plumstead, which turned out to be his home. He was soon identified as Charles Munday, a twenty-two-year-old assistant chemist in the Woolwich Arsenal.

M now had the outline of a Soviet spy ring. Charles Munday, the chemist, and George Whomack, the middle-aged man involved in the first operation, both worked in the Woolwich Arsenal and were presumably responsible for getting stolen material out of the complex. Olga ran the safe house. Glading took photographs and supplied negatives to his Soviet controller, which were then passed on to Moscow. But if M ordered the arrest of Glading, Munday and Whomack now, the prosecution would rest on the strength of Olga's evidence and the testimony of the MI5 watchers. It might be enough. It might not. M felt that he needed more.

Several days later, Olga received a call from Glading. He sounded tense. He said that he wanted to have lunch the next day. Without giving away anything specific on the phone, Glading intimated that a new job was in the offing and it could be bigger than the last. Olga agreed to the meeting, hung up and dialled M's number.

The following day, Glading arrived at the Windsor Castle pub in Notting Hill, west London, carrying a suitcase. It contained his photographic equipment. He wanted to do another job, not the next week or tomorrow, but that very evening. This time Glading planned to take the photographs at Olga's safe house. He told her to be back at the flat before six o'clock to help set up the camera. After that he would go to Charing Cross Station to pick up the stolen material.

At last, M decided to strike. He would collapse the house of cards that he had built up so meticulously around Olga over the past six years. He instructed Special Branch to make the arrests that evening.

At quarter past eight, Glading was greeted on the concourse of Charing Cross Station by a middle-aged man carrying a paper parcel. They walked together towards the exit while a team of plainclothes policemen closed in on them, an implosion in slow motion, and when the middle-aged man handed over the parcel the officers made the arrest. Percy Glading had flown too close to the sun. As he was led away by the police, he said nothing.

Back at the safe house, Olga was expecting to see Glading walk in the door; instead, her younger brother, Richard Gray, recently qualified as a policeman, bounded in. He told her to pack up her things and took her off to a hotel in East Horsley, Surrey, a different kind of safe house, where she would lie low until the trial.

Olga's career as an undercover MI5 agent had entered its final phase. So much espionage work ends in a fog of uncertainty and irresolution. Olga's penetration of the Communist underground was about to reach a sharp conclusion, one that would be played out before the world.

29

MISS X

_____

'Sample of the tempting sort of bait successfully used to catch spies by His Majesty's Government has now been on view in London's ancient, soot-blackened Bow Street Police Court for several weeks, officially tagged "Miss X",' began _Time_ magazine's breathless account of Olga's first public appearance, the preliminary hearing against Percy Glading and the other members of what became known as the Woolwich Arsenal spy ring. 'This slim, bobbed-hair blonde, English to judge from her accent, arrived curvesomely sheathed in clinging black, kept shifting her handsome fur piece with the sinuosity of Mae West, as she testified before a bug-eyed judge.' The 'bug-eyed judge,' otherwise known as Mr Fry, ruled that the case should go for trial, and a date was set for the Old Bailey.

This preliminary hearing was widely reported in Britain and throughout North America. Glading and his accomplices may have been the ones on trial, but it soon became clear that they were not the main attraction. Olga was hailed in one report as 'Britain's counter-espionage heroine'. The _Washington Post_ thought her 'stylish'. The _Atlanta Constitution_ admired her 'black two-piece ensemble and a smart halo hat'. She was 'slim', 'blonde' and 'trim', according to the Associated Press, and had a 'cultured' voice. 'Fair-haired, and attractive,' added the *Manchester Guardian*. *Time* was more matter-of-fact, describing Olga as 'exceptionally pretty'.

Here was 'a real spy hunt that outdid fiction thrillers', as the *Chicago Tribune* put it. The *New York Times* also noted the similarity between the events unfolding in Bow Street Police Court and so 'many fictional trials'. In the form of Olga Gray, or 'Miss X', reality had trumped the collective imagination. 'Was there ever a more dramatic role, in actual life, for any modern young woman to play?' the *Atlanta Constitution* demanded to know. 'Not even Oppenheim, master of fictional international intrigue, ever concocted a more fascinating scene than that of this girl sitting in the witness chair at historic Bow Street court and telling of the dangerous existence she led in order to protect her country's secrets. It is doubtful if there are any young women of this modern age who do not feel some envy of this girl of mystery. To sit within the world spotlight and to tell, in her educated voice and confident manner, the story of her work as an espionage agent – it must be a thrill! And, to modern youth, what is there more to be desired than a thrill?'

Yet for Olga this was not 'a thrill'. It was gruelling to explain in forensic detail what she had done to an inscrutable audience of lawyers, journalists, members of the public and, crucially, the man that she had betrayed. The scene being played out in court may have looked like something that belonged to spy fiction, yet beneath the surface, in the realm of motivation and sacrifice and the crushing burden of having to lie repeatedly to someone you like, the reality of spying and the fiction that had grown up around it were worlds apart. Olga's experience of espionage had long ago left behind anything that she had read about in a book or seen in a film. At one point Olga's barrister 'asked her if she would like to sit down'. Just one journalist picked up on the tension in court between Olga Gray and Percy Glading.

'Big, blue eyes are her chief personal attraction,' wrote the *Atlanta Constitution*'s correspondent, 'and they gaze intently at counsel for the crown as he puts a long series of questions to her. Unwavering, they occasionally turn to the man in the dock, P. E. Glading.' He added, pointedly, 'Glading does not meet her glances.'

What made this so much harder for Olga was her sense that she was now on the run and that Moscow was out to get her. Indeed one Scottish Communist angrily told M/5 at around this time that he 'would not be surprised to hear that "Miss X" had been hit on the head with a stick'. Olga did not leave the court as a conquering hero; instead, she 'was whisked away through a door behind the witness stand' and out into a police van, before being transferred to the hotel where her brother had been installed as her bodyguard.

Olga was visited in this hotel by her sister Marjorie, who recalled: 'I wanted to get some shopping in the village, but she begged me not to go.' Olga could no longer bear to be alone. 'Then I read all the newspaper accounts and suddenly realised what my sister had done. It was incredible – I just couldn't believe it.'

In just under a month Olga would have to go through the whole thing again, only this time at the Old Bailey, where there would be far more scrutiny of her character. If she messed up, became muddled, revealed a detail that she was not supposed to about M and MI5, or just cracked under the pressure, the Crown's case could collapse, for she was set to be the prosecution's principal witness. The success of M's investigation of Glading rested on Olga's ability to perform in court.

On 14 March, 1938, the trial began at the Old Bailey of Percy Glading and his three accomplices, Albert Williams, George Whomack and Charles Munday, all previously employed at the Woolwich Arsenal. The four men were charged with offences under Section 1c of the Official Secrets Act of 1911, concerning information that might be useful to an enemy. Britain may not have been at war with the Soviet Union, but it was agreed in court that the meaning of the act could apply to any country with which Britain might later be at war. These four were accused of stealing plans for an anti-submarine bomb fuse, an anti-tank mine pistol, a pressure-bar apparatus designed to test detonators, a 200-page manual on explosives and the blueprints for a fourteen-inch naval gun, and of taking photographs of these, before passing some to representatives of an 'enemy' nation. Everyone in court knew that this meant the Soviet Union. But in an attempt to limit the diplomatic fallout, efforts were made to keep mentions of Moscow to a minimum.

Although Glading had gone to great lengths to leave no finger-prints on the photographic apparatus, either by wiping it down or by using gloves, just before leaving for Charing Cross Station one of the bulbs in the safe house had blown. He had replaced it without cleaning up afterwards. Scotland Yard's fingerprint department found evidence of what they called Glading's 'nasty fingers' on an arc light switch, its shade and the replacement bulb. This was enough to link him definitively to the equipment.

The police also produced in court the suitcase with a false bottom that had been used, they alleged, to smuggle documents into and out of the Woolwich Arsenal. But the police had made one mistake. Immediately after arresting Percy Glading they had gone to search his house without a warrant. This had the effect of placing more weight on Olga's testimony.

Percy Glading's defence was led by Denis Pritt, KC, a skilful bar-rister and Soviet stooge. He understood the need to undermine Olga, so began by asking for her name to be released. This was met with strong resistance. 'Spy Fighters Guard Name of "Miss X",' was the headline in one American newspaper, with the subheading: 'Identity of Blond Lure One of Best Kept Secrets in British Empire'. Hopefully, this was an exaggeration. Vivian Hancock-Nunn, who was friendly with the left-wing lawyers representing Glading, reported to M that they already knew Olga's name, and in one report of the trial she was referred to, in print, as 'Miss G'.

Pritt tried to pick holes in Olga's evidence, but the MI5 agent stood firm. Having gone through the story repeatedly with M beforehand, Olga gave an assured and consistent account of what she had done over the last six years, and what she had seen and heard. M's agent did not fluff her lines, nor did she omit any vital details. In remarkably little time the case was concluded.

As was reported all over the world, Percy Glading was found guilty. He was sentenced to six years penal servitude, meaning hard labour. Albert Williams received four years. George Whomack, the only one to present the judge with 'difficulty' given 'the comparatively small part' he had played, was sentenced to three years in prison. Charles Munday was discharged because no evidence had been presented against him.

The presiding Mr Justice Hawke declared that Glading had acted 'with the sole and vulgar motive of obtaining money'. This was not true. Glading had been driven by his own ego and a desire for revenge, after losing his job, but underlying all this was a personal commitment to an ideology. Glading was a committed Communist who had openly placed his political beliefs before his country's interests.

At first this suggests a failure of imagination by the judge. Perhaps it was evidence of the reverse. In the spy novels and films that Mr Justice Hawke had undoubtedly seen and read, it was a trope that spies were driven by either patriotism or money. It would take the exposure of Kim Philby and the rest of the Cambridge Spies more than a decade later for this assumption to change, and for the British public and its judiciary to accept that a spy could be driven mainly by what George Orwell called 'that un-English thing, an idea'.

The judge may have been wrong about Glading, but he was right about Olga. On the day of the sentencing she had come in to the

Old Bailey and was sitting alone in a nearby room, with a guard on the door, smoking and reading magazines, when the judge mentioned her in his closing remarks.

'I do not propose to call her into court,' he said of Olga, 'but I think that young woman must be possessed of extraordinary courage, and I think she has done a great service to her country.' Even the defence would later confide to Vivian Hancock-Nunn that they had made 'the closest enquiries possible regarding Miss X's morals, but all the results were in her favour' – which, incidentally, militates against the idea that she was having an affair with Glading.

Olga Gray had triumphed. The Corinthian Casuals had scored a goal against the run of play. Olga would later be described in an official MI5 history as the government's 'leading pre-war penetration agent in the CPGB'. She had done everything she had been asked to do and much more, and had done so exceptionally well. In the process she had broken up a professional Soviet spy ring. Now her career as an undercover agent was over.

Shortly after the trial Olga was taken out for a lavish meal at the Ritz Restaurant by an MI5 officer, probably one of M's superiors, Jasper Harker, who thanked her for her work and gave her a cheque for £500. This was the equivalent of just under four years' wages as an MI5 agent. But it would be an unhappy send-off for M/12.

In the wake of the trial, Olga had begun to feel invincible. Almost at once she began to miss the work. She wanted to keep going as an agent, yet this was no longer practical. Too many people knew her identity. Spying can be addictive. Now M's agent would have to go cold turkey.

Olga also found it strange that she had been taken out to dinner by Harker rather than M. Perhaps her spymaster was worried that she might be under surveillance by the Soviets. More likely, he wanted to make a clean break. Although he may not have cut himself off from her entirely, he knew that it would be hard to turn their relationship into a casual friendship. Their bond as spymaster and spy had had the intensity of an affair. Now it was time to move on.

Olga drove an ambulance during the Blitz and continued her career as a secretary, taking a series of high-powered jobs. Towards the end of the war, she would find herself one day on the London Underground standing next to a good-looking Canadian Air Force officer. He gazed at her. She looked back at him. He asked her what time it was. Olga looked to his wrist and saw that he was already wearing a watch.

His name was Stanley Simons, and soon after picking up Olga on the Tube he got down on one knee. Their wedding was in Chelsea. Ten months later Olga became a mother. She and her new family then emigrated to Canada where she began a new and very different life.

MONA

The Woolwich Arsenal case was a moment of triumph for M. His transformation from jazz-playing animal enthusiast and family misfit to successful MI5 spymaster appeared to be complete. Fifteen years earlier he had been challenged by Sir George Makgill to take on the Red Menace. Here was his answer. Breaking up this Soviet spy ring, a network that had been primed to steal vital industrial and military secrets for years, was the great MI5 success story of the 1930s. Yet behind the scenes, unknown to the public, the greater achievement was the extent of his agents' infiltration of the British Communist movement.

In MI5 a certain mystique was starting to form around M's section. As well as being the most independent, economical and unconventional of MI5 sections, it was one of the most effective. The Woolwich Arsenal case was a vindication of M's tradecraft, especially his preference for long-term penetration agents and for taking on women.

The weeks that followed might have been a moment to bask in this success, but there was no time for that. The reaction to the trial in Communist circles had been explosive. Olga's performance in court confirmed that MI5 was able to get agents inside the movement. Their assumption was that there must be more. The Communists were determined to root them out – all of them.

'An organised "spy hunt" is to take place with as little delay as possible,' reported M's man in Liverpool. Any Party members who had been reluctant in the past to go canvassing now came under suspicion, as did those who sent their children to religious schools or did not socialise with other Party members. M also heard about the reaction in London. Indeed, the best intelligence he received about the Communist spy hunts in the wake of Glading's conviction came from the unlikeliest source. After more than six years of struggling to be taken seriously within the Party, remarkably his female agent M/2 had been taken on as a secretary at the Communist Party headquarters on King Street, the same office in which Olga had worked before her breakdown.

M/2 was now providing MI5 with regular, accurate intelligence about what she called 'the most exhaustive investigations, enquiries and heresy hunts', all of which had been set up to uncover people like her. Over the months that followed, M/2 produced a considerable haul of information. As well as being the most resilient of M's agents, having gone for so long without penetrating the Communist movement, she had suddenly become one of the most prolific.

Yet M/2 rarely appears in later accounts of MI5's work during the 1930s. This is partly because her name has never been revealed. That can now change.

From a recent official history of MI5 there is little doubt that during the late 1930s this particular agent belonged to a trade union called the Association of Women Clerks and Secretaries (AWCS). By going through her declassified reports, it also becomes clear that M/2 made it on to the executive committee of this union. This may not sound like much, but it is enough to open a door onto her identity.

Almost every Communist who made it onto the executive

committee of a trade union like this one would also join the relevant Communist 'fraction'. A fraction was a secret cell of Communists on a particular committee who gathered before each session and agreed on how they were going to vote in the forthcoming meeting. Although there is no evidence of there being a Communist fraction on the AWCS executive committee, we can presume that such a thing existed, and that M's agent would have been required to join it.

Although it is still theoretical, this edges us closer to M/2's identity. The point of a Communist fraction was to influence voting on a particular committee. So, by looking at the voting records of the AWCS executive committee on issues of interest to the Communists, it might be possible to build up a list of women who belonged to this Communist fraction, one of whom could be M/2.

At the Working Class Movement Library in Manchester there is a collection of AWCS papers, including a little-known history of this trade union. Among many other details this gives the names of several prominent Communists who sat on the executive committee during the 1930s. One of these was a Mrs Williams – who could not have been M/2 because she was too old (and too prominent). Crucially, this archival collection also holds the voting records of the AWCS executive committee during the 1930s. During the period that M/2 was active on this committee, there were forty-eight different women who voted with the strident Communist Mrs Williams, for one reason or another. Some of those would have done so simply because they thought she was talking sense, others because they belonged to the same Communist fraction. One of these forty-eight women may have been M/2.

Most of these names can be ruled out as M/2 on the basis of other details gleaned from her MI5 reports, such as her approximate age and when she joined and left this trade union. This leaves nine possible candidates.

How to whittle these nine names down to one? This is the trickiest part of the puzzle (and one that took me some time to work out). But there is a way to do it.

If you map the locations mentioned by M/2 in her reports to M and correlate these with the dates when these reports were made, an interesting pattern slowly emerges. It seems that in the years before 1938, M/2 was living south of the River Thames, perhaps near Stockwell or Brixton – as most of her reports before this date mention places close to or inside this area. After this date, however, she appears to have been based in Hammersmith.

In London today most councils have a local history centre that holds a complete set of annual electoral registers for the surrounding boroughs. By visiting enough of these centres dotted around the capital, it is possible to work out roughly where these nine women who might have been M/2 lived, and when. It turns out that just one of the nine candidates for M/2 lived in Stockwell until 1938, after which she moved to Hammersmith. Her initials were M. M.

When she was at school, M. M. was twice awarded 'Honours' in the Royal Drawing Society Certificates. We know that M/2 was a good sketcher; indeed, some of her drawings have survived in MI5 files.

M. M. worked on the China Campaign Committee in 1939. So did M/2.

M. M. attended the International Peace Campaign in 1938. As did M/2.

We also know that after the start of the war M. M. was an air raid warden in Hammersmith. M/2 had the same job in the same place at the same time.

The agent known as M/2 can now be revealed as an enterprising, brave and selfless woman called Mona Maund. Her name also explains M's codename: M. M., with her two Ms, was M/2.

Similar to Olga Gray and Vivian Hancock-Nunn, Mona Maund had almost certainly come to M's attention through the good offices of the Conservative Party. Her father, Captain Maund, was a staunch Conservative and at one time High Sheriff of Worcester. Like so many of M's agents, Mona Maund had had an interrupted childhood. Her mother died when Mona was just four years old. For the rest of her life, she was particularly close to her father, who referred to her touchingly in his will as 'my darling daughter' and 'my best of all God-sent daughters'. Indeed, Maund's career as one of M's agents may have finished in 1940, not, it seems, because she was exposed as a spy, but as a result of her father moving into a nursing home in Worcester. She moved back there to look after him.

Mona Maund's great skill as an agent was her extraordinary perseverance, as well as her ability to persuade so many Communist Party members to see past her right-wing background – even if this had taken several years to achieve.

It is striking that M chose to use agents like Maund, from resolutely right-wing families, to penetrate left-wing groups. Moscow Centre often asked successful upper-middle-class Englishmen to masquerade as, well, successful upper-middle-class Englishmen. Yet few of these agents were ever fully trusted by their controllers, even after they had defected to the Soviet Union. By contrast, M liked to recruit Tories or Fascists and turn them into Communists. The transformation was harder to achieve and it required superior tradecraft, yet the payoff was significant: he had no cause to question their loyalty.

Mona Maund was a doting daughter and a resilient spy, yet the most valuable intelligence she passed on to MI5, and it was priceless, would go to waste. When the police searched Percy Glading's house after his arrest in 1938, they found a diary that listed six names. As MI6's Valentine Vivian pointed out, two of these names actually referred to the same person – a young Communist called Melita Norwood. Also, in Charles

Munday's flat, a slip of paper was found that had Norwood's address on it. Clearly, Melita Norwood was important. She was also Honorary Secretary of the AWCS Cricklewood Branch. Mona Maund was Honorary Secretary of the AWCS Central Branch. The two women knew each other.

'This girl is a rather mysterious character,' wrote Maund about Melita Norwood. 'She is quite an active person in her trade union but a certain amount of mystery seems to surround her actual Communist Party activities. She has a husband about whom nothing is known except that he looks rather like Charlie Chaplin.' Maund then supplied M with the crucial detail: 'it is also certain that she is doing some especially important Party work'. This 'Party work' was so important, she added, that Norwood had told her comrades 'she will not be able to undertake any open Party work for some little time'.

This was not all that Mona Maund provided on Melita Norwood. 'Suppose you can draw and paint,' M later wrote. 'What an advantage this will prove to be!' Although he was a hopeless sketcher himself, M urged his agents to make drawings of their targets. Having provided excellent intelligence on Melita Norwood and a character sketch of this woman, Maund made an actual sketch of her. Her likeness was so striking that it was later reproduced in an official history of MI5 next to a photograph of Norwood. But Maund would have hoped for much more from her intelligence than that it would be used many years later to illustrate a book.

M had passed Maund's reports about Melita Norwood to the head of B Division, Jasper Harker, a handsome former Indian policeman who was rumoured among the MI5 secretaries to have either no toes or 'very small feet'. He was also known to be not very bright. Harker examined the reports carefully. He then decided not to have Melita Norwood investigated.

It later emerged that Norwood had been recruited as an NKVD

agent by either Theodor Maly or Arnold Deutsch in 1937 – just a year before Mona Maund's reports. Norwood went on to spend most of her career as a secretary at the British Non-Ferrous Metals Research Association, which coordinated British nuclear projects, where she used her position to pass on to Moscow Centre an avalanche of atomic secrets. She became one of the most successful Soviet agents in Britain with the longest record of service. She was finally exposed at the age of eighty-nine, in 1999, after the collapse of the Soviet Union. 'I've been rather a naughty girl,' she said, when her cover was finally blown, which endeared her to some. But there was nothing charming about what she had done. Melita Norwood is seen today as having had a greater impact on the Cold War than any other Soviet agent active in Britain.

Although there may have been relatively few officers working for MI5 when Harker made his disastrous decision not to follow up on Mona Maund's reports on Norwood, and, yes, it was not possible for MI5 to pursue every lead produced by the Glading case, this was the most important. MI5's ability to prevent espionage depended on both the intelligence it received and the quality of its analysis. In this instance, the two were woefully mismatched. Jasper Harker's failure to exploit this intelligence about Melita Norwood was a blunder of Homeric proportions. The greatest intelligence coup to come from M's most persistent agent ultimately came to nothing.

'WHAT A VERY BEAUTIFUL VIEW'

On 12 March, 1938, just two days before Percy Glading and his accomplices were sentenced, German troops marched into Austria in what was euphemistically called the Anschluss, meaning the 'connection' or 'annexation'. Even if the troops were welcomed by many Austrians, this was an invasion in all but name. The territorial expansion Hitler had set out in his memoir *Mein Kampf* was now under way. Spain looked set to become another nation in which a democratically elected government was to be replaced by a dictator, now that the Spanish Civil War had swung decisively to the Fascists. By the summer of 1938, the greatest threat to world peace did not come from Moscow but from right-wing dictators. As the *News Chronicle* put it, 'sooner or later the democracies will have to stand'.

Earlier that year an MI5 source inside the German embassy in London, the aristocratic diplomat Wolfgang zu Putlitz, reported that German espionage operations against Britain had begun. The days of cooperation between German and British intelligence were a distant memory. MI5 needed to infiltrate pro-Nazi organisations in the capital, and do so fast.

M's response was to take on two new agents, both of whom were unlike any others he had recruited: they were German. Their job was to penetrate the German expatriate community in London and try to win over Nazis and Nazi sympathisers. The trouble was, one of M's new agents was gay and had refused to join the Hitler Youth. The other was a passionate opponent of Nazism who had recently married a Jew. But if M could teach British Fascists to pass themselves off as Communists, perhaps he could get these two to disguise themselves as devout Nazis.

One was Harold Kurtz, codenamed M/H, a twenty-five-year-old German later given the nickname 'The Porpoise' on account of the way he liked to leave the bathroom soaked in water after his ablutions each morning. Kurtz would go on to write distinguished biographies of the Empress Eugenie and Marshal Ney. He was bad with money, smoked as if it was good for him and was fond of drink. He was also a pronounced Anglophile desperate for British citizenship, which is what M promised when taking him on.

The same was broadly true of M's other new agent, Friedl Gaertner, a stunning divorcée who had recently arrived in London after her sister's marriage to Ian Menzies, brother of the senior MI6 officer and future 'C', Stewart Menzies. Friedl Gaertner's sister had met Ian Menzies after he saw her perform at the London Casino. At the time she had been wearing nothing but a diaphanous pink body stocking. When Stewart Menzies met Friedl, he tried to recruit her as an MI6 agent, asking her to go back to Nazi Germany on his behalf, but she refused.

'Though willing to work,' explained Stewart Menzies, 'her whole heart is set on living over here.' So he suggested that she work for MI5 instead and put her in touch with M.

After their first meeting, M described Friedl Gaertner as 'an extremely level-headed and intelligent person' whose 'one aim and object in life is to secure a permit to work in this country and to remain here', adding that 'there is no doubt whatever about her very considerable personal attractiveness'.

This gave M an idea. He suggested that she should pose, in every sense of the word, 'as a sort of super high-class mannequin', that is, model, who was new to London and who wanted to help the Nazi cause. After taking the weekend to think about it, Friedl Gaertner agreed to work for MI5. But she drew the line at pretending to be a model. Instead, M, or 'Michael', as she called him, found her a job as a secretary for Dennis Wheatley, his novelist friend. Once he was happy with her cover, a version of the one he had first given Olga, M the spymaster launched her and Kurtz at the German community in London.

M wanted to take on many more agents, but he did not have the resources. He later bemoaned his 'financial starvation' at this time and the government's failure to take 'a more courageous attitude'. Because of a lack of funds, it seems, he also lost the exclusive services of E. G. Mandeville-Roe, or M/R, by then a trusted figure in several extremist right-wing groups with close ties to Nazi Germany. Instead, Mandeville-Roe began to combine his work for MI5 with espionage for the Board of Deputies of British Jews, which was quite a turnaround for a man who had recently railed in print against 'the Ghetto descendants of Throgmorton Street'.

M was stretching himself perilously thin and was now running far too many agents. He later warned that 'no officer can efficiently look after more than eight agents', adding that 'six is probably a better number'. By the summer of 1938, M had over a dozen in play. This was hazardous, both from their point of view and from his.

'I shall always endeavour to be available,' M wrote to one agent, adding elsewhere that an MI5 officer must 'be at the beck-and-call of the agent – not the agent at the beck-and-call of the officer'. The danger attached to this, one rarely acknowledged, was that M might lose sight of himself.

'The officer will have to be continually adapting himself to agents who vary very much in character and personality,' M later warned, when describing his craft. 'This is one of the most important items in regard to the handling of agents, for while the officer must always adapt himself to the agent, and not the agent to the officer, the latter must be constantly on his guard in order to see that he does not become that terrible creature, one who is "all things to all men".'

This is a curious line, one that stands out from M's other writings on espionage. He had been running his stable of agents for most of the last fourteen years, almost without pause. The need to mould himself to so many different personalities during that period must have left him in danger of losing touch with himself, or knowing exactly what he believed in.

On top of all this came the mounting threat of war, which had escalated suddenly over the summer. By early September 1938 the Munich Crisis, as it was later known, began to approach its nerve-racking crescendo. Hitler continued to call for the partition of Czechoslovakia and the transfer of the Sudetenland to Nazi Germany, refusing all talk of compromise.

M section was understaffed and overworked. The movement M had once belonged to had become the greatest threat to world peace. War seemed to be imminent. In London there were rushed marriages. Trenches were dug in parks to serve as makeshift air raid shelters. Children were evacuated from the capital, air raid wardens were recruited and millions of gas masks were distributed as the crisis intensified. Almost twenty years after the end of the last war, Britain appeared to be just days away from another bloody conflict against Germany.

At the height of this crisis, M produced a stark reassessment of his old friend William Joyce. One of M's informants, probably John Hirst, another comrade from his days in the British Fascists, no longer felt that 'Joyce's loyalty can be relied upon. He [Hirst] thinks that Joyce has been keeping in constant touch with the NSDAP [Nazi Party] over the last week or so.' M's agent had even heard Joyce declare that 'if there is war with Germany I will be shot rather than take any part in it on behalf of Britain'. At this point, tears had run down Joyce's cheeks, rolling over his scar, before he went on shakily, 'but I am convinced that we shall one day see Germany the master of Europe'.

'Joyce's personality, which is always highly emotional, has become more hysterical during recent weeks,' added M, who had finally accepted, it seemed, that his erstwhile brother-in-arms could pose a threat to national security. The following day a warrant was taken out to intercept Joyce's post. This bore fruit almost at once.

The day after the Munich Agreement was signed and the Sudetenland was ceded to Germany, MI5 intercepted a suspicious letter addressed to Joyce. It came from Ernst Bauer, who was known to MI5 as a Nazi spy.

The following month Joyce's business partner, Angus MacNab, went to Belgium and got drunk with a stranger who was, unfortunately for him, an MI6 informant. MacNab revealed that he was on his way to Cologne to meet the same Ernst Bauer. The following morning, displaying all the tradecraft of a goldfish, MacNab asked the MI6 informant if, by any chance, he had mentioned the name 'Bauer' last night, because if he had, this had been a mistake. The informant replied that indeed he had.

'For God's sake,' said MacNab, 'forget that I ever mentioned such a man or such a name.' Understandably, this plea had the opposite effect. A report of this exchange made its way to MI5, and MacNab's colleague, William Joyce, was added to a list of Britons to be rounded up in the event of a war.

In the weeks after the Munich Crisis, as a necklace of barrage balloons, or 'blimps', was installed around London to force the German bombers higher when they attacked, M looked frantically for more agents to launch at Fascist organisations. He even turned to Vivian Hancock-Nunn. Having already asked Eric Roberts and Jimmy

Dickson to do the same, M instructed this gentleman barrister to reinvent himself as a Fascist and in late 1938 Hancock-Nunn duly joined an extreme right-wing organisation called The Link.

In his new guise as an enthusiastic Fascist, the country squire went off to have lunch with the man who ran The Link, Admiral Sir Barry Domvile, previously Director of Naval Intelligence. Domvile encouraged Hancock-Nunn to visit Nazi Germany with The Link, promising him 'personal introductions to the principal Party leaders'. Although the MI5 agent did not take him up on this offer, the following year one of M's other agents did.

In July 1939, a new agent codenamed 'M/T' made her way to Nazi Germany on a trip organised by The Link. On 2 August, the group went to visit Berchtesgaden, in the Bavarian Alps, to admire from a distance the *Kehlsteinhaus,* or Eagle's Nest, where Hitler liked to stay. As they took in the view, their coach was boarded by two uniformed men. They began to shout. To her horror, M's agent realised that they were yelling out her name.

'I must admit that for a moment I got a bit of a fright,' she wrote, which may have been an understatement. 'I was asked to come out of the coach, which I did, and was then taken up to the house and inside; after waiting in a room for a while I was taken into another room where Hitler was sitting in an arm chair. Another man came into the room and spoke to him, and also acted as interpreter for us.'

M/T had been working for M as an agent for less than a year. She had no training and very little experience. Her name has never been revealed, but it is not hard to work out.

In one report she described herself as the wife of 'Leonard Robert XXXX', adding that her father-in-law was a German-born British citizen with a German-sounding name. Although her name has been officially redacted, it is possible to see that it was roughly five letters long. On that trip there were just nine women with names that sounded remotely German: Fraus Kunze, Frederich, Heler, Kemper and Goetze as well as Mrs Rusge, Mrs Volkerborm, Mrs Stramer and Mrs Tesch. Just one of these women was married to a 'Leonard Robert', and her surname was five letters long. This was Mrs Tesch. Although her father-in-law was a *Danish*-born British citizen, in every other respect Kathleen Tesch perfectly matches the description of M/T. Her husband, Leonard Robert Tesch, was a legendary bug enthusiast, the founder of the Amateur Entomologists' Society, and thus a man well known to M.

Kathleen Tesch, or M/T, was a tiny housewife who was particularly fond of dogs. She came across as an entirely ordinary and unassuming member of the public, the daughter of a Yorkshire pithead engineer who lived in the quiet Home Counties village of Whaddon where she was best known for her imaginative costumes at the local village fete. M saw other qualities in her, and recruited her as an undercover agent for MI5. Now she was in Nazi Germany sitting opposite the man who was about to start another world war. Her only disappointment was that he hardly noticed her.

'Hitler seemed to be quite unaware that I was in the room,' complained Tesch, 'and he strongly impressed me as a man who lives in a <u>dream</u> world entirely his own. I cannot say whether it was his normal mood or not, but I thought at the time that if a hundred people had been in the room he would not have known. He looks much older and more care-worn than his photographs appear; and though this may sound a silly description of him, I can only describe him as he appeared to me – as a man who is one moment burnt up with a kind of fire, and the next absolutely spent and unaware of anything. A good deal of the time was spent in complete silence which I tried to break by making such idiotic remarks as "What a very beautiful view." To be candid, I felt rather uncomfortable, not because of the importance, but because they seemed to know very much more about me than I did about them!'

They knew a certain amount about her, but not that she was

working for MI5. Had it emerged that Kathleen Tesch was really a British government agent, it is unlikely that she would have made it out of Nazi Germany. The reason she had been hauled off the coach and presented to Hitler like this was simply that her name, Tesch, was 'a very honoured one in Germany'. Apparently, Hitler wanted to relay this information to M's agent in person. When he came out of his daze, Hitler managed to present Tesch with an autographed copy of *Mein Kampf* embossed with a silver eagle. She returned to the coach, no doubt a little shaken.

Given what we know today about Hitler's drug use, it is possible that Kathleen Tesch had met him in a lull between injections. But even without the drugs, it is not surprising that Hitler should have come across as preoccupied during early August 1939. Several weeks after presenting this MI5 agent with a signed copy of his book, the German leader formalised an alliance that made the outbreak of war almost inevitable.

32

CRISIS

On 23 August, 1939, the Nazi diplomat Joachim von Ribbentrop, a man known to the British press as 'Von Brickendrop', on account of his gaffes at diplomatic events, dropped a different kind of brick. Just days after negotiations had broken down about a possible military alliance among Britain, France and the USSR, the man who had once hosted MI5's Guy Liddell in Berlin flew out to Moscow to sign what became known as the Molotov–Ribbentrop Pact, an agreement between Hitler and Stalin to the effect that neither Germany nor the Soviet Union would attack each other and, secretly, that Poland would be divided between them. This was less than a year after the Munich Agreement. Communism was now allied to Fascism. In the political tug-of-war between the Right and the Left, the axiomatic conflict of the age, the two opposing teams had just agreed to pull in the same direction. It was absurd and terrifying in equal measure. The greatest obstacle to German territorial expansion had been removed, suddenly, and now it seemed to be just a matter of time before war broke out.

As they had done during the Munich Crisis, less than a year earlier, piles of sand started to appear at street corners in London to fill up sandbags or put out fires once the bombing began. More men were seen walking around in uniform. There were more gas masks, more helmets and more bayonets. Searchlights began to sweep the capital's horizon at night. Museum staff packed away their beloved treasures and many Londoners made plans to leave. These were twilight days. As Virginia Woolf wrote, it felt 'like waiting a doctor's verdict'.

An equally busy scene was being played out in the offices of M Section in Dolphin Square. Earlier that summer M had at last been able to add two officers to his unit. One was Jimmy Dickson, the civil servant who had spent the last fifteen years as M's most trusted agent. Now he would be running agents himself. The other addition was the stepson of M's friend Dennis Wheatley, the renowned novelist. This was Bill Younger, recently an undergraduate at Oxford where he had carried out several jobs for M. Like most of M's agents, Younger had been held back in childhood, having suffered from polio that stunted his growth and left him with a withered arm; he also continued M's tradition of working with authors. Dickson had produced five thrillers by the time he joined M Section, while Younger, aged just twenty-two, had already had two collections of poetry published.

In the hours after the Molotov–Ribbentrop Pact was announced, M, Dickson and Younger, the three officers of M Section, were being inundated with intelligence. The best of it came from Friedl Gaertner, the beautiful divorcée, who had reported on the day before the pact was signed that Hitler and Stalin had secretly agreed to carve up Poland and that London would not be flattened by the Luftwaffe at the start of war.

She was right. As well as carrying out what M described as 'excellent work in connection with German organisations in this country', Gaertner had secured the trust of the Nazi Party in London, to the extent that she was asked around this time to become a spy for the Abwehr, the German military intelligence department. This was exactly what M had hoped for when he had taken her on only a year ago. It marked the genesis of Friedl Gaertner's career as a British double agent codenamed 'GELATINE'.

As Gelatine, Gaertner would become one of the many cogs in MI5's intricate and hugely successful Double Cross deception, in which German agents were turned by MI5 and used to feed misleading information back to Berlin. Dusko Popov, a Serbian playboy turned MI5 double agent codenamed 'TRICYCLE', apparently on account of his preference for three in a bed, was besotted with Gaertner, and described her as 'highly regarded by the Germans'. Later on in the war, her credibility as a German agent allowed MI5 to feed inaccurate information to Berlin about where V-1 and V-2 rockets were landing, which helped to save many British civilian lives.

In those dying days of August 1939, M Section was also receiving a glut of intelligence about the reaction to the Molotov–Ribbentrop Pact from British Communists. One of M's best sources on this was M/8, an agent who had been reporting to him on and off for the last fifteen years but who was coming into his own only now. M/8 was Tom Driberg, the flamboyant *Express* columnist and future Labour politician and peer. Although Driberg was the unlikeliest of M's agents, being promiscuously gay, indiscreet and famous, he was now one of his most valuable sources.

Another important agent was M/4, M's long-serving Liverpudlian, one of the few comrades in his local branch who seemed capable of understanding what had happened. 'I have been able to explain to confused members the apparent change in Soviet policy,' this MI5 agent reported, later adding that he was 'in demand as a speaker at branch meetings specially called to clarify the programme of the CPGB and its attitude to the war'. The District Organiser for Merseyside would soon take M/4 aside to tell him that he was 'very pleased' with his work and that he had 'shown a deep political understanding of Marxism as applied to the present situation'. It should come as no surprise that M/4 could give such a coherent account of Moscow's volte face, given that he had spent most of his adult life pretending to be someone other than himself.

There was also confusion on the Right, unless, that was, you spoke to William Joyce. In the wake of Stalin and Hitler's extraordinary pact, Joyce pronounced himself 'very clear' that 'the greatest struggle in history was now doomed to take place' and that 'I wanted to play a clear and definite part.' Unfortunately for him, that was unlikely to happen. For many months he had been on a Home Office list of pro-Nazi extremists who were to be arrested as soon as war broke out. Before that took place, however, something very unusual happened.

At around midnight on 24 August, 1939, Joyce received a telephone call. According to his sister, who was in the room at the time, the man on the other end of the line told him that the 'Defence Regulations would become effective in two more days and that his detention order had already been signed'. It was a short conversation, she remembered, lasting less than a minute. Little more than a day later, on 26 August, William Joyce and his wife, Meg, fled to Berlin.

William Joyce would spend the rest of the war broadcasting splenetic Nazi propaganda back into Britain and became known as 'Lord Haw-Haw,' infamous for his broadcasts that started with him saying 'Jairminny calling, Jairminny calling' . . .

Joyce, or Lord Haw-Haw, as he had become, may not have been the only Briton doing propaganda work for the Nazis, but he was the most effective. By the end of 1939, according to a Mass Observation survey, M's former comrade, the man who had married the girl that he had once loved, had as many as six million regular listeners in Britain while a staggering eighteen million people tuned in occasionally to hear him. Goebbels referred to Joyce as the best horse in his stable, and at one point during the war he was branded by a prominent *Daily Mirror* columnist as 'the biggest danger to the nation'.

Yet perhaps the most remarkable part of William Joyce's transformation into Lord Haw-Haw was how he had escaped to Berlin in the first place, given that he was on a list of twenty-three individuals to be arrested by the British police. The official who renewed his passport shortly before his departure must take some of the blame, as should those who waved him through customs and immigration. However, most of the responsibility for Joyce's escape lies with the man who tipped him off on the phone.

So who was he?

The answer was revealed to MI5 less than a month after Joyce had made it to Berlin. Joyce's sister, Joan, who had helped her brother pack, explained what had happened to a member of the Nordic League, an extreme right-wing organisation. Except this man was no ordinary fanatic. The individual she confided in turned out to be an undercover policeman.

Joan Joyce told him that a 'secret service' officer 'had advised William to leave England to avoid being arrested'. She then let slip a vital detail. This 'secret service' officer had also visited one of her other brothers, Quentin, then in prison. She provided a date and a time for the prison visit. It was the morning of 19 September.

Records show that on the morning in question, Quentin Joyce was visited by just one officer from MI5.

His name was Maxwell Knight.

Ever since M had joined MI5, in 1931, there had been a danger that his past was not yet history, and that his connection to British Fascism might one day come to haunt him. By making that call, M had been mainly responsible for Joyce's escape. This was not a forgivable oversight on his part; he had gone out of his way to warn his former comrade.

The years that M had spent with the British Fascists had finally become his nemesis, but not for political or ideological reasons. Although M had joined the BF at a formative point in his life and had poured himself into this fledgling movement, because he believed in its mission to save the country from international Communism, the version of Fascism that he had signed up to was significantly different from its more extreme incarnation under Mosley. M's membership in the BF had certainly edged him further to the Right, and he remained throughout his life a man who 'did not rate democracy very highly,' according to a former official MI5 historian. Yet by 1939 he was not a Fascist, in the contemporary understanding of the term. The most troubling legacy of M's time in this extremist group was not political, it was social. He had been caught up in the web of friendships that he had made long ago. While he may have felt a lingering guilt about what had happened to Joyce fifteen years earlier outside Lambeth Baths, M was driven mainly by a sense of friendship. He made that call out of personal loyalty.

Only the year before, in 1938, E. M. Forster had suggested provocatively, and to great effect, that 'if I had to choose between betraying my country and betraying my friend, I hope I should have the guts to betray my country'. M and Joyce lived in an age when for many people the friends one chose in life mattered more than an inherited attachment to one's country. M was bound to his comrades in the BF and K both by the choices they had made in life and what they had experienced in each other's company. These men had fought together, burgled together, marched together, drunk together, even kidnapped together. In the case of M and Joyce, they had loved the same woman. Some of M's previous associates had become agents of his at MI5; others had formed the nucleus of the new Fascist movement. If he could help it, M would prefer not to betray any of them.

Yet the Prime Minister's declaration of war on 3 September, 1939 changed the complexion of these relationships. War presented M with the most profound challenge of his life. For years he had believed that the men and women he had got to know among the British Fascists were, for the most part, on the side of the angels.

Now he had to decide whether he was willing to destroy this understanding of them and the movement that they belonged to. It was like being asked to kill off a part of himself. What made this so difficult was not just the bond he felt towards some of these people but the premium he had always placed on loyalty. The man that he had long aspired to be – that blurry composite of his father and his brother, of Richard Hannay and Bulldog Drummond, the zookeepers he had looked up to as a boy, the poachers, the naturalists, the sea captains, the spies – that man did not betray his friends. Not under any circumstances. But neither did he turn against his country. Never before had M imagined that he might have to decide between the two.

Now the particular course of his life, the nature of his profession and the outbreak of war had combined to produce a punishing test of character. Maxwell Knight would have to choose between his friends and his country.

PART III

THE ENEMY WITHIN

MRS MACKIE INVESTIGATES

'Gloomy, darkened and lifeless buildings looked like menacing cliffs. The streets between them were black gorges. Cars moved slowly in the thick darkness, like ghostly shadows. Like magic birds with a red eye on their tail. Quiet. Gloomy. Watchful. Fantastical. A scene from Dante's Inferno,' wrote Ivan Maisky, the Soviet Ambassador to Britain, of the scene in the capital each night following the start of the Second World War. 'That is how London lies low, waiting for the raids of the German bombers.'

Although the city was not pulverised by the Luftwaffe in the immediate aftermath of the Prime Minister's declaration of war on 3 September, 1939, as many had feared, very quickly it had begun to look and sound like a city at war. People spoke a little louder than they had done in the days before. Windows were now latticed with tape. Cinemas were locked up, and the streets had crazy white lines meandering over them to guide cars and pedestrians during the blackout. Tens of thousands of women and children had been evacuated from the capital, making London a more masculine metropolis, which, in turn, triggered an influx of prostitutes.

All over the country the first few weeks of the war were

characterised by uncertainty: uncertainty about where to live, what job to take, how long it might all last and, ultimately, uncertainty about whether this war was really necessary. For some the answer came easily – yes, and that was all there was to it. Others paused before reaching the same conclusion. Yet for a respectable number of people the decision to wage war against Germany had been a mistake. There was little of the jingoistic certainty which had accompanied the start of the last war, when young men all over the country had rushed to enlist. Not everyone in Britain saw this conflict in terms of democracy standing up to dictatorship, or as one nation's heroic attempt to resist a murderous tyrant. Instead there were those who positioned it within the ongoing struggle between Right and Left, which had dominated European politics over the last decade, and who felt that a strong Germany was an essential protection against the Soviet Union. They also worried that a prolonged period of total war would cause a lurch to the Left in domestic politics.

After an initial muddle, the British Communist Party denounced the conflict as an 'Imperialists' War' and urged all workers to have nothing to do with it. Mosley's Fascists immediately labelled it a 'Jews' War'. They too called for resistance. At both extremes of the British political spectrum there were calls for peace, and from a clutch of Liberal, pacifist and religious groups, such as the Peace Pledge Union. Thousands of anti-war pamphlets were printed in the first few weeks of the war. Pacifist slogans appeared on walls. There were also times when Neville Chamberlain, the Prime Minister, gave the distinct impression that he had cold feet about a fight to the death against the Nazi war machine.

'One begins to wonder whether we are really at war at all,' despaired Guy Liddell, Deputy Director of MI5's B Division, who was not the only one in the Office to resent this hesitant, nebulous atmosphere. Liddell wanted all anti-war publications shut down and the immediate internment of the 70,000 Germans living in Britain.

He felt that 'enemy aliens', as they were then known, must be locked up and then 'called upon to show cause why they should be released'. Not the other way around. This was the policy stipulated in the War Book, and it was roughly what had happened during the last war.

The Home Office refused. Inspired by what Liddell dismissed as 'old-fashioned liberalism', senior Home Office officials took a principled stand at the start of the war against the prosecution of anti-war publications and the mass internment of enemy aliens. 'Our tradition is that while orders issued by the duly constituted authority must be obeyed,' wrote Sir Alexander Maxwell, the donnish Permanent Secretary at the Home Office, 'every civilian is at liberty to show, if he can, that such orders are silly or mischievous and the duly constituted authorities are composed of fools or rogues.' Although Maxwell accepted that this gentler approach might backfire, because it could encourage those 'who desire revolution, or desire to impede the war effort', he insisted that this 'risk is the cardinal distinction between democracy and totalitarianism'. The Home Office would rather lose the war nobly than sanction an all-out attack on civil liberties.

MI5 could only offer strongly worded protests as the Home Office pursued its alternative policy on enemy aliens, which was to set up one-man tribunals all over the country and review the case of each German national individually. This was both enormously fair and unbelievably time-consuming. After several months it would lead to the internment of 569 Germans. A further 6,800 were told to observe a curfew and stay away from certain parts of the country, while the remainder, some 64,000 people, were given no restrictions at all.

MI5's Guy Liddell called this 'laughable'. 'The liberty of the subject, freedom of speech etc. were all very well in peacetime,' he wrote, 'but were no use in fighting the Nazis. There seemed to be a complete failure to realise the power of the totalitarian state and the energy with which the Germans were fighting a total war.' Already there was a fundamental rift in Whitehall, and it reflected a similar division throughout the country. The Home Office saw the war as a clash of principles, yet for MI5 this was a bloody fight for survival and it began at home, as the example of Poland and Czechoslovakia had shown.

With the war less than a month old, reports had come in from Poland to suggest that the Nazi invasion had been assisted, in part, by ethnic Germans living inside Poland. Some of these stories were accurate. The *Volksdeutscher Selbstschutz,* a series of paramilitary units made up of Germans resident in Poland, had indeed committed acts of sabotage during the invasion and had even taken on armed Polish units. The German occupation of the Sudetenland the year before had been assisted very slightly by the *Sudetendeutsches Freikorps,* a similar paramilitary organisation for ethnic Germans living beyond the borders of Nazi Germany. For MI5, this raised the spectre of there being inside Britain already a so-called Fifth Column.

This term had been coined several years earlier by General Franco, during the Spanish Civil War, when he referred to his 'Fifth Column' of sympathisers in Madrid, living among the enemy. Now, in Britain, *Fifth Column* became shorthand for a supposed network of Germans living in Britain who were ready to rise up in the event of a Nazi invasion to carry out sabotage, espionage and perhaps launch attacks against British forces.

This was a familiar fear. Although it had not been referred to back then as a Fifth Column, in the years before the First World War millions of Britons became convinced that there were hundreds of German spies living secretly among them. The hysteria followed the publication of various novels and speculative newspaper articles by the likes of William Le Queux, whose best-seller *The Invasion of 1910* cemented this idea of expatriate Germans forming a readymade net-work of potential spies. Indeed, the spy fever had been so intense in 1909 that the government had felt compelled to respond. It had asked a young Vernon Kell and one other officer to set up the Secret Service

Bureau, which later divided into MI6 and MI5. MI5 had been born out of spy fever, and it was easy for those in the Home Office, in September 1939, to imagine that its fear of a Fifth Column in Britain was inspired by little more than institutional prejudice.

This was part of the reason why those in the Home Office refused to authorise the mass internment of enemy aliens that MI5 had called for. As a result, Kell, Liddell and the rest of MI5 were swamped with work relating to the new one-man tribunals, which, in turn, made it harder for them to concentrate on combating German espionage. MI5 also had growing pains to contend with. During the early stages of the war, Kell's department doubled in size. At the same time its staff struggled to adapt to their new wartime headquarters in Wormwood Scrubs, a former prison block.

M's situation was rather different. He continued to run his section from a palatial housing development overlooking the River Thames, and his staff of three officers remained unchanged. Captain Knight, as he now was, would have to make do with just Jimmy Dickson and Bill Younger. Yet with the small injection of funds he had received several months earlier, M had been able to take on several new agents. These included 'M/C', a female typist in the mould of Mona Maund and Olga Gray. M/C had managed to get a job as a secretary at BUF National Headquarters and over the following months she would supply M with a valuable stream of material on Fascist activities. But he needed more.

Following the outbreak of war, M Section found itself responsible for dealing with individual cases of suspected espionage as well as monitoring the Communist underground and penetrating all extremist political organisations on the Right. As usual, M would have to do a lot with very little. But the stakes were higher now. His choice of precisely where to deploy his agents, when and how to instruct them could be the difference between his uncovering a Fifth Column and there being a successful German invasion.

M had to think very carefully before deciding where to direct one of his newest agents, Marjorie Mackie, codenamed 'M/Y', a middle-aged single mother from Essex who was short and broad and had remarkable sky-blue eyes. Mackie's only son had recently joined the merchant navy. Before the war she had made a living doing public cooking demonstrations for a well-known flour company. Like a modern-day television chef, only without the cameras, she baked bread and pies while chatting to an audience of passing shoppers, a job that seemed to combine her two great skills in life: cooking and talking. Yet the legacy of this work, even if she did not recognise it in herself, was an exaggerated manner. Mrs Mackie would often come across in conversation as the kind of person who was willing to embellish a story if she felt her audience was losing interest. She could try too hard to be believed, a quality that did not bode well in her new job as a government agent.

M wanted Mrs Mackie to infiltrate the Right Club, a secretive anti-Semitic group committed to undermining the war effort and spreading the idea that this conflict was part of a global Jewish-Communist-Masonic conspiracy. M had reason to believe that the Right Club was developing its own network of agents – just as a Fifth Column might do. This rumour almost certainly came to him from one of his two agents already inside the group, John Hirst and Eric Roberts. Yet neither man was at all close to the figure at the heart of the Right Club. This was where Mrs Mackie came in.

The Hon. Captain Archibald Ramsay, MP, usually known as 'Jock', was a former officer in the Coldstream Guards and a Conservative backbencher whose outlook was essentially Fascist. He had set up the Right Club earlier that year in response to the looming possibility of Britain and Germany going to war, an event which he felt was a terrible mistake. Yet he was not anti-war on humanitarian grounds. Instead Ramsay thought that Britain and

Germany should be allies in the struggle against Jews, Masons and Communists.

This moustachioed, balding politician had belonged in the early 1930s to various right-wing and anti-Communist groups, including the Christian Protest Movement, which campaigned against the persecution of Christians in the Soviet Union. Its Assistant Secretary back then had been Mrs Mackie. This was why M had taken her on. Mackie's first job for MI5 was to get back in touch with Captain Ramsay and to find out what he was up to.

'I telephoned to Mrs Ramsay,' wrote Mrs Mackie, 'and asked her if I could see her and Captain Ramsay and renew our acquaintance. She invited me to tea.'

The conversation that followed was 'violently anti-Semitic and anti-Masonic,' explained Mackie. The former cookery demonstrator played along, nodding when necessary and otherwise trying to persuade Mrs Ramsay that her views were just as extreme as her husband's.

It worked. The following month Mackie was invited to join the Right Club, and in late September 1939 she finally got to speak to Captain Ramsay himself. What she heard was extraordinary.

Ramsay told this MI5 informant that Right Club members, his agents effectively, had infiltrated not only every leading right-wing group but also Whitehall. 'He told me that he had most of the Government Departments covered with the exception of the Foreign Office and the Censorship Department. He added, "If you could help us here it would be very useful."'

'I made no promise,' she told M, but Mackie led Ramsay to believe 'that I had many friends in military circles who would use their influence on my behalf'.

Captain Ramsay was not only building up a network of agents inside the British government, but, according to Mrs Mackie, he was making tentative plans for a right-wing coup. M had also begun to receive disturbing intelligence from within the Communist movement, including one report suggesting 'that instructions have now been received from Moscow to go right ahead with all plans for creating a revolution in this country when the time is ripe'.

There seemed to be danger from homegrown Fascists and homegrown Communists, as well as the growing threat of a Nazi invasion. At the same time, M had a more personal crisis to contend with. Just four days after Captain Ramsay had told Mrs Mackie to find a job in the Foreign Office or Censorship, a Special Branch report came into the Office to suggest that M, of all people, had tipped off William Joyce about his imminent arrest. By then Joyce's broadcasts from Berlin were being discussed in the press.

M responded immediately. While he conceded that he had spoken to Joyce on the phone shortly before his escape, 'there was no question of Joyce having been warned or given any improper information'.

Yet M offered no plausible explanation as to why Joan Joyce would have made this up. She knew that M was trying to get one of her other brothers, Quentin, released from prison and she had no incentive to slander this MI5 officer. If this had been a lie, it was an elaborate one that served no purpose. It is hard to say which of his colleagues actually believed M's denial. Yet, by that stage of the war, the Office was overwhelmed with more pressing work and this matter was left alone.

The first month of the war had been a strange, discomforting time for M. He had received ominous intelligence about plans being made by Captain Ramsay and the Right Club, and had seen reports describing Communist and Fascist plots for a coup. In the background came the drone of his former comrade, Lord Haw-Haw, as he made broadcasts from Berlin. It was impossible for M to know what the fallout from his telephone call might be, but this did at least force him to confront his relationship with Joyce and perhaps with British Fascism more generally.

Most of M's identity as a young man had been bound up in his experiences with K and the BF. The reinvention of this movement as a pro-Nazi phenomenon must have been painful for him and confusing; it was a shift that ate into his understanding of himself and his past, as well as his amour propre. It also challenged his sense of what this war was about. Many people, including those who, like him, had once been involved in the Makgill Organisation, men whom M respected, admired and liked, saw this as part of an ongoing conflict between the Right and the Left in which Britain would be better advised to side with Germany. For others the war belonged to a struggle between dictatorship and democracy, and steps should be taken to limit the freedoms of those people in Britain who sympathised with Hitler and the forces of dictatorship. Maxwell Knight was not a man given to long expressive outpourings of his innermost feelings, either in conversation or on the page, so there is no direct account of his political position at this time. Indeed he was so accustomed to presenting different sides of himself to his many agents that keeping his interior world hidden came naturally. Instead, we are left with the record of what he did.

Inasmuch as this tells us anything, it suggests that by the start of October 1939 this MI5 spymaster, like so many others with connections to the Right, was still undecided about how he saw the war, or indeed the threat of homegrown Fascism. Politically the BUF was by then something of a joke, and there was no prospect of a truly popular Fascist uprising in Britain, yet the danger was that radicalised British Fascists, for whom ideology was more important than nationality, may have already decided to work for Nazi Germany. M's dilemma was centred on just how serious that threat really was.

34

THE FASHION DESIGNER

On 4 October, 1939, the day before Hitler flew out to the
newly occupied capital of Poland for a victory parade, Marjorie
Mackie began her job in Military Censorship. Her contact at the
Right Club who had encouraged her to apply for this position,
Mrs Ramsay, was thrilled. Mackie now worked in the same complex
as MI5, one of the few government departments in which the Right
Club had no agents.

Very soon after Mackie had started her new job, Mrs Ramsay
asked her whether she had been able to meet any MI5 staff. For once,
the MI5 agent was able to tell the truth. Yes, she replied, she had
met several people who worked for the service.

She then told Mrs Ramsay that this happened occasionally in the
shared canteen.

Mrs Ramsay was impressed.

'Yes, I think when it comes to a showdown,' she said, 'you will
have work to do.'

Showdown. This language must have been familiar to M. 'The
Showdown' was similar to 'The Day', which had once been predicted
by his friends in the British Fascists, when the Communists would

try to seize power and the Fascists would nobly rise up to stop them. But there was a critical difference between the Showdown and The Day. The current crop of right-wing extremists, including Mosley and Ramsay, had little intention of handing back power once they had seen off the Communists. They wanted to run the country themselves.

It was not long before Mrs Mackie was invited to join the Right Club's 'Inner Circle'. In one of the subsequent meetings, she was told about the group's red leather-bound ledger that contained details of every Right Club member, a list including at least eleven MPs, almost as many peers, the Duke of Wellington, Lord Carnegie – husband of Edward VII's granddaughter, Princess Maud – Lord Redesdale – father of the Mitford sisters – Harold Mitchell, MP – later a vice chairman of the Conservative Party – as well as one German princess, one Russian prince and at least one MI6 agent, Arthur Loveday, who had joined for ideological rather than operational reasons. The calibre of these members was a reminder of just how many well-connected and politically influential figures remained unsure, either privately or publicly, about the need to take on Hitler.

Yet for now Mrs Mackie did not know who was on that list of Right Club members. It was only as she earned the trust of Captain Ramsay and others that she was introduced to more members of the group. One of these was a woman about whom her spymaster had already heard a great deal. This was Captain Ramsay's unofficial secretary, an aristocratic Russian-born fashion designer called Anna Wolkoff.

Earlier that year Wolkoff had been described in one MI5 report as 'a staunch Nazi propagandist'. Since then four separate warnings about her had been received by the Office. One described her 'displaying pro-Nazi, pro-Communist and anti-British tendencies to a degree which exceeds that of wrong-headed stupidity and may be dangerous'. All suggested that she might be working for the Nazis.

But it was still possible that she was just an angry anti-Communist, which would make sense given what had happened to her family.

Anna Wolkoff's father, Admiral Wolkoff, previously an aide-de-camp to Nicholas II, the last tsar of Russia, had been posted to London as naval attaché in 1917, shortly before the Bolshevik Revolution. He and his wife were never able to return to the land of their birth. Instead, they took on a small café in South Kensington, the Russian Tea Rooms, and read impotently about the destruction of the society that they had known all their lives. The Wolkoffs' daughter, Anna, became a fashion designer, and at one point in the 1930s was doing well. She opened a shop on Conduit Street, her clothes were being worn by the likes of Princess Marina of Kent and Wallis Simpson and one of her outfits was photographed by Cecil Beaton for *Vogue*. But her company's finances were shambolic, and shortly before the war began her business had collapsed.

By the time she was introduced to Mrs Mackie, in December 1939, Anna Wolkoff had been forced to move back in with her parents. Wolkoff was still furious about the demise of her company, and had concocted a bizarre Jewish conspiracy theory to explain what had happened. She had also taken to calling herself Anna 'de' Wolkoff. This small adjustment is telling. It reflected her growing sense that nobody was taking her seriously. Wolkoff felt entitled to a job just as she felt entitled to have her views heard. This was one of the reasons why she and several friends from the Right Club had begun to put up 'sticky-back' posters at night during the blackout, so-called because one side was covered in adhesive gum. These contained sarcastic, usually anti-Semitic messages designed to undermine the war effort. Sometimes Anna Wolkoff and her sticky-back gang went to cinemas to boo at newsreel footage of Churchill or any other pro-war MP. She was angry about the war and sympathetic to Hitler, but beneath it all was an opinionated individual who wanted to feel important again.

When Mrs Mackie told Anna Wolkoff that she had taken a job in Military Censorship, the fashion designer's response was characteristically spiky. She told Mackie that she could easily get uncensored messages out of the country using her many diplomatic contacts. Wolkoff added that she was planning to get a job in the Ministry of Information's Censorship Department and that an old family friend might pull a few strings for her.

That friend was Admiral Sir Reginald 'Blinker' Hall, the ex-Conservative politician who had set up the Economic League – the organisation that had employed K during the 1924 General Election. Admiral Hall was a prominent figure from M's past and a man he would ordinarily trust. Hall had got to know Anna's father when he had been the Russian naval attaché. Since then he had supported her application for British naturalisation, describing the Wolkoff clan as 'a fine example to others'. M was about to reach a rather different conclusion.

By the time M's agent had been introduced to Anna Wolkoff, M appears to have undergone a profound change. His wife, Lois, had moved away from the capital and for the first time in his adult life he appears to have been without his collection of animals. In anticipation of London being flattened by the Luftwaffe, an estimated 400,000 animals had been put down during the first few weeks of the war, most of them cats. Outside veterinary hospitals one would see piles of animal corpses covered by tarpaulins. Although M never wrote about the fate of his pets during the early stages of the war, by the end of September 1939 he and Lois were no longer living in the flat on Sloane Street. Some of his pets would have been taken in by his long-serving daily, Mrs Leather, while others were no doubt passed on to friends, but the rest were probably put down.

This left M in a cold and unfamiliar world, and he must have felt strangely cut off from his past. At about the same time, he experienced a political and moral shift in his outlook. Perhaps the change came over him suddenly. One secretary described him wandering around with one of his black cigarettes in his mouth, being 'suddenly immobilised by a plan of action which came into his head' and 'standing with a pair of drumsticks in his hand while he worked out the details'. Or else it crept up on him in the wake of Joyce's departure and the outbreak of war. Either way, in October 1939, he told a British Fascist that 'there was little difference between Communism and present day National Socialism'.

This may not sound like much, but to a man who had long seen international Communism as the great existential threat to his country, and whose former comrades now identified themselves with National Socialism, this was a huge departure. M had come to see the war as a struggle between democracy and dictatorship. In principle, this MI5 spymaster had resolved to turn against his Fascist past. Now he had to decide how far he was willing to go.

35

THE MYSTIC

During the first few months of 1940, M launched a fresh assault on the Fascist movement. He took on four new officers and at least six new agents. All were directed against right-wing targets. The scale and intensity of this harked back to his days working for the Makgill Organisation when he had dispatched Fascist agents into the Communist Party. Now he was facing the other way, the stakes were higher and he had less time. The Phoney War, or *Sitzkrieg,* in which there was no major offensive in Western Europe, was unlikely to go on much longer. M's challenge was to get inside Britain's Fifth Column of Nazi sympathisers as quickly as possible. First, he had to find it.

M did not have time to recruit new agents who could patiently work their way up within extremist right-wing groups. He had little choice but to approach current and former Fascists and persuade them to work for MI5. This required all his considerable tradecraft: his charm, his wit, his understanding of human frailty and his ability to lie.

Needing better intelligence on Neil Francis-Hawkins, a senior figure in the British Union of Fascists, M approached this man's brother-in-law, Arnold Bristol, and told him that Francis-Hawkins was actually a Communist agent. Bristol was shocked, and agreed to report to M.

Francis-Hawkins later described the idea that he was working for Moscow as 'ludicrous,' which it was. It was a simple trick, and not one that M would have been proud of. But his country was running out of time and so was he.

Other new additions to M Section included 'M/B', 'M/D' and 'M/M' – all well-connected in Fascist circles, all unidentified to this day – and 'M/A', who was probably a right-wing taxi driver from Brighton. Another of M's new recruits was 'M/I', a Belgian called Hélène de Munck, who had spent most of the last few years working for Henry and Mary Hope, later Lord and Lady Rankeillour, as a nanny. By the start of 1940, this twenty-five-year-old was no longer working for the Hopes and had described herself soon after the start of the war as a 'mannequin', that is, a model. But she appears to have been out of work. She also wanted British citizenship, which was what M promised when he took her on.

The other woman working for M who had once been described as a mannequin was Friedl Gaertner, whose looks had helped her win over key Nazis in London. Hélène de Munck had model looks, but she would not be using them to tease secrets out of middle-aged German men. Instead, M wanted her to penetrate the mostly female gang of Right Club members that had formed around Anna Wolkoff. Her entrée to this group was that she had once met Anna's father.

M's instructions to Hélène de Munck were to visit the Russian Tea Rooms, the café in South Kensington run by the Wolkoff family, and there to renew her friendship with Admiral Wolkoff. Typical clientele at the café included 'several aristocratic Russian speaking ladies', noted M, probably from first-hand experience, 'a couple of French-talking individuals' and 'a few elderly Englishmen [were] regular customers, since they had their reserves of bottles put in front of them'. Above an open fireplace was a portrait of the deposed Tsar Nicholas II. Downstairs in the kitchen was a cook who had been working in the Russian embassy in 1917 at the time of the revolution and had been kept on by the Soviets before Admiral Wolkoff managed to poach him. It was the old man's solitary revenge on the Soviet Union.

This cook made excellent Russian pastries, or *pirozhki,* and was famous for his *tyanuchki,* a potent blend of milk, cream and sugar. The caviar was also very good, as customers at the Russian Tea Rooms were told by the charismatic *maitre d'hôtel,* Admiral Wolkoff himself, who was no doubt pleased to see Hélène de Munck when she came to visit unexpectedly in February 1940.

'I noticed that there was a group of people who met there very often,' reported de Munck, after several further visits. 'They generally sat together at the same table and talked in low voices. The group consisted mainly of women, but occasionally there was a man or two.' This was Anna Wolkoff and her clique. Hélène de Munck was unable to find a way in.

The MI5 officer that de Munck passed this on to was not M but one of his new additions to M Section, the Hon. John Bingham, later the seventh Earl of Clanmorris. Bingham was an impoverished Irish aristocrat who would later become the physical model for George Smiley in the Le Carré novels. He was soon known to everyone in M Section as 'the Hon. John': although he was a married father of one, Bingham had a reputation as a Don Juan. Hélène de Munck was probably the first agent he had been told to run and without doubt the most attractive.

M would always urge each of his officers to 'set himself the task of getting to know his agent most thoroughly', and that it was 'a thing much to be desired' for the officer to become a 'firm personal friend' of the agent. Yet he did not recommend they start sleeping together.

Very soon after they began to work together, Bingham and de Munck were 'in the throes of a reckless affair'. It was M's responsibility to stop this kind of thing, but the subject of sex seemed to scramble his radar. 'It is difficult to imagine anything more terrifying than for an officer to become landed with a woman-agent who suffers from an overdose of Sex,' he once wrote, a sentiment that may not have been shared by Bingham. 'But as it is to be hoped that no such person would be chosen for the work, there is no need to go further into this point.' The danger was that this affair would end, and with it de Munck's desire to work for MI5. M must have realised this, yet he did nothing.

Meanwhile, Mrs Mackie had come under suspicion. Shortly after de Munck had begun to frequent the Russian Tea Rooms, Mackie endured what she called 'practically three hours of third degree' from Captain Ramsay and his wife, who wanted to know just how extreme her political views actually were. To pass this test she must have released a torrent of anti-Semitic bilge.

It worked, and over the next few weeks Mrs Mackie became an even more trusted member of the Right Club. She even acquired a nickname: 'the little Storm Trooper'. To anyone else in the country this was an insult. In the Right Club it was high praise. Rather than make herself invisible, as M's agents usually did, the talkative Mrs Mackie began to dominate the group around Wolkoff. 'Anna Wolkoff used to tell her mysterious information she had got,' recalled one of her friends, 'and Mrs Mackie used also to give her a bit of mysterious information back, and it used to sound like a competition.' This was perfect for the MI5 agent, and no doubt she encouraged it. Wolkoff's characteristic desire to outdo the little Storm Trooper made her more inclined to brag, which provided Mackie with more intelligence to pass on to M. The problem was that not all of it was necessarily true.

Although Mrs Mackie was by now an accepted member of this right-wing gang, she was excluded from some conversations. In

February 1940, Mackie was within earshot of Wolkoff when a friend addressed her in French, 'as it was considered that those standing near would not understand'. Wolkoff's friend had taken one look at Mackie and presumed that this working-class mother from Essex would not speak French. Mackie later reported, with some satisfaction, that she had been able to understand the conversation perfectly and that Wolkoff had been asked, in French, for 'information about Sir Vernon Kell'.

The fact that Anna Wolkoff knew the name of the Director of MI5 was impressive, yet the idea that she was personally acquainted with Kell was remarkable. 'Anna Wolkoff claims to have met some members of Sir Vernon's family,' Mackie went on, 'and she is to endeavour to renew the acquaintance.'

It is not often that an individual under investigation by MI5 applies for a job at MI5. But this is more or less what happened on 22 February, 1940, when Anna Wolkoff wrote to Kell, reminding him of a dinner thrown by Mark Pepys, the Earl of Cottenham, now an MI5 officer, at which they had met. Apparently, Wolkoff and Kell had had much in common, especially when 'a certain subject' came up. This was probably Communism and the threat of the Soviet Union. The rest of the letter was taken up by Wolkoff explaining to Kell that she was now unemployed, living at home and looking for a job. The implication was clear.

The previous day, M had received a report on Anna Wolkoff that changed the way she was seen, and underlined why she must not under any circumstance be offered a job in the Office. Until then, MI5 had seen her as a propagandist. Now, it seemed that she was involved in espionage.

'Wolkoff is in contact with the Belgian Embassy,' reported Mrs Mackie, who had been told that the Second Secretary of the Belgian Embassy, Jean Nieuwenhuys, had agreed to send Wolkoff's messages to Berlin. He would use the Belgian diplomatic pouch to get these letters to a Monsieur Price, a friend of Wolkoff in Brussels, who was to forward them on to Nazi Germany. Theoretically, this gave the Right Club a means of communicating with the Nazis in Berlin.

That was not all. Mackie had also discovered the name of the club's contact in the German capital. To say that this figure was well known to M would be the understatement of his career. Wolkoff wanted to get letters out to William Joyce.

First M had to find out whether this system actually worked. Were Wolkoff and the other members of the Right Club really in touch with Berlin? M remembered that one of the other women in Wolkoff's cabal had earlier given Mackie a letter addressed to Monsieur Price in Brussels and asked her to use her position in Military Censorship to get this to Belgium uncensored. This gave M an idea.

He made arrangements for the letter to be sent. 'If by any chance a reply is received (in God's good time),' he wrote, 'we shall at least know that the system works.'

Before he could find out whether it did, John Bingham had good news. His agent – and mistress – had been approached by Anna Wolkoff and introduced to her group. Now it was time for Hélène de Munck to use her special powers.

M always urged his agents to make judgements about 'the character and temperament' of their subjects and to observe their 'personal characteristics, strength and frailties'. With this in mind, Mrs Mackie had noticed earlier that 'Wolkoff, like many Russians, was extremely superstitious,' wrote M, after reading a report from Mackie. 'She was interested in spiritualism, clairvoyance, astrology, and in fact anything to do with the Occult.' So was Mackie, who would later throw drinks parties, or soirées, as she liked to call them, which ended with a séance. Indeed, many of M's female agents had an interest in spiritualism. Mona Maund bequeathed her estate to a spiritualist association. Another of his agents, Joan Miller, wrote about consulting clairvoyants. Yet Hélène de Munck was the only one with a skill that could be made to sound like evidence of some kind of hidden spiritual prowess.

The Belgian nanny possessed 'to a remarkable degree the ability to read characters from hand-writing,' explained M – what we would call graphology. Now he planned to harness these powers to the British war effort. De Munck was instructed to tell Wolkoff all about 'the Occult, and gradually to introduce her own interest in character-reading'. 'She was told to elevate her ability from the fairly material level of the formation of handwriting into the realms of psychic phenomena.'

Anna Wolkoff 'swallowed this bait avidly'. She asked de Munck to read her character based on a sample of her own handwriting. This was 'a splendid opportunity' for the MI5 agent 'to cement her friendship with Wolkoff, for the latter was extremely susceptible to flattery'.

Hélène de Munck produced a reading of Wolkoff's character that was 'suitably edited and embellished' by Bingham and M. Wolkoff was so impressed by de Munck's – and Bingham's and M's – gushing portrait of herself that she asked for readings of her friends' hand-writing. This was an excellent opening for M. 'It was possible for us to increase Anna's confidence in some of her colleagues,' he wrote, 'and to decrease it in respect of others, according to the way in which we wished to direct her feelings.'

The idea of *directing* her feelings is striking. Counterespionage is supposed to be centred on observation, not manipulation. The investigation of Anna Wolkoff had already reached the point when M might be able to steer his target in a particular direction, or even engineer a situation in which she was likely to incriminate herself.

Hélène de Munck's hold on Wolkoff also allowed M to remove any suspicion Wolkoff may have had about Mrs Mackie. When the Belgian nanny was given a sample of Mackie's handwriting, she gave it a glowing write-up. This was just one of the ways in which having two agents inside the same group was useful. Another was the potential for corroboration in court. The danger, from M's point of view, was that these two agents might somehow find out about each other.

For M, a basic principle of agent running had always been that his operatives must be kept in the dark about one another. 'This is not necessarily due to any personal mistrust or reservations in respect of an agent,' he explained. 'It is to safeguard all the agents concerned against certain very human temptations, such as the temptation to glance too much at another person,' he went on, 'or even at times to exchange a humorous, surreptitious wink.' 'The temptation to indulge in them is very real, and very strong,' he added, sounding like a man writing from personal experience. Again his long history as both spy and spymaster informed his handling of the situation. For as long as it was practicable, M would try to keep Mrs Mackie and Hélène de Munck unaware of the fact that they were both working for MI5.

M had successfully penetrated to the heart of the Right Club, thanks to the skilful work of his two new female agents. But he had nothing to show for it. There had been no arrests, nor were any imminent. M had not yet found the fabled Fifth Column.

Meanwhile, the tension between Britain and Germany was beginning to be ratcheted up. Although there had been no full-scale engagements between these two warring nations, isolated attacks had been reported with casualties on both sides. More worrying was that Ribbentrop, the German foreign minister, had recently flown out to Rome to discuss with Mussolini a possible military alliance.

Lois Knight, M's second wife. 'If only he could have been honest with me – about everything.' COURTESY OF TONY TAYLOR.

Vernon Kell, founding director of
MI5, a man skeptical of M's plan to use
female agents. NATIONAL ARCHIVES, KEW.

M during the war, not
long after the arrests of
Tyler Kent and Anna
Wolkoff. HARRY SMITH.

Guy Liddell, a key
MI5 ally. GETTY IMAGES.

William Joyce, or 'Lord Haw-Haw', Maxwell Knight's nemesis. Getty Images.

Percy Glading, the unemployed former factory worker who starred in Stalin's efforts to rebuild the Red Navy.

Tyler Kent, the US Embassy official, shortly after his release from jail.

Anna Wolkoff, the aristocratic fashion designer who believed the world was not taking her seriously.

Marjorie Mackie, another unsung heroine of M Section, and one of M's most important wartime agents. COURTESY OF STEPHEN MACKIE.

David Cornwell, better known as John Le Carré, who worked under M in MI5 and used him as the inspiration for Jack Brotherhood in *A Perfect Spy*: a 'tweedy, unscalable English mountain'. GETTY IMAGES.

One of the only photographs of an M agent at work: Tom Driberg, or M/8, in Moscow, gulling secrets out of Guy Burgess. GETTY IMAGES.

Knight with Erica the fox.

M's house in Camberley as painted by John Bingham, thought to have been the physical model for Le Carré's Smiley character. HARRY SMITH.

Knight
entertaining
a friend.

Knight with Willie the woodpecker. Photograph by Ron Francis,
reproduced by the kind permission of Surrey Heath Museum.

The retired spymaster. National Archives, Kew.

36

A SMOKESCREEN

In spite of Britain being at war with Nazi Germany, the membership of the British Union of Fascists actually grew during the first few months of 1940. Many of these new recruits were men and women who wanted Britain to join the Fascist bloc rather than fight against it. 'No war was being conducted by Germany against this country,' argued Captain Ramsay, leader of the Right Club. Like many others on the Right, he was emboldened by the lack of any major German offensive against Britain and he continued to call for peace. Yet the reports coming in to M suggested that Ramsay and his ilk were after much more than an end to hostilities.

M knew that Mosley had recently been heard to say in private that 'our time is approaching' and 'reward and victory were in sight'. Senior Fascists had been instructed to be near their telephones when the 'showdown' began. M had been told as well about an extremist Fascist cell within the Fellowship of the Services, a group for active servicemen, which was centred on Charles Geary, a former member of the British Fascists and one of M's old comrades from K. Another ex-BF man, John Hirst, reported 'that Geary was trying to recruit from among the members of the Fellowship of the Services extremists who would be prepared under certain circumstances to resort to violence in the event of a political upheaval in this country'.

In a purely democratic sense the homegrown Fascist movement was irrelevant, as it had been for several years, yet it was increasingly clear that some members of this radical fringe were either willing to help the enemy or had begun to do so already. Anna Wolkoff and her clique in the Right Club, meanwhile, were trying to carry out espionage. But M did not have enough evidence for a prosecution. If he could show that they all belonged to the same undercover network, however, that would change.

M was also aware that Wolkoff was spending time with a 'young man employed in the United States Embassy'. Mrs Mackie had told her spymaster that this was not a romantic relationship, and 'that this man is definitely pro-German'. This was curious. M needed to find out the name of Anna Wolkoff's new American friend and the nature of their non-romantic relationship. Of course, the easiest way to do this was to ask Wolkoff herself.

On the afternoon of 19 March, 1940, M sat down in a room in the War Office with Vernon Kell and Anna Wolkoff. Her brother, Alexander, had been told by a friend – presumably one with an MI5 connection – that Anna should tone down her anti-war activities. At around the same time, Alexander Wolkoff's application for British citizenship had been denied. Anna thought that he was being punished for her activities. She had written a furious note to Kell demanding an explanation. His response was to call her in for an interview, where she met both the Director of MI5 and a 'Captain King', one of M's favourite aliases.

'It was a real pleasure to cross swords with someone of Miss Wolkoff's calibre,' wrote M afterwards. 'She is an extremely clever woman with a considerable amount of superficial charm. She is also a first-class liar.'

Wolkoff began by trying to overwhelm Kell and M 'with thanks for having granted her an interview', before following up with a customary blast of name dropping. She told the two MI5 officers about the drinks party she had attended the night before with Prince Schubatow and advice she had received from Admiral Hall. She then admitted to being a 'stickyback performer', meaning she put up anti-war posters at night. But this was not a contrite confession, as far as M could tell, merely 'a smoke screen'. Her real purpose, he surmised, was 'to obtain information as to the intention of the authorities' regarding her and her associates.

The MI5 men gave away nothing. Wolkoff went on the offensive, trying to pressure them into revealing what they knew about her. 'I hope I am right in saying she did not get any change out of the interview,' wrote M, 'and I trust in due course that I shall receive some reports as to exactly what version she puts round among her friends.'

Before that could happen, Wolkoff wrote to M directly.

'Dear Captain King,' she began, 'thinking over my interview this afternoon on my way back, I remembered that I said to my brother: "If this sort of nonsense goes on, I *shall* simply write to . . . . . . (you know whom I mean)." I mention this for your information as it may be of use to you.'

This information was of no use to M. The letter was a threat. She wanted him and MI5 to back off. The person she planned to contact if MI5 continued its investigation into her was probably Admiral Hall, a man with powerful connections within British intelligence, but this is not clear. Like many others on the Right, Wolkoff believed that MI5 should be on her side. The fact that she was friendly with the likes of Vernon Kell, Reginald Hall and Mark Pepys, all of whom were either working for or connected to MI5, only emboldened her. Wolkoff believed that she was above investigation by them because she belonged to their social milieu. Later that year a different

Fascist appealed against her detention by producing an account of her genealogy, or, as she put it, her 'pedigree'. Nobody from 'good respectable stock', she insisted, could pose a threat to national security. 'There are rogues in every class of society,' she was told, and her appeal was turned down.

Barely twenty-four hours after M had received Wolkoff's menacing note, he read Hélène de Munck's account of a long conversation with the same woman. 'She had some idea that I could teach her to see the future,' began de Munck. 'The early part of the interview was devoted by Anna to staring at a piece of silver in a glass of water with this in view.' Once they had finished trying to predict the future, Wolkoff told de Munck that there were Right Club agents hidden throughout Whitehall, all of whom were ready 'to work against the Jews'. She also mentioned a document she wanted to smuggle into the country from Belgium.

At this point Anna Wolkoff asked the Belgian nanny if she would bring this item into the country during her next trip to Brussels. Just as Olga Gray had played coy when asked to be a Comintern courier, de Munck was admirably vague in her reply. She told Wolkoff that she would think about it.

This was promising. It took M one step closer to being able to put together a case against Wolkoff and the Right Club. He had also begun to learn more about the American embassy official who was spending time with Wolkoff. Mrs Mackie had reported that this man was now in a position to provide details of the inner workings of MI5, and towards the end of March 1940 she reported that he was called 'John Kent'.

This was not his real name, but it was close enough. M would soon have a sense of what Kent had in his possession that made him of such interest to Anna Wolkoff and the Right Club.

A LETTER TO AN OLD FRIEND

Collectors tend to fall into one of several categories. There are completists, who want a full set of whatever it is they are interested in, hoarders, who like to gather as many examples as they can of a particular type of object, and perfectionists, who seek out only the best. Tyler Kent displayed elements of all three. The range and quality of his illegal collection mattered to him, but so did the incredible size of it.

The son of a senior American diplomat, Tyler Kent was something of a dandy. He came from a prominent Southern family and had arrived in London, in October 1939, to start a new job as a cipher clerk at the US Embassy. Yet deep down he felt this position was beneath him. Kent had been educated at Princeton, the Sorbonne, Madrid University and George Washington University; he spoke Russian, French, Spanish and Italian; he had grown up in China, Germany, Ireland, England, Bermuda and Switzerland. Though a citizen of the world, he presented himself as a fastidiously patriotic American. Malcolm Muggeridge later described him as 'one of those intensely gentlemanly Americans who wear well-cut tailor-made suits, with waistcoat and watch-chain, drink wine instead of high-balls, and easily become furiously indignant. They always strike me as being somehow a little mad.' Kent was not mad, yet by the time he had arrived in London he was on a secret crusade.

After joining the US State Department in 1934, he had pushed for a lowly job in Moscow – an unusual choice given his impressive qualifications. His boss out there, the US Ambassador to the Soviet Union, William C. Bullitt, did not take to him. 'The sooner you shoot him the better,' Bullitt would later say of Kent. 'I hope you will shoot him, and shoot him soon. I mean it.'

Kent may not have seen eye to eye with Bullitt, but the main reason for the disillusionment he began to feel in Moscow concerned the confidential messages going into and out of the US Embassy. After several years in the Soviet Union, Kent had become certain that the United States was manoeuvring itself into a diplomatic cul-de-sac that made its involvement in the next European war all but certain. Senior American diplomats were, he said, 'actively taking part in the formation of hostile coalitions in Europe, and all sorts of things of that nature, which they, of course, had no mandate to do'. He was so angry about this that he began to do something that he himself had no mandate to do: collect classified diplomatic correspondence.

Soon after the outbreak of war in 1939, Kent was told that he would be transferred to London. Rather than risk smuggling his collection of stolen documents out of the Soviet Union, he had them burned. On his arrival in Britain he began to build up a fresh collection of material pilfered from the Code Room of the US Embassy.

The communications that Kent was now gathering in London were not only more sensitive than what he was used to seeing in Moscow, but easier to steal. The US Ambassador to Britain, Joseph Kennedy, father of the future US President John F. Kennedy, and a man whose sympathies were closer to Berlin than London, liked to have copies of important documents made for his own private collection.

'Part of my function was to make these copies,' explained Kent. 'It was quite simple to slip in an extra carbon.' He made each facsimile on embassy notepaper so that nobody could doubt its provenance when, or if, he came to share this collection with the world.

After just six months in London, Tyler Kent had stolen or copied more than a thousand confidential documents. He kept these items in his flat in neat labelled folders with titles like 'Germany', 'Turkey' or his favourite: 'Churchill'. By the start of April 1940, he even had in his collection copies of four of the eleven messages that had passed between Winston Churchill, then First Lord of the Admiralty, and the US President, Franklin D. Roosevelt.

This exchange between Churchill and Roosevelt would amount to just fifteen telegrams in total, yet it contained enough to suggest that the American president was colluding with Churchill to help Britain win the war, despite America's neutrality. These messages show Churchill offering to share secret military technology with the US Navy to help it police American territorial waters, all to Britain's military advantage. Roosevelt, meanwhile, comes across as having decided long ago to bring America into the war. The political ramifications of these telegrams being made public were seismic.

M was unaware of Tyler Kent's stash of documents. But he knew that this man had been seen in the company of a suspected Nazi agent soon after his arrival in Britain. In October 1939, a team of MI5 watchers had been following Ludwig Matthias, a businessman from Stockholm, following a tip-off from the Swedish police. Kent was one of the first men seen to meet Matthias. This alleged German spy then took an envelope from Kent. It was roughly ten inches by six inches and was described as 'bulky'.

Ordinarily, a suspicious meeting like this between a suspected Nazi agent and a US diplomat would be reported immediately to the US Embassy. MI5 had gone out of its way until then to maintain good relations with American officials. But on this occasion they held back. MI5 wanted to see where the Tyler Kent trail might lead.

The dilemma now facing Kent, in early 1940, was what to do with his enormous collection of stolen material. The publication of the telegrams between Churchill and Roosevelt would strengthen the American isolationist movement immeasurably and 'do incalculable harm to the Allies', as M later wrote, but only if this correspondence was conveyed to an individual or organisation that was willing to use it against British interests. Kent understood this. He knew that if he played his cards in a certain way he could change the direction of the war.

One danger was that Kent would share his material with the Germans. Towards the end of February 1940, he had asked for a transfer to Berlin. Perhaps he had been ordered to do this by Ludwig Matthias, the suspected Gestapo agent. Yet his transfer request was turned down.

Another possibility was that Kent would use these stolen papers to launch a new career in journalism. In March 1939, he had contacted an old friend, Barry Dennis, Editor in Chief of the International News Service, one of the world's largest telegraphic agencies. Dennis had informally offered him a job as a foreign correspondent. Publishing these papers would be a sensational way to start his journalistic career.

Kent would later claim that he had only ever planned to be a patriotic whistleblower, and that he worried the American people 'were not being adequately informed, or if they were informed, they were informed in the sense of being told half-truths instead of the strict truth'. He wanted the facts 'brought to the attention of say, the American Senators'. Some of the statements he made are reminiscent today of American whistleblowers such as Daniel Ellsberg or Edward Snowden. The difference is that these two had always known roughly what they planned to do with their material. By April 1940, Tyler Kent appeared to be dangerously undecided, or was he waiting for instructions from his spymaster?

One of the few people that Kent had spoken to in London about his collection was Anna Wolkoff. She had been introduced to him by a mutual acquaintance at the Russian Tea Rooms. Kent described Wolkoff as 'a smart woman, fun to talk to, but plain as hell'. Even if he had found her attractive, he had just begun an intense affair with Mrs Irene Danischewsky (the aunt of the actress Dame Helen Mirren). Instead, Kent and Wolkoff clicked on the subject of politics. Both were anti-war and anti-Semitic. They began to meet more frequently. Kent showed her some of the documents in his collection. Wolkoff excitedly passed on details of what she had seen to her friends in the Right Club, including Mrs Mackie, and from here the information went back to MI5.

M knew that Anna Wolkoff was receiving valuable intelligence from somewhere, but he was not yet aware of Kent's archive. Nor had he got any further in his attempt to prove that the Right Club was communicating with Berlin. Nothing had come of the test letter. By the start of April 1940, M had two agents at the heart of an extremist group that had access to secret intelligence and might, or might not, be trying to establish a Fifth Column in Britain.

That was all.

He needed a break. Anything, really, that would allow him to prove in court that the Right Club had a means of communicating with the enemy.

Just when he needed it most, a member of the Right Club was asked to commit an act of espionage.

J. McGuirk Hughes was an ex-Makgill agent who had spent most of the last decade working as the BUF Director of Intelligence. He also had close ties to Special Branch and may have been taken on by M as his agent codenamed 'M/J'. His precise relationship with M is ambiguous, and no doubt it went through several permutations. Much clearer is that on 9 April, 1940, J. McGuirk Hughes approached Lord Ronald Graham, 'Ronnie' to his chums, the younger son of the Duke of Montrose, an officer in the Right Club and a man described by M as 'pleasant, politically stupid, but quite honest'.

Hughes began by asking Lord Ronald to send a letter to William Joyce in Berlin.

If he agreed to do this, the young aristocrat would be guilty of communicating with the enemy and under a strict interpretation of the law he could then be classed as an enemy agent. It is unlikely that he was aware of this. Nor did he have any idea that copies of the letter Hughes was so keen for him to send would soon be, or already were, in the possession of MI5 and Special Branch.

Lord Ronald agreed to the plan. He told Hughes that he would ask a friend of his at the Spanish embassy, the Duke of Alba, to send the letter to Berlin via the diplomatic pouch. But then he had second thoughts.

At the time, he was trying to get a commission in the Royal Naval Volunteer Reserve. Wisely, he concluded that sending letters to the enemy might not improve his chances of getting it. Instead, Lord Ronald took Hughes to the Russian Tea Rooms, where he introduced him to someone with less to lose: Anna Wolkoff. Hughes asked Wolkoff 'if she would like to do something against the Jews'. He had never met this woman before, yet he seemed to know exactly which of her buttons to press.

Wolkoff replied at once that she would very much like to do something 'against the Jews'.

Hughes produced an envelope addressed to 'Herr W. B. Joyce, Rundfunkhaus, Berlin' and asked her to send it. Without finding it too much of a coincidence that Hughes should have on his person a letter addressed to the one man in Berlin that she had already tried to contact, Wolkoff agreed.

Very soon after, right on cue, Hélène de Munck came in for dinner. She mentioned to Admiral Wolkoff that she had a friend at the Romanian Legation who would soon be leaving for mainland Europe. The admiral passed this on to his daughter, who came over at once to ask de Munck whether it was true.

It was, she replied.

'Why didn't you tell me this before?'

Good question. De Munck replied that she had not thought it important.

Wolkoff asked whether her Romanian friend might be able to get a letter out to Germany.

'I replied that I thought he might be able to,' recalled de Munck, 'as he had sometimes been good enough to take letters for me to an uncle who lives in Romania.'

Wolkoff reached into her bag, pulled out the sealed envelope addressed to Joyce, and handed it over to the former nanny. She told de Munck to pass it on to her friend so that he could send it to Berlin. Wolkoff then asked whether she could meet this mysterious Romanian.

'I explained that I could not very well ask him to compromise himself by meeting strangers, and I thought he would be much more likely to take the letter as a personal favour to me.'

Wolkoff accepted this.

That night Hélène de Munck passed the letter to M, who had it and its contents photographed. The next day Wolkoff asked whether she could add a few lines to the message.

'I replied that it might be difficult to contact my Legation friend, but that I would do my best and let her have it as soon as possible.'

That night de Munck got the letter back from M and arranged for Wolkoff to come round the following morning.

Shortly before nine in the morning on 11 April, 1940, Anna Wolkoff arrived at Hélène de Munck's flat where she opened the envelope. Eyeing its contents with interest, de Munck said that her Romanian friend would probably want to know what was in the letter before agreeing to take it.

'Well, look at it,' replied Wolkoff, holding it out to her.

De Munck reached forward and took 'a single sheet of quarto paper covered with a code consisting of letters and figures. It was typewritten and there was a diagram at the bottom of the back page. The only portion of the document which was *en clair* was a short passage typed in German.'

She complained that it meant nothing to her.

'Neither does it mean anything to me,' said Wolkoff. 'But I know what the letter is about.'

Wolkoff explained that it was an account of Jewish activities in Britain for Lord Haw-Haw to use in future broadcasts, adding, with a characteristic flourish, that in Berlin this would be 'like a bombshell'.

Rather than add a message to the original document, Wolkoff took a fresh sheet of paper and sat down at de Munck's typewriter – the same machine that the MI5 agent had probably used to produce reports about her – and typed out a few inconsequential lines in German asking for a repeat of a particular broadcast about Freemasons, one of her pet obsessions. She signed off 'P. J...!' This was short for 'Perish Judah', so that Joyce would know this message had come from the Right Club. She also drew the group emblem of an eagle and snake.

'She resealed the letter in an envelope which she had brought with her,' wrote de Munck, 'handed it back to me, and left the flat at about 9.15 a.m.' Later that day the MI5 agent handed the package to M, who had it photographed by Special Branch and arranged for the text to be passed on to the Government Code and Cypher School for decoding. 'Certain arrangements were then made' for the letter to be sent to Joyce in Berlin.

M needed it to reach the German capital so that he could show in court that Wolkoff had successfully communicated with the enemy. Fortunately for him, the coded letter contained a line asking Joyce to acknowledge that he had received the note by referring in a future broadcast to 'Carlyle'. If Lord Haw-Haw used this word in the coming weeks, then it would be possible to frame a prosecution against Wolkoff. This would allow M to charge at least one Nazi sympathiser: but that might be all.

CARLYLE

On 9 April, 1940, the same day that Anna Wolkoff was handed a letter addressed to William Joyce, German forces launched a surprise attack on Denmark and Norway.

The Phoney War was over. In London more people began to be seen carrying around their gas masks. The streets in the capital were eerily empty that night as everyone gathered round their radios. All over the country the mood had changed. Bullish indifference started to be replaced by caution and, for some, a creeping, contagious anxiety. MI5 began to be bombarded with reports from wary members of the public. Some had seen pigeons flying in a suspicious manner that they took to be German courier pigeons; others, marks on telegraph posts that could be coded signals for German invaders.

As spy fever rose, MI5 saw reports from Norway to suggest that Germans living in Norway, as well as pro-Nazi Norwegians and Danes, may have committed acts of sabotage, subversion, propaganda and espionage to assist the invading Nazis. How else to explain the crushing nature of the German advance? If there had been a Fifth Column in those countries, as some newspaper reports suggested, it would be naïve to think that Berlin had not tried to set up a similar network in Britain.

As the Germans continued to punch north through Norway, Anna Wolkoff saw more of Tyler Kent. He showed her further documents from his collection, including an item from the Churchill–Roosevelt correspondence.

'May I have this?' asked Wolkoff, holding up the message.

Kent asked if she was going to show it to Captain Ramsay, the Conservative MP and leader of the Right Club.

Wolkoff replied that she was. Kent offered no objection.

Tyler Kent agreed to let Captain Ramsay see his documents on the understanding that the politician would use them to raise a question in Parliament about Churchill's correspondence with Roosevelt. At last, the American cipher clerk had decided to play his hand. In doing so, he hoped to kill off any chance there was of America coming into the war unprovoked. But it may not have been Kent who had made this decision.

Years later it emerged that Kent was not working for German intelligence, but nor was he a patriotic whistleblower. He appears to have been working for Moscow Centre. The NKVD agent Guy Burgess later attested to this. Other scraps of evidence all point in the same direction. The alleged Gestapo agent that Kent had been seen to meet, Ludwig Matthias, was Jewish and anti-Nazi and was far more likely to have been working for Moscow than Berlin. It is also striking that the material gathered by Kent from the US Embassy had very little value to the Germans, but was of considerable interest to the Soviets.

Regardless of what his motivation may have been, Tyler Kent had just lit the fuse on a series of events which could seriously damage the prospects of America joining the war. M still had no evidence of espionage. He gave instructions for Hélène de Munck to tell Wolkoff that she was going to Belgium and to ask the fashion designer whether she still needed a document smuggled in from Belgium. She did not. But she had another job for de Munck in Brussels. Wolkoff asked her to meet 'our principal agent in Belgium' and to use her spiritual powers to work out whether this man could be trusted.

Belgium was MI6 territory. For M to send one of his agents there was a risk, but one that by this stage of the war he was willing to take. On 16 April, 1940, the former nanny flew to Brussels where, as Wolkoff had instructed, she met Nieuwenhuys, the Second Secretary of the Belgian Embassy, who had agreed earlier to be part of the chain of people relaying uncensored messages from London to Berlin. Four days later Hélène de Munck was back in London, where she assured Wolkoff that in her spiritual opinion Nieuwenhuys could be trusted.

Only two days after de Munck's return from Belgium, Mrs Mackie reported that someone living at No. 47 Gloucester Place was supplying Wolkoff with 'confidential information about members of the British Intelligence Service', including Guy Liddell. One of the residents at this address was the American embassy official Tyler Kent.

This was M's clearest indication yet that Kent was sharing with Wolkoff, and presumably others, 'information which [he] had no right to be conveying to any person outside the United States Government Service'.

Then M had another breakthrough. During one of his broadcasts, Joyce decided to turn against the French. 'Where is their Shakespeare?' he fumed. 'Who is their Carlyle?'

Carlyle.

This was the agreed code word to show that Joyce had received the letter first presented to Wolkoff by J. McGuirk Hughes. Wolkoff could now be classed as an enemy agent.

M did not waste any time. He compiled a comprehensive report linking Tyler Kent to Anna Wolkoff, Captain Ramsay and the Right Club. 'It seems urgently necessary for something to be done about this man,' he wrote on 4 May, 1940, meaning Kent. He then suggested that Liddell, who had good contacts at the US Embassy, should take this report to the Americans.

But he did not.

By now the Security Service was, in the words of its former official historian, 'close to collapse'. Following the German invasions of Norway and Denmark, it received from government departments more than 8,000 vetting and security requests *each week*. Liddell was struggling to stay on top of this, just as he was failing to get anywhere in his attempt to persuade the Home Office to reconsider its stance on the mass internment of enemy aliens and homegrown political extremists. MI5 was no longer alone on this. The Joint Intelligence Committee, a relatively new body dominated by senior intelligence officials from across Whitehall and the armed forces, was 'strongly of the opinion that something more should be done.'

The Home Office would not budge. If there was an MI5 investigation that could be used to strengthen the case for the internment of those who might belong to a Fifth Column, then it was in Liddell's and MI5's interests to make sure that it did. This was perhaps why Liddell sat on M's report about Kent rather than pass it on to the American embassy.

Just days later, on 10 May, 1940, on a gloriously sunny morning in London, German forces poured into Belgium and Holland. The day began with news of the Blitzkrieg. It ended with the installation in No. 10 Downing Street of Winston Churchill.

VICTORY AT ALL COSTS

The morning after Churchill became Prime Minister, the Director of MI5 wrote to the Home Office asking for the immediate internment of the BUF leadership and all members of extremist right-wing groups. This amounted to roughly five hundred people in total. 'It will be interesting,' wrote Liddell, 'to see if the Home Office are prepared to swallow this pill.'

It was not. Liddell's boss, Jasper Harker, was summoned to the Home Office that evening and told as much. As a sop to MI5, the Home Office agreed to the internment of male enemy aliens aged sixteen to sixty-five years living in a county adjacent to the south and east coasts of Britain, and to placing tighter restrictions on non-enemy aliens. Yet even these mild measures elicited a flurry of complaints from the British public. 'An elephant keeper in Bertram Hills Circus at Southampton is a German,' noted Liddell, wearily. 'They do not know what to do with the elephants.'

By this stage, Guy Liddell did not have 'the slightest doubt' that the BUF would be willing to help the Germans in the event of an invasion. 'There were after all some quite intelligent people in this office who had given careful study to the matter and that was their considered view,' he wrote, referring here mainly to M.

Liddell, M and a growing number of MI5 officers were 'very concerned' about the Home Office position. Relations between the two departments had become, according to one MI5 historian, 'severely strained'. The following day Jimmy Dickson and Francis Aikin-Sneath, a former schoolteacher who had been taken on by MI5 to help investigate British Fascism, were asked to put together a report showing precisely why the BUF was a hostile association. The plan was for M, Kell and the heads of both the Metropolitan Police and Special Branch to present this document once it was finished to the Home Secretary. Just hours after Dickson and Aikin-Sneath had been put to work, Churchill stood up in Parliament to deliver one of the great speeches of the twentieth century, one that seemed to sum up the mood inside MI5 better than that of the Home Office:

> I have nothing to offer but blood, toil, tears and sweat. We have before us an ordeal of the most grievous kind. We have before us many, many long months of struggle and of suffering. You ask, what is our policy? I can say: It is to wage war, by sea, land and air, with all our might and with all the strength that God can give us; to wage war against a monstrous tyranny, never surpassed in the dark lamentable catalogue of human crime. That is our policy. You ask, what is our aim? I can answer in one word: It is victory, victory at all costs, victory in spite of terror, victory, however long and hard the road may be; for without victory, there is no survival.

That night, in west London, Anna Wolkoff made omelettes with Mrs Mackie and Joan Miller, the society girl working at MI5 who had recently been brought into M's investigation of the Right Club. If they did discuss Churchill's speech, Mackie did not mention it in her report. Instead she focused on what Wolkoff told her, once Miller had left, about the dinner she had attended several nights earlier at the glamorous L'Escargot Restaurant in Soho. It was not the food or the setting that had excited her so much as the company.

Wolkoff explained that there had been four people at that dinner: Tyler Kent, herself, another Right Club member called Enid Riddell and an Italian referred to by Wolkoff as 'Mr Macaroni'. Apparently, she gave most people nicknames like this. 'It was a joke,' explained Kent much later. Mrs Mackie tried to find out who Mr Macaroni was, but all she could get out of Wolkoff was that he had a 'name like a tin of fruit'.

Three days later, Wolkoff obtained another secret message from the Churchill–Roosevelt correspondence. This telegram had come into the US Embassy that very morning and was the US President's reply to Churchill's request, on 15 May, for some fifty 'of your older destroyers,' 'several hundred of the latest types of aircraft' and 'anti-aircraft equipment and ammunition'. Churchill had also asked Roosevelt to send a naval squadron to Ireland, for fear of a possible German invasion. In return he had offered the use of the British port of Singapore to help the Americans 'keep that Japanese dog quiet in the Pacific'.

Roosevelt replied that 'it would be possible to hand over 40 or 50 destroyers of the old type, but this is subject to the special approval of Congress, which would be difficult to obtain at present'. This was the genesis of the 'Destroyers for Bases' deal, also known as 'Lend-Lease', in which the United States would swap fifty ageing American warships for leases on various outlying British bases. Despite heavy opposition from both Congress and the US Navy, Roosevelt would force the deal through. The first destroyers were delivered (full of supplies) in September of that year. But on 16 May, 1940, when Wolkoff first read Roosevelt's message, its meaning was less clear.

Later that day, Wolkoff and Mackie stumbled through the

blackout to a private residence in Chelsea where they posted an envelope through the door. Inside was a copy of Roosevelt's message to Churchill, the one that had been received in London earlier that day. This house was the home of 'Mr Macaroni', who was in fact Francesco Marigliano, the Duca Del Monte – which explains the line about tinned fruit. Del Monte was an experienced Italian diplomat and close friend of Mussolini who had in the past couriered secret messages between Rome and London. He was connected to Italian intelligence. 'It is understood,' wrote Mackie shortly afterwards, 'that the Italians were very pleased with this information.'

One week later, a message arrived in Berlin from the German Ambassador in Rome. It gave an accurate precis of Roosevelt's message about destroyers. The German Ambassador explained that his information came from an 'unimpeachable source'. By passing this classified document to an Italian diplomat, at a time when Italy was a military ally of Nazi Germany, Anna Wolkoff had committed a flagrant act of espionage.

The following day, Canning, the head of Special Branch, and M went to see a Home Office Assistant Secretary, Sir Ernest Holderness. They were accompanied by an MI5 lawyer, Toby Pilcher (whose father would have been known to M because he, too, had belonged to the British Fascists in the 1920s). The meeting went well. Holderness asked how many homegrown Fascists MI5 would like to see interned.

'We said that as a maximum about 500, though if absolutely necessary we would be prepared to modify this.' Holderness then went to present the MI5 case to the Home Secretary.

A message came back from the Home Office later that day. They were absolutely opposed to MI5's plans for mass internment, arguing that there was no evidence of any Fifth Column activity in Britain.

Churchill's position was pointedly different. Less than twenty-four hours later, on Saturday, 18 May, the War Cabinet met to discuss the question of British political extremists. 'Action should also be taken against Communists and Fascists,' urged Churchill, 'and very considerable numbers should be put in protective or preventive internment, including their leaders.' His views seemed to be perfectly aligned with M's. The Cabinet agreed with him. But again, the Home Office demurred.

'During wartime,' wrote M, 'there will always come a point in an investigation where an agent must be sacrificed in order to achieve satisfactory results; and the Intelligence Officer in charge of the case must face the responsibility of deciding the exact point at which such sacrifice must be made.' M decided that this moment had come. Just hours after that Cabinet meeting, M went to meet Herschel Johnson, a senior official at the US Embassy.

M told him that an American embassy official had been stealing documents and passing them on to an extremist right-wing organisation that was suspected of espionage. He then took Johnson through the association between Wolkoff and Kent, adding that Kent had been seen the year before in the company of Ludwig Matthias, a suspected Gestapo agent.

Johnson was 'profoundly shocked', wrote M. He was also furious that MI5 had waited until now to tell them about Tyler Kent. He demanded to know why they had been kept in the dark for so long. M replied that nothing had been found to confirm that Matthias was actually a spy.

Perhaps wanting to change the subject, M handed over his written summary of MI5's case against Tyler Kent and Anna Wolkoff. Johnson would have been justified in telling the MI5 officer at this point that he could handle the situation from here, before showing him politely to the door. Instead, he agreed to M's request. The MI5 spymaster wanted to do more than staunch the flow of secrets from the US Embassy. Rather than have the Americans deal with Kent internally, as they might have done, M wanted a synchronised double arrest of Kent and Wolkoff.

This was partly a practical measure, but mainly it was to increase the impact of these arrests and to draw out the connection between Wolkoff and Kent. If the Americans agreed to waive Kent's diplomatic immunity, M could arrange for his arrest to take place at the same time as Wolkoff's on Monday morning.

M saw Johnson again the next day, Sunday. By then, the US Ambassador, Joe Kennedy, who had been out of town for the weekend, had been briefed. He, too, was livid about being kept out of the loop for so long. But he agreed to M's request.

All that remained was for the State Department in Washington, DC, to confirm the removal of Kent's diplomatic immunity. The problem was that Kent himself was due to work in the Code Room that night, just as the message waiving his immunity would come in. Johnson 'will act with great care,' reported M, 'in order to see that there is no leakage which might get back to Tyler Kent'. It was agreed that the arrests of Kent and Wolkoff would go ahead the next day.

THE RAID

By Monday, 20 May, 1940, Holland had fallen, Belgium was on the brink and France looked set to follow. Britain was surely next. Indeed Hitler would soon issue Directive No. 16, regarding the German invasion of Britain, which included plans for 67,000 German troops to land by sea on the south coast of England, supported by waves of parachutists, before securing London. After this, the Nazi clean-up operation would begin. With this in mind the *Reichssicherheitshauptamt*, or Reich Security Head Office, would compile a list of several thousand prominent Britons, the so-called Black Book, who were to be rounded up in the wake of the German invasion and delivered to the Gestapo. They would either be imprisoned or shot. One of the names on that list was: 'Captain M. King, Whitehall'.

Londoners had been bombarded over the last month not with bombs but with the news of Allied losses, reversals, defeats, retreats and surrenders. German forces appeared to be better equipped than their opponents, they had superior tactics and they were better led. As one MI5 officer wrote, 'the news has been so bad that it made me feel physically sick'. Even more unsettling was the idea that there were people in Britain willing to assist the invading German forces.

M made his way to the Home Office early on that Monday morning while most Londoners were having their breakfast. He showed his pass to the sentries outside the main entrance and continued into a building that must have felt like enemy territory. He was there to pick up a detention order for Anna Wolkoff that had been signed by the Home Secretary. Usually, this would be passed on to the police at Scotland Yard, yet his agent, Mrs Mackie, had heard that the Right Club had sympathisers among the senior ranks of the police. M was not prepared to take the risk.

From the Home Office, the MI5 spymaster made the short journey to Scotland Yard, where he met Sir Norman Kendal, the Assistant Commissioner (Crime), who was to decide whether there was sufficient evidence to have Kent arrested. Also in the room was Joe Kennedy, the US Ambassador, whose fiery red hair matched his temper that morning. Kennedy assured M and Kendal that Kent's diplomatic immunity had been waived, adding that he wanted Kent to be taken into custody right away. Kendal ruled that the arrest could go ahead.

At this point, M should have felt a pang of uncertainty. After all, none of his agents had actually been inside Kent's flat to see this material. Mrs Mackie had merely been told by Anna Wolkoff, who was prone to exaggeration, like Mackie herself, that Kent had a number of confidential documents. But it seems that M knew precisely what the police would discover in Kent's home, and where.

The author Paul Willetts has argued persuasively that M may have crept into Kent's rooms in the weeks before Kendal authorised this arrest. It would not have been hard. The flat was always unlocked when Kent was out, and the MI5 watchers could have easily told M when he was at work. This was also entirely in character for M. Ever since those raids on the Glasgow headquarters of the Communist Party, in 1925, he had displayed a remarkable eagerness to break into other people's homes. This was a man who revered the 'old-fashioned poacher', praising him as 'a field naturalist of a high order'. One woman who worked under M recalled being ordered to break into the homes of suspected spies, adding that 'M certainly never minded taking a risk.' Willetts has also shown that in one of M's reports he refers to having 'examined' 'many' of the papers in Kent's flat. It is hard to think when he could have done this other than during the weeks leading up to the day of the arrests.

Presumably feeling confident about what they were going to find, M decided that he would lead the raid on Tyler Kent's flat. He placed Jimmy Dickson in charge of the near-simultaneous arrest of Anna Wolkoff. Once he had all the right paperwork, M set off for the US Embassy with three policemen. Meanwhile, Dickson got together two policemen and a female officer and prepared for the journey to South Kensington.

Tyler Kent was approaching the end of his night shift when M arrived at the US Embassy, which was beyond the jurisdiction of the British police, so no arrest could take place there. It was just after seven o'clock in the morning. M found the Second Secretary, Franklin Gowen, and they waited until Kent finished his shift at around eight o'clock.

The dandyish cipher clerk then emerged into a bright, summery day. He was spotted immediately by a team of MI5 watchers. This was not the first time they had followed him home like this after a night shift, and they knew that if today was like any other he would soon be in bed with his mistress, Irene Danischewsky. Keeping a suitable distance, they followed him back to No. 47 Gloucester Place. Not long after, the two lovers were alone in the flat.

As things progressed in Kent's bedroom, M and the others piled into a police car and drove to the flat. The door to the boarding house was opened by a maid. She asked them to wait as she fetched her employer. Instead, they rushed in, one following the maid, the others heading for the stairs. On the landing they found the landlady, who pointed them towards Kent's door. They knocked several times. Kent refused to let them in. Inspector Pearson prepared to charge the door, and for a moment all was still.

M was moments away from plugging an intelligence leak at the US Embassy, but this raid could amount to much more than that, and he knew it. It seems that M already had a sense of how the arrests of Tyler Kent and Anna Wolkoff could be used to achieve a more radical outcome, one that might banish forever the ghost of his Fascist past.

Inspector Pearson crashed into the door, and it gave way. The men rushed in to find Tyler Kent in his pyjama bottoms. Pearson identified himself and explained why they were there. One of the other policemen went for the door to the bathroom. Kent could not prevent him from opening it, to reveal his mistress wearing just a pyjama shirt.

The lovers got dressed.

M fired off his first round of questions at Kent.

Was there anything in the flat that belonged to the US Embassy? Did he know Anna Wolkoff? Was her loyalty to Russia or to the United Kingdom?

Kent turned to Gowen, his fellow American, and asked whether he should respond.

'Answer everything,' came the reply.

He did so, but he revealed nothing.

Kent began by claiming to have no items in the flat that belonged to the American government, a particularly inept lie given that a team of policemen was then conducting a search. This set the tone for the interrogations that followed. Kent's attitude throughout was detached and prickly. At times he seemed to take pleasure in evading the meaning of the questions aimed at him.

It took the policemen seconds rather than minutes to find Kent's collection of more than 1,500 documents. The police also discovered a set of keys for the US Embassy Code Room that Kent had had cut, in case he was transferred to a different job, and a considerable sum of money. Yet the key piece of evidence, from M's point of view, was a leather-bound ledger secured by a simple brass lock, the Right Club's Red Book. The man from MI5 forced it open to reveal a complete list of Right Club members, including details of who had paid what and when.

The testimony of Mrs Mackie and Hélène de Munck would link Anna Wolkoff to Tyler Kent, yet this vital document connected Kent to the Right Club and Captain Ramsay, and in turn Ramsay could be linked to Sir Oswald Mosley. This list of Right Club members did not prove any wrongdoing on their part, but it was invaluable for anyone trying to suggest or imply the existence of a Fifth Column in Britain.

Kent was arrested. Danichewsky was not. The American was led downstairs by the policemen and driven back to the US Embassy. There was no room in the car for his collection of papers, so a passing taxi was used to bring them to the embassy where they were lugged into the Ambassador's office. Kent was locked up in a room nearby.

Now Kennedy had a chance to go through the material. Burning with indignation, he agreed that these papers had come from the Code Room. Indeed Kennedy would later describe Kent's collection as 'vital' and that 'in the event of its being passed on to Germany, the most disastrous consequences would ensue'.

Then Kent was called in. The ambassador began by reminding him of his family's history. Given all this, 'one would not expect you to let us all down'.

'In what way?' asked Kent.

'You don't think you have?' snapped Kennedy. 'What did you think you were doing with our codes and telegrams?'

'It was only for my information.'

After a brief consultation, M took over.

'The situation as I see it is this,' began the MI5 officer. 'I think it is just as well you should know you can be proved to have been associating with this woman, Anna Wolkoff.'

'I don't deny that.'

'I am in a position to prove that she has a channel of communication with Germany, that she has used that channel of communication with Germany, that she is a person of hostile associations, that she is involved in pro-German propaganda, to say the least,' said M. 'As your Ambassador has just said, you have been found with documents in your private rooms to which he considers you have no proper title. You would be a very silly man if you did not realise that certain conclusions might be drawn from that situation, and it is for you to offer the explanation, not us.'

Kent said nothing.

'What is this?' asked M, holding the ledger that contained details of the Right Club membership.

'I don't know,' said Kent.

'Who gave it to you?'

'I think probably if you opened it you could find out.'

'Who has the key?'

'I haven't any idea.'

Kent offered nothing to M, who soon concluded that this man was 'either a fool or a rogue' and 'nothing very useful is to be got by carrying on this conversation'. Instead, the well-tailored clerk was led off to Cannon Row Police Station.

M had long been of the opinion that 'what the suspect says in the first excitement of interrogation is often the very thing that gets him six months hard'. Kent had revealed nothing, other than his determination to clam up. M would not be able to frame his prosecution around a full or partial confession from him. Instead, the onus would have to be on other evidence.

At eleven thirty that morning, just as Tyler Kent was being grilled by Joe Kennedy and M, Jimmy Dickson formally detained Anna Wolkoff and took her to Rochester Row Police Station. Both arrests had gone as planned, yet the prosecution of these two would not be for some months.

Using superb tradecraft, M had manoeuvred two of his female agents into the heart of a hostile spy ring and had stopped a potentially devastating leak of information to the enemy. But his work was not finished.

THE MEETING

The following evening, Tuesday, 21 May, 1940, M attended a meeting at the Home Office. Gathered round a table was his immediate superior in MI5, Guy Liddell, and the two most senior figures in the Home Office – the Home Secretary, Sir John Anderson, and the Permanent Secretary at the Home Office, Sir Alexander Maxwell – as well as the head of the British Army, Chief of the Imperial General Staff, General Sir Alan Brooke and, finally, the Director of MI5, Major-General Sir Vernon Kell. At an early stage the Home Secretary trotted out the line he had been using since the start of the war, namely, he felt there was no evidence that the British Fascists were prepared to assist the Germans if there was an invasion. He referred to an article by Sir Oswald Mosley in which the BUF leader had apparently 'appealed to the patriotism of its members'.

At this point M intervened.

'M. explained that this was merely an example of how insincere Mosley really was,' recorded Liddell, 'and how many of his supporters simply regarded utterances of that kind as a figure of speech. He then went on to describe something of the underground activities of the BUF and also of the recent case against Tyler Kent involving

[Captain] Ramsay. Anderson agreed that the case against Ramsay was rather serious but he did not seem to think that it involved the BUF.'

At this point in the meeting, M could have agreed with the Home Secretary. It was the polite thing to do, the sensible thing to do and perhaps the most accurate thing to do. It was what the majority of his Fascist friends, past and present, would have done in his position, and it was probably what he himself might have chosen to do had a similar situation arisen several years earlier. The link between the BUF and the Kent-Wolkoff-Ramsay affair was tangential, not direct.

M chose otherwise. He pushed back against the Home Secretary. Using his intimate knowledge of the movement, he made the case in the strongest terms for the internment of all senior British Fascists, referring not only to the arrests of Kent and Wolkoff but to the list of Right Club members contained in the secret ledger. 'M. explained to him [Anderson] that Maule Ramsay and Mosley were in constant touch with one another and that many members of the Right Club were also members of the BUF.'

The meeting lasted just under two hours. 'M. was extremely good,' wrote Liddell, 'and made all his points very quietly and forcibly.'

By the end of it, thought Liddell, Sir John Anderson was 'considerably shaken'. 'He asked us for further evidence on certain points which he required for the Cabinet meeting which was to take place tomorrow evening.'

That meeting was chaired by Churchill, who pushed for a new clause, 1a, to be added to the existing Regulation 18b of the Defence (General) Regulations 1939. This would allow for the detention without trial of any British citizen thought to pose a threat to national security as a result of their membership in an organisation that might be under foreign control or influence – such as the BUF, the Right Club or any other extremist right-wing group. This new clause was not put before Parliament but was approved by the Cabinet, including the Home Secretary, that same evening. No public announcement was made. This was to ensure an element of surprise when the arrests began, as they did the next day.

Over the next three months, Sir Oswald Mosley, Captain Ramsay and more than 1,000 senior British Fascists were arrested and imprisoned without trial. According to the Home Office, more than 700 of these men and women belonged to the BUF, an organisation that was soon outlawed by the Home Secretary. On the day that these arrests began, 23 May, 1940, Parliament also passed the Treachery Act, which made it easier for the death sentence to be delivered in cases of espionage or sabotage. Just four days later the Home Defence (Security) Executive was established to look into questions concerning the so-called Fifth Column.

Two weeks after that, in the wake of Dunkirk, Churchill dismissed MI5's most senior officer, Sir Vernon Kell, who had been in charge of this department since its creation in 1909. His long-serving deputy, Sir Eric Holt-Wilson, resigned in protest. Part of the reason for Kell's removal was that he had agreed too easily to the Home Office position on mass internment. With Kell and Holt-Wilson out of the picture, it was agreed at an MI5 board meeting that 'our policy with regard to enemy aliens should be their wholesale internment followed by their removal from the country as and when this might become possible. Our object is to clear the ground as far as possible in the event of an invasion of this country.' Very soon after, the British Joint Chiefs of Staff ordered the internment of all male enemy aliens between the ages of 18 and 70 years. By the end of July, as the Battle of Britain began and Hitler's plans to invade Britain reached an advanced stage, roughly 27,000 Germans and Italians – for Italy was now at war with Britain – were detained in camps across England and some were sent to Canada and Australia.

Before considering the legality of this mass internment, of both homegrown Fascists and enemy aliens, or the question of whether it was justified, we should ask *how* this had come about.

'It seems that the Prime Minister takes a strong view about the internment of all Fifth Columnists at this moment,' wrote Liddell, shortly after the critical Cabinet meeting of 22 May, in which the key 1a clause was approved. 'He has left the Home Secretary in no doubt about his views. What seems to have moved him more than anything was the Tyler Kent case.'

This last sentence is telling. The arrests of Kent and Wolkoff played a pivotal role in the decision to order mass internment. But why did Churchill know so much about this particular case? And for what reason did he imagine that it strengthened the case for having senior Fascists locked up, exactly as M had argued?

The answer appears to lie in the identity of the man who told Guy Liddell about the importance Churchill had attached to the Kent-Wolkoff case. This was the Prime Minister's close friend and *homme d'affaires:* Desmond Morton.

Desmond Morton, the bad-tempered Old Etonian with the bullet lodged in his chest, M's former spymaster at MI6, had become Churchill's most trusted adviser on national security. Indeed, the head of MI6 was said to be 'mortified' by the extent to which Churchill now relied on Desmond Morton.

Morton's influence would wane, yet by May 1940 he was at the peak of his powers. Desmond Morton was the conduit between the Prime Minister and MI5 who was capable of exerting huge influence on Churchill regarding national security. At the same time, Morton remained a 'great contact' of M, 'to whom he had direct access'.

It is not a wild leap to imagine that as German forces poured into the Low Countries, M chose to bypass his superiors in MI5 and that he presented Morton with his own analysis of the threat posed by the BUF and the Right Club, and the need for mass internment of political extremists, and that Morton used this to lobby the Prime Minister. The way Churchill stressed the need for Communists and Fascists to be interned, in terms that M might have used, as early as 18 May, several days before the arrest of Wolkoff and Kent, only reinforces the idea that M was in touch with Morton and that his version of the situation was being passed on directly to Churchill.

It is also possible that this channel of communication accelerated the departure of Kell and Holt-Wilson. Just two days after they had gone, it was Desmond Morton who urged MI5 not to compromise with the Home Office as these two had done. M's channel of communication with Morton would have underlined to the Prime Minister's office the gulf between more hawkish MI5 officers such as Liddell and himself and the two elderly men at the helm.

Even if M had not been feeding information to Morton, his decision to synchronise the arrests of Kent and Wolkoff, his presentation of the case against them and his pressing of the Home Secretary for the mass internment of senior Fascists contributed decisively to the implementation of 18b(1a).

Beyond any doubt is the effect of this particular legislation on Fascism in Britain. Most of the senior Fascists who were interned during the war would be tarred for the rest of their lives by this detention. Although they were never tried, and their sentences were custodial rather than punitive, in postwar Britain the idea that they had done something that *might* have been treacherous or disloyal proved to be toxic.

When Neil Francis-Hawkins, a senior BUF figure, tried to return to his job at the Medical Supply Association shortly after the war, more than a hundred employees walked out in protest. He was forced to find work elsewhere. Many other Fascists had similar experiences. The *Daily Worker* and the Communist Party kept an eye on who was being released from detention, frequently calling for strikes if a Fascist was set to resume his or her pre-war job. Mosley was unable to successfully relaunch his political career after the war. Fascism was never again a legitimate voice in British politics. The wartime detention of so many senior figures after the introduction of 18b(1a) ensured the death of organised Fascism in Britain.

The origin of this legislation is easy to pin down: it was the moment in 1937 when MI5, using intelligence from M's agents, pushed for an amendment to the War Book. This new clause proposed the internment of any British citizen thought to pose a threat to public safety or national security. The implementation of 18b(1a) three years later was realistic partly because of this earlier clause, also because the government already had details of who belonged to these extremist groups. Much of that intelligence had been patiently accumulated by MI5 and, in particular, by M Section. The end of British Fascism had been made possible by the diligent, selfless work of M's agents, including Eric Roberts, E. G. Mandeville-Roe, Claud Sykes, John Hirst, Kathleen Tesch, Friedl Gaertner, Harold Kurtz, Vivian Hancock-Nunn, Jimmy Dickson, Hélène de Munck and Marjorie Mackie. Without their intelligence, gathered during thousands of hours of painstaking and often boring undercover work, it would have been extremely hard, perhaps impossible, to execute the order in May 1940 to detain all senior British Fascists.

Much of the credit should go to M. By running these agents, by presenting the Wolkoff-Kent case in the way that he did and, presumably, by lobbying Morton, he had played a key role in the introduction of the legislation that killed off British Fascism. The man who had helped to nurture this movement so soon after its birth in the 1920s had been instrumental in its demise. M had chosen his country over his friends, patriotism over personal loyalty and, by doing so, he had overcome his past.

In August 1940, M told a senior Fascist during a long interrogation that he had spent fifteen years getting to know the Communist and Fascist movements in Britain. 'I'd like to impress on you one thing,' said M. 'I have no very particular biases one way or another.' This was perhaps the first time in his life that Maxwell Knight had been able to say such a thing and to mean it, and for it to be true.

42

THE TRIAL

The trials of Tyler Kent and Anna Wolkoff began in an almost empty court room at the Old Bailey just days before the US presidential election of 1940. Even the police were barred. Members of the press were allowed in only for the sentencing, which took place more than five months after the defendants had been arrested and two days after President Roosevelt had secured his third term in office.

Breckinridge Long, then the US Assistant Secretary of State, described the trial as 'almost a major catastrophe' for the president, and would refuse permission for one of Roosevelt's telegrams to Churchill to be read out in court. Long worried that this message 'might implicate the chief'. It is not hard to see why. The Churchill–Roosevelt correspondence to which Tyler Kent had had access showed the president acting without congressional approval and apparently engaging in an undeclared war against Germany. The timing of this trial, and the decision to hold it *in camera,* was partly procedural but mainly political. Roosevelt was not the only one who would come out of this badly. Even today there are papers relating to the consecutive trials of Kent and Wolkoff that have either been lost or have not been released because of their sensitive nature.

We do know, however, that Tyler Kent arrived at the Old Bailey looking 'dapper', as a reporter from the *Daily Sketch* put it, a 'typical American former University man', also that the trial was interrupted by air raid sirens. By this point in the war, the Blitz was under way. The Crown prosecution, led by Solicitor General Sir William Jowitt and assisted by George McClure, who had handled the prosecution of the Soviet agent Percy Glading two years earlier in the same court, depended on detailed testimony from both Hélène de Munck and Marjorie Mackie. Although these trials were held behind closed doors, this would mark the beginning of the end for both MI5 agents. For one of them, at least, it was a fitting send-off.

Marjorie Mackie had often struggled in life to be taken seriously and believed. Now she had been asked to testify before the highest court in the land as a key witness in what was arguably Britain's major wartime spy scandal. It was the ultimate test of her credibility, and one that she passed.

M sounded as proud as a parent when he recorded that the police officers who took statements from Mackie and de Munck 'complimented each of the two women on their detached attitude, and their extremely accurate memories', and that the Crown prosecution 'congratulated all the agents concerned – not only on their work as agents, but on the manner in which they gave their evidence in Court – little of which was even questioned, let alone discredited'.

This was not for want of trying. Wolkoff instructed her defence to argue that Hélène de Munck was a 'drug fiend'. Joan Miller also suggested that the Belgian nanny had a problem with drugs. It is impossible to know whether this was true, but these allegations in court did not undermine her testimony. Evidence was also provided by the US Embassy's Second Secretary Franklin Gowen as well as Guy Liddell, M and other MI5 officers. Wolkoff called as character witnesses Admiral Sir Reginald Hall, Captain Ramsay and Sir

Oswald Mosley, who arrived from Brixton prison looking dishevelled and angry. Their evidence had little or no effect on the jury.

By passing on Roosevelt's message to an Italian diplomat, Anna Wolkoff had committed an act of espionage. Yet this was not brought up in court. Instead, her decision to add several lines to a message intended for William Joyce was used to frame her as a 'foreign agent', loosely defined as 'any person who is or has been or is reasonably suspected of being or having been employed by a foreign power either directly or indirectly for the purpose of committing any act either within or without the United Kingdom prejudicial to the safety or interests of the State'. There was no suggestion that Wolkoff was actually in the pay of a foreign power, but in the eyes of the law this one act was enough for her to be classed as a spy.

This changed the case against Kent. Although he had not been shown to be in direct contact with either Berlin or Rome, or indeed Moscow, he had passed on information to a 'foreign agent', that is, Wolkoff. Despite detailed attempts by Kent's lawyer, Maurice Healy, KC, to argue that his client's offences had taken place within the precincts of the US Embassy and were therefore extraterritorial and beyond the jurisdiction of that court, or that his diplomatic immunity applied when he was arrested and his flat was searched, the jury took less than half an hour to find Kent guilty on five counts under the Official Secrets Act and one count of larceny. A separate jury found Wolkoff guilty on two counts under the Official Secrets Act and one under the Defence (General) Regulations. The press was then called in to watch Mr Justice Tucker sentence Kent to seven years of penal servitude. Wolkoff received ten.

That is a wrinkle-free account of the two trials, and it is striking that neither jury took very long to reach their verdicts. They might have taken longer, and possibly reached different conclusions, had the full facts of the case been put before them.

When the hearings began, two people intimately connected to

these trials were hundreds of miles away from London. One was the US Ambassador, Joe Kennedy, who left the country only hours before the trial began. Another was J. McGuirk Hughes, who had presented Wolkoff with the encoded letter to Joyce.

The reason for Kennedy's hasty departure may have concerned the question of Kent's diplomatic immunity. There are different accounts of when this was formally waived by the State Department. Most likely this did not happen until shortly after the raid on Kent's flat, which would make his arrest and the subsequent search of his property unlawful.

It was vital to the prosecution that Kennedy could not be called, and the same was true of Hughes. The last man to be summoned by Wolkoff's defence was the unfortunate process server who had been given the job of serving Hughes with a subpoena. For many years Hughes's actual whereabouts during that trial were a mystery, until the historian Bryan Clough tracked down his granddaughter. She explained that her grandfather had been told that his life was in danger and he must fly to Scotland. This had happened just before the start of the trial. Hughes was one of the only people named in court who could have explained the origins of the coded letter that was sent to Joyce. The other was M.

So where did this letter come from – and why should it matter?

'The lawyer told me that Hughes sent this message as a plan to test Miss Wolkoff,' explained one of Wolkoff's character witnesses. In her account, the letter had originated with Hughes.

M gave a different explanation. He revealed in an internal MI5 note that this coded letter had been written by Joyce's close friend and fellow extremist Angus MacNab.

So why did M fail to mention MacNab in court or have him charged with espionage? This same question was asked by the Home Office Advisory Committee several years later.

'The real reason why MacNab was not prosecuted,' came the reply from MI5, 'was that an agent had to be protected.'

That is all we have. Either MacNab was an MI5 agent, or the agent referred to here was J. McGuirk Hughes. In any event, the idea for this letter does not appear to have originated with MacNab. More likely, M was involved from the start. There is no question that Wolkoff was guilty of espionage, but it is also clear that M had carefully arranged a situation in which she was given the opportunity to carry out this act and that she was encouraged to do so.

'The agent provocateur is a most loathsome figure,' said one Colonel Labouchere, head of a government intelligence agency during the First World War, 'whose employment can never be justified under any circumstances whatever.' Despite this, Labouchere employed several. Almost nobody in MI5, Special Branch or any other government agency relished the use of agents provocateurs, yet they were employed repeatedly against British civilians during both world wars.

In the years immediately after the Wolkoff-Kent trial, there were many other occasions in which an MI5 officer decided that, on the basis of reliable evidence, an individual was likely to commit a treacherous or disloyal act. Rather than wait for that person to commit the crime, a government agent would be dispatched to provide the suspect with the opportunity to incriminate themselves.

Perhaps the finest wartime agent provocateur employed by MI5 was Eric Roberts, who was first taken on by M as a seventeen-year-old. Roberts left M Section early in the war to join a separate MI5 unit and would spend the next few years posing as an undercover Gestapo officer on the lookout for new recruits. At least one MI5 officer had scruples about Roberts's work, calling it a 'serious form of provocation'.

'In a very mild sense it is,' replied Guy Liddell, 'but in the absence of any other methods I do think it is desirable to ascertain something about evilly-intentioned persons.'

This sentiment was shared exactly by M. In his desire to neutralise British Fascism he had taken shortcuts. Asking Hughes to present Wolkoff with a letter to Joyce was a provocation. Making sure that during the trial Hughes was many miles away in Scotland, if this is what he did, allowed him to obscure the nature of the trap that he had laid. By sending Hélène de Munck to Belgium, M had been operating in MI6 territory, as they would soon find out – which led to another inter-agency row. By slipping into Kent's flat before the raid, as he appears to have done, M had also committed an act of trespass, and it is possible that he had Kent unlawfully arrested. Yet perhaps the most serious departure from his role as an MI5 officer was his decision to lobby Churchill's trusted adviser Desmond Morton, as he appears to have done in May 1940. 'The duties of a Security Service end with the supply of accurate information,' wrote Kell. 'It should have no executive function.' By pushing for the detention of so many senior British Fascists, M had not broken any laws, but he had ignored one of MI5's guiding principles.

He would argue that the end justified his means, and the wartime threat of Nazi invasion changed everything. His underlying desire to stop the flow of intelligence from the US Embassy to Berlin is understandable and legitimate, but was it reasonable to argue in May 1940, as he did, that there could be a Fifth Column in Britain?

By that point in the war, a smattering of intelligence suggested that the German advance in not only Poland but Denmark, Norway, Belgium, Holland and France *might* have been assisted by German nationals and those sympathetic to the Nazi regime. Soon after the invasion of Holland, the Nazi Party publicly thanked the leader of the Dutch Fascist party for his assistance. On balance, it probably *was* reasonable to conclude in May 1940 that the German advance in some of these territories could have been accelerated by so-called

Fifth Columnists. M's agents had encountered people in Britain who wanted Germany to win the war, as well as those gathering arms or making plans to seize power in the event of an emergency. M did not have evidence of a Fifth Column of saboteurs and agents in the pay of the Nazis – because this did not exist – but he was unable to rule it out. Indeed, given the reports he had received, it would have been irresponsible if he had done.

While it was reasonable to think, in May 1940, that there might have been a Fifth Column in Britain, it does not follow that the government was right to order the mass internment of enemy aliens and homegrown Fascists. Yet given what was known by MI5 at the time, and the threat of German invasion, the temporary internment of political extremists probably was justified. Locking up so many enemy aliens was not. The difficulty was that these two very different groups – the enemy aliens and the homegrown Fascists – were frequently lumped together during discussions of a potential Fifth Column.

The government's understanding of homegrown Fascism was informed by a detailed intelligence picture that had been built up over many years by MI5, Special Branch and various police constabularies. The decision to intern so many enemy aliens, however, was based on not much more than a handful of reports from mainland Europe, and was influenced by the historic fear of Germans living in Britain. Indeed, throughout history whenever an entire ethnic group is cordoned off like this it inevitably stems from a failure of intelligence. MI5 pushed for the internment of homegrown Fascists because they knew so much about them; it called for the internment of Germans and Italians for the opposite reason: they knew so little.

Accurate, verifiable information is the seawall against historical prejudice. In the case of enemy aliens in Britain during the summer of 1940, that wall was breached, leading to the wholesale internment of thousands of innocent people, including many German Jewish refugees who were eager to help the British war effort. The most tragic unintended consequence of this mass internment of enemy aliens concerned the men and women on board the transport vessel *Arandora Star,* then bound for Canada. On 2 July, 1940, this ship was torpedoed, resulting in the deaths of many British seamen and military guards, a small number of German prisoners of war and more than seven hundred German and Italian civilians who had been living in Britain at the outbreak of war.

As the panic of these months subsided and the threat of Hitler's invasion fell away, thousands of these enemy aliens were released. After the first year of detention, more than 12,000 had been set free.

The rate of release for the right-wing extremists held under 18b was slower. All had the right of appeal before the Home Office Advisory Committee. Although MI5 was able to supply evidence to this committee from anonymous agents, which could not be verified, the process was largely fair. Detailed records were kept of each hearing and by the end of 1944 just sixty-five extremists were still interned under 18b. For all its deficiencies, and there were many, the mass detention of these homegrown Fascists, which had been triggered by the Kent-Wolkoff affair, helped to remove the possibility of a Fifth Column in Britain. It also reinforced the resolve to fight. Above all it killed off British Fascism.

KNIGHT'S BLACK AGENTS

Very little in M's experience of the rest of the war would come close to that first year of the conflict, either in its intensity or its historical impact. After Germany's invasion of the Soviet Union in 1941, the Communist Party put its weight behind the war effort. British Fascism by then had been all but extinguished. German espionage was contained. Indeed, by 1941, thanks to the Double Cross deception, in which captured German agents were used to relay false information back to Berlin, MI5 'actively ran and controlled the German espionage system in this country [Britain]'. Just one German spy evaded detection. After less than five months in the country he ran out of money and committed suicide.

Even as the scale of the threat to British security was reduced, the size of M's section continued to grow. Four officers had been added to his office shortly before the arrests of Kent and Wolkoff, and several months later M took on another five. In the space of just over a year, M Section had gone from one officer – M himself – to twelve. Most of these new recruits had no experience of running agents. M's response was to take an almost unprecedented step in the history of MI5.

'There was nothing in the way of a regular "course",' wrote the new head of MI5 and the first to be called Director General, Sir David Petrie, in 1941. Hitherto training 'was acquired in the school of experience'. 'The only thing to do,' echoed Liddell, 'is to start in at the bottom rung.' During the summer of 1940, M broke with MI5 tradition by giving his new officers basic training. 'I was given permission to conduct a sort of "school" at Wormwood Scrubs,' he explained. 'I think it can be justly claimed that this little school achieved its object.'

Preparing this new course also forced Major Knight, as he now was, to set out on paper the rudiments of his tradecraft. Over the years that followed, M would often be asked to regurgitate what he had learned, and this changed the way that future MI5 spymasters were trained. For the first time, his career was starting to be retrospective and some of his principles of agent running began to be enshrined in MI5.

Having so many officers working in his section also required M to learn the art of running a large office, which did not come easily. One of his blind spots was sex. Guy Liddell later described the atmosphere in M Section as 'deplorable, both from the sex point of view and organisationally'. By this he meant that too many people were having affairs. As well as John Bingham, Jimmy Dickson had a string of relationships with female MI5 staff. Another problem, wrote one secretary, was 'M's attitude to paperwork'. This 'was representative of his general disinclination to involve himself in the trappings of bureaucracy'. Liddell also noted a 'laxity of control in financial matters'.

Yet what M lacked in organisation, discipline and financial prudence he made up for with charisma and an absolute mastery of his craft. His record as a spymaster inside MI5 was without equal. Bingham described him as a 'tremendous leader', adding that 'we would follow him anywhere'. 'We adored him for he made serious work great fun – a unique quality.' When the bombs began to fall on London in September 1940, Bingham recalled how M 'clucked round like a mother hen for he regarded us as his family'. He also tried to protect his officers from the scrutiny of MI5 Headquarters on St James's Street. As a result, wrote Nigel West, his unit was 'held in some awe by personnel based in St James's Street because of its mystery and the amount of autonomy granted to it'.

M Section sounded like an exclusive members' club, which was pretty much how officer recruitment worked. Sometimes an existing member of M's staff proposed a new officer, such as Tony Gillson, the playboy and racehorse owner, yet each addition had to be personally approved by M, the one-man membership committee. Other additions were old friends of his like Guy Poston, whom he had known since he was a boy growing up in Mitcham, or Henry Brocklehurst, 'an explorer of world-wide experience with the most amazing number of personal contacts, which ranged literally from personal friendship with the Royal Family to cockney coffee-house keepers in the East End of London'. Other new officers had more in common with the agents that M liked to take on. They were quietly watchful and quick-witted, and often came to see him as a father figure. In many cases they had carried through childhood some kind of handicap. Bill Younger had been crippled by polio, John Bingham was short-sighted and had a squint, Jimmy Dickson had a weak heart. Perhaps this helped to bring them together.

M's officers soon had a nickname for themselves. They were 'Knight's Black Agents', after the lines from Shakespeare's *Macbeth*:

> Light thickens, and the crow
> Makes wing to th' rooky wood.
> Good things of day begin to droop and drowse;
> Whiles night's black agents to their preys do rouse.
> Thou marvel'st at my words: but hold thee still.
> Things bad begun make strong themselves by ill.

There is a hint in this last line of the swagger of M's elite unit, and a sense that they might do more or less what they pleased. In one sense they really could. MI5 was not recognised by law, so there were no legal limits to the range of its powers. Although its officers took their unwritten responsibilities seriously and they rarely lost sight of their role to provide other branches of government with reliable intelligence, there were times when corners were cut. Most notably during the panic that had gripped the country in spring 1940. One particular incident from this period would haunt M and two of his agents for the rest of the war.

Ben Greene was a gentle giant, an enormously tall man who was also a Quaker, a committed pacifist and a cousin of Graham Greene. During the first few months of the war, he had become a prominent campaigner for a negotiated peace with Germany. Ben Greene belonged to the British Council for a Christian Settlement in Europe and had joined the Peace Pledge Union and the British People's Party. Each of these bodies had attracted well-meaning pacifists like him as well as some much less benign Fascists. Several months into the war, MI5 received a complaint from a magistrate who believed that Ben Greene's real sympathies lay with Hitler. M was told to investigate. Soon after the Nazi invasion of Norway and Denmark he laid a trap.

M engineered a situation in which two of his agents, Harold Kurtz and Friedl Gaertner, sat down for dinner with Greene and during the meal asked him to post a letter to Germany, hinting that this would go to a Nazi official. This happened less than three weeks after Anna Wolkoff had taken a similar bait. It had worked in her case because she was anti-war and pro-Hitler. Although Greene was a pacifist to his core, he was not a supporter of Nazism and he refused to take the letter.

M's ruse had failed to show that Greene owed any allegiance to Berlin, yet he was one of the first men to be rounded up in May

1940 after the introduction of Defence Regulation 18b(1a). Greene appealed immediately. The case against him was based on reports made by or attributed to Harold Kurtz, and after a year and a half in prison Greene was told that the Home Office had rejected Kurtz's evidence and he was released.

Greene's response was to sue the Home Office for libel and false imprisonment. Although he was unsuccessful, and was ordered to pay costs of £1,243, it was a moral victory. The Greene clan would later exact a further revenge on the MI5 agent at the heart of this scandal when his cousin Graham Greene named a villain in *The Third Man* 'Kurtz'.

Had Harold Kurtz lied? M was always deeply protective of his agents and assured his colleagues that the Home Office's rejection of Kurtz's evidence was part of its ongoing assault on MI5. This was a widely held view. Liddell, for one, was convinced that in April 1940 Kurtz had been 'present at a treasonable conversation with Greene', and that this gentle giant had been released only because Kurtz's memory had proved to be hazy on several details.

Yet after the war Ben Greene claimed to have been approached by a former MI5 officer who told him that they had forged one of the documents used against him. The same officer suggested that some of his colleagues 'had become very uneasy at the part they were required to play in the case of some of the detentions,' wrote Greene, and that this former officer 'was particularly uneasy about the part he had played in mine'.

M once suggested that 'what is fatal in good detective work is to twist the facts so that they line up with the theory'. He also told his agents that 'if you are going to tell a lie, tell a good one and above all stick to it'. For M and his agents to do their job well, they were required to be not only models of truth and integrity when called before a judge, but fraudulent fantasists when out in the field. Perhaps the real surprise here should be that these two competing drives did not overlap more often. In all likelihood, Kurtz had either embellished Greene's statements or had made them up entirely, or this was done by an MI5 officer. We will probably never know.

The Ben Greene case did not reflect well on either M or his agents, yet the effect of this on his career was later exaggerated out of all proportion. Long after M's death it was claimed that this detention of Greene effectively ended M's time at MI5. The problem with this theory is that M remained in his job for almost two decades after this incident, which is a long time to spend treading water. Nor was it true that M was solely responsible for providing the Home Office with evidence against Greene. The case was written up by a different MI5 officer, S. H. Noakes. When representatives of MI5 were asked to appear before the Home Office Advisory Committee, it was both M and Noakes who came to see them. The meeting that followed was written up by Noakes, and Noakes rather than M was contacted by the Home Office when they decided to release Greene.

Nor are there any clear indications that M's superiors in MI5 turned against him on account of this case. Shortly before the conclusion of Greene's libel action, M was even made an Officer of the Order of the British Empire (OBE) in the 1943 King's Birthday Honours. More recently, a retired senior MI5 officer has described the Ben Greene incident as obviously 'a low point' in M's career, 'but not the only mistake made over internments or post-war purges' and probably not one that 'had a long-term impact on his reputation'.

Other investigations involving M's officers and his stable of agents were more successful. In late 1941, Irma Stapleton, a worker in a munitions factory in Staffordshire, was approached by an undercover Abwehr officer asking her to smuggle a twenty-two-millimetre Oerlikon shell out of the factory. She did so, and handed it over to the man she presumed to be a German spy. Instead, he was one of M's officers, John Bingham. Stapleton was sentenced to ten years in jail.

After an official in the Portuguese embassy, Rogerio Menezes, was identified by intercepted German radio communications as a Nazi spy, M gave Bingham the job of posing as a Nazi officer again and winning his trust. The Hon. John did so with great skill. Soon there was enough evidence to secure the young diplomat's conviction. Although Menezes was sentenced to death as an enemy agent, this was later commuted to penal servitude for life.

There was also the case of Norah Briscoe and Molly Hiscox, the latter a founding member of the extreme right-wing group The Link, who had come to MI5's attention after she wrote to Hitler to let him know that 'I have unlimited trust in you.' Briscoe was a typist in the Production Executive of the War Cabinet. She told several friends, in 1941, that she had access to important documents and wanted to send some to Germany. One of the people present when she suggested this was an M agent, John Hirst. He encouraged her to go ahead with the plan and put her in contact with Harold Kurtz, who had been told by M to play the part of a German agent.

Kurtz performed his role with restraint and composure. To avoid any possible accusation of exaggeration, M bugged the room in which Kurtz was to meet the putative spies. Briscoe produced a pile of documents for him to pass on to Berlin. The arrest was made. Briscoe and Hiscox were both sentenced to five years in jail.

The rest of M's wartime work resembled a succession of opening chapters. Very few cases kept him and his section occupied for more than a few months, and they usually resulted in an arrest, were taken over by the police or the initial lead proved to be inaccurate. M did some work for Special Operations Executive (SOE) on its internal security. He continued to run agents inside the Communist Party and other left-wing groups. He also interviewed Fascists who had been detained, in the hope of learning more about hidden right-wing networks within Britain. This produced an important cache of intelligence. The only danger here was that some of these detained

Fascists might recognise him. They were certainly intrigued as to how this officer knew so much about British Fascism. In Brixton prison, M's interrogations 'were the favourite topic of conversation' among the Fascists, as was M's real identity. The men who knew him by sight were kept away from the others for this reason. Otherwise he made a point of interviewing some men in civilian dress and others in full military get-up. According to one historian, M's 'ruses were remarkably effective, and his identity never became known to the men at Brixton'. Having struggled in the past to make himself anonymous, it seems that M had at last become a master dissembler.

M's section also did important work on security for the D-Day landings. Most of this involved breaking in to factories that were producing specialist material for the invasion, on the principle that if one of M's men could get in, so could an enemy agent. Burglary and illegal entry remained this spymaster's signature dish. On most occasions his men were able to slip into these plants undetected, after which the factory manager, usually indignant about the idea of MI5 breaking into his plant, was told to have security tightened up.

As the war progressed, M and his staff also began to spend more time in an MI5 safe house in Camberley, Surrey, not far from London, which allowed him to build up his collection of pets again. Soon there was a Himalayan monkey sleeping in the conservatory of this safe house and elsewhere a dim-witted Great Dane called Gloria, several white ferrets, Mr Socks the Pekinese dog, a ginger cat and a host of other creatures, many of them handed on to M by people who no longer knew what to do with them or, in the case of a springer spaniel called Ben, because their owner had been killed on active duty. It is easy to imagine the equilibrium returning to M's life as his home filled up once more with animals.

On 8 May, 1945, the German Instrument of Surrender was signed in Berlin. The war in Europe was over. European Fascism had been defeated. In the days that followed, M recalled listening to one of his favourite jazz recordings: the trombonist Jack Teagarden playing 'Junk Man', a sunny, carefree number that might have been written with that moment in mind. Yet this phase of his life still had a few more months to run.

'That boy will either do something very great in the world, or he will finish on the end of a rope' had been the canny judgement on William Joyce from one of his schoolteachers.

The man known to most Britons as Lord Haw-Haw had been arrested in Germany soon after Victory in Europe (VE) Day and then flown back to Britain to face trial on three counts of high treason. In September 1945, Mr Justice Tucker, who had presided over the Kent-Wolkoff trials, heard arguments centred on Joyce's nationality and whether he owed loyalty to the British Crown when he began to broadcast from Berlin. After a legal debate of byzantine complexity, it was established that although Joyce was now a German citizen, when he had started to broadcast from Germany as Lord Haw-Haw he had been an American citizen, having been born in New York, who was living in Germany under British protection. This peculiar status snaked back to 1933 and his fateful decision to lie about his nationality to get a British passport. As such, he had owed allegiance to Britain when making the first of his broadcasts as Lord Haw-Haw.

Joyce had come of age in an era when ideology and friendship seemed to trump nationality. British law, however, was rooted in an older tradition. His technical allegiance outweighed his ideological preference, and Joyce was found guilty on one count of high treason. This carried a mandatory capital sentence.

On the morning of 3 January, 1946, a small crowd gathered outside Wandsworth Prison. Shortly after nine o'clock a notice was pinned to the door. William Joyce had been hanged.

It is tempting to wonder whether M paid one final visit to Joyce in the days leading up to his death, and to speculate on what might have been said, but it is unlikely that he would have done this. Early on in the war this MI5 spymaster appears to have severed his personal connection to William Joyce and everything he represented. Now the man who symbolised for M not only the potential of the movement he had once joined, but its capacity for betrayal, subversion and treachery, was dead. A chapter in M's life had closed. His focus could go back to where it had been at the beginning of his career.

44

THE COMINTERN IS NOT DEAD

'In dealing with Communism in particular, it should be borne in mind that the Russians are past-masters at the art of long-term policy,' wrote M in 1945, prophetically. 'It is not unusual for a Soviet agent to be "planted" in some position in order to carry out work which will probably not fructify for a matter of years.' 'The Russians are very patient,' he was also quoted as saying at around the same time. 'They will recruit a young man at university with Communist views, tell him to dissociate himself from the Party, watch him, and keep him on ice for years. Then one day they will come to him and say: "Now we want you to do this. . . ."'

M was correct, and uncannily so. Although most of the Cambridge Spies, such as Kim Philby, were recruited as graduates, their intellectual conversions to Communism took place at university. As M had predicted, each one was told to distance himself from the Party and would only become active later. M was able to guess what his opposite numbers in Moscow Centre might be doing because it was what he would have done himself. He shared his concerns about Soviet sleeper agents with various colleagues, including John Curry, who was then researching the first history of MI5. He even alluded to them in his summary of M Section's wartime exploits. What he did not record, however, because it was scandalous and he had no proof, was the name of the MI5 officer whom he believed to be a Soviet agent. Which is a shame, really, because he was right.

M's suspicions had been aroused four years before the end of the war when one of his agents, Tom Driberg, had been expelled from the Communist Party after being accused of working for MI5. This had been a major operational setback. Driberg was a long-standing Party member and, although he was by no means a senior figure, he had access to many high-profile Communists and was 'perhaps the best informed of all' M's sources on the Left. Far more worrying, however, was the nature of Driberg's dismissal. He had been accused of being 'M/8', a term that was only used in MI5 reports.

The Office had a leak. M launched an investigation to find out who it was, and although this was formally inconclusive he reached his own verdict.

The following year another of M's agents, Norman Himsworth, was accused of working for MI5 by a senior Communist who read back to him sections of a report that he had written for M. This confirmed that the Communist Party had access to some MI5 files. In July 1943, Celia Luke, then employed in the MI5 Registry, confessed to passing on classified information to the Party. She had taken the place of another MI5 secretary who had also been leaking information to the Party before her. So there had been two consecutive Communist moles inside the Office. The more recent of these, Luke, claimed to have identified Driberg – but M thought she was lying.

In 1940, there had been a change in MI5's overall approach to recruitment. Previously suspicious of intellectuals, MI5 had begun to take on talented lawyers and academic high-flyers, including an erudite art historian called Anthony Blunt.

'He was convinced that it was Blunt who had exposed Driberg,' recalled M's nephew, Harry Smith, who lived with his uncle for much of his childhood. Indeed M was not the only one to suspect Blunt of being an agent. Eric Roberts suspected that Tony, as he was known (also Blunt's NKVD codename), was an agent, except he thought Blunt was working for the Germans. Roger Hollis was also suspicious of Blunt.

'But he did not have any evidence,' said Smith of his uncle, 'otherwise he would have had Blunt prosecuted.' Instead, M's suspicion of Blunt was based on little more than an instinctive feeling that this man was hiding something more than his sexuality. M had by then spent most of his adult life honing his ability to get the measure of people, be they prospective agents or officers. Although he could sometimes get too close to them, as he had done with Joyce, M was usually a wise judge of character and could tell when someone was not what he or she claimed to be.

We know now that Blunt was the only Soviet agent inside MI5. Celia Luke and the other female secretary were passing information to the British Communist Party, but it was Blunt who was working for the NKVD and who had identified Driberg, as he later explained in an interview with Nigel West.

In the same month that Celia Luke was dismissed from MI5, the senior Communist Douglas Springhall was convicted under the Official Secrets Act. This came in the wake of Moscow's announcement that the Comintern had been disbanded.

M's response was to write a report titled 'The Comintern Is Not Dead'. This document has never been released, but we can guess what its underlying message may have been. M was increasingly worried that his fellow MI5 officers had failed to recognise the continued threat of international Communism. He sent copies of his paper to senior colleagues, including Guy Liddell and Roger Hollis. Both were broadly in agreement. 'Neither Hollis nor I think that there is any evidence to show that the policy of the Soviet Government and the Comintern has changed one iota,' wrote Liddell. 'Whether the instructions come by courier or through the Embassy makes no difference. There is no doubt that the Russians are taking every possible advantage of the present situation to dig themselves in and that they will cause us a great deal of trouble when the war is over.' Yet Liddell did not bring himself to imagine that one of Moscow's most valued agents might be his former assistant and close friend Anthony Blunt.

Although Guy Liddell recognised the danger of Soviet espionage, he understood that little could be done until after the war. MI5's resources were concentrated on defeating Nazi Germany. The Soviet Union had become a vital wartime ally and there was no appetite in government for headline-grabbing convictions of Soviet spies.

Others were more sceptical when they read 'The Comintern Is Not Dead'. M was renowned within the Office for his dislike of Communism. By this stage in his life he could sometimes come across as increasingly wary of the new-fangled, left-leaning world in which he found himself. Some of his colleagues in MI5 thought 'The Comintern Is Not Dead' was merely an expression of M's pre-war prejudice against the Soviet Union.

Indeed, by the end of the Second World War few British intelligence officers believed that Moscow Centre had either the desire or the capability to penetrate the upper reaches of Whitehall, let alone MI5 and MI6. 'In our insularity,' wrote the historian Hugh Trevor-Roper, then serving in MI6, 'we had not yet caught up with the ideologies of the Continent or appreciated their distorting effects on the minds of men.' Most of M's colleagues found it difficult to believe that any reasonable, intelligent Englishman could be persuaded by the dry precepts of Marxism to betray his country. MI5's press officer, Derek Tangye, described the Office at that time as an organisation that was 'bewildered when faced by the naughty deceit of the Russians', except for 'one, small, ignored corner of the organisation'. That was M Section.

Following the Labour Party's landslide victory of 1945, the new Prime Minister, Clement Attlee, installed an outsider as Director General of MI5, a former police chief constable called Percy Sillitoe. He did not flood left-wing organisations with long-term agents, nor did he treat Communist subversion and Soviet espionage as a priority. Instead, MI5 concentrated on the threat posed by two Zionist terrorist groups, Irgun and the Stern Gang, as there were indications after the attacks on the King David Hotel in Jerusalem and the British embassy in Rome that these groups would be targeting the British mainland next. Nor could MI5 ignore the possibility that Fascism might one day rise from the dead.

M's section continued to be responsible for running MI5 agents inside left-wing organisations, but his outfit became leaner in these postwar years and it began to lose some of its prized independence. M was increasingly desk-bound, which was difficult for someone who so relished being outside. He was in his late forties now, the point in his career when he might have begun to angle for one of the top jobs. Yet he was in no position to do so. M had never mastered the internal politics of MI5, whether it was lobbying for a new job or for more resources. He was listened to, and he commanded respect on account of his record, but he did not have a network of trusted allies in senior positions from whom he could now call in favours.

The price to pay for those years of glorious isolation on Sloane Street, followed by Dolphin Square, was that M would never make it to the top of MI5 – but there is nothing to suggest that he had ever wanted this. Instead, he aspired to keep doing what he did best: spotting, recruiting and running agents. He gloried in the craft of his profession and the knowledge that he and his stable of informants were helping to protect the country from the Soviet Union.

What did M believe in by this stage in his life? He wanted to save Britain from Communism, but what had changed over the last few years, the painful journey that he had been required to take, was his understanding that it was possible to take this too far.

If some of M's younger colleagues thought his obsession with Moscow was old-fashioned, others felt his methods were out-of-date. Following the success of wartime Ultra signals from Bletchley Park, there was a new feeling that the future lay with signals intelligence rather than what Liddell called 'the old cloak and dagger' of human intelligence, that is, taking on and running agents. MI5 now had four microphones inside the Communist Party headquarters on King Street, codenamed 'Table', 'North', 'King' and 'Lascar', which produced reams of accurate intelligence from deep inside the Party. Relying on agents to gather information was more labour-intensive than using a hidden listening device and, of course, riskier. Its product had to be fed through another layer of subjective interpretation. But the need to run human sources against left-wing targets did not disappear in the years after the war, and it would soon be more pressing than ever.

Three years after the British scientist Alan Nunn May was convicted under the Official Secrets Act of passing atomic secrets to Moscow, the Soviet Union successfully tested its first atomic bomb. This was a near-replica of the American bomb which had been detonated at Los Alamos in 1945. Another British atomic scientist, Klaus Fuchs, was revealed to be a Soviet agent, and shortly after that Bruno Pontecorvo, a colleague of Fuchs, disappeared, only to resurface later in the Soviet Union. Meanwhile, China became a Communist republic and Communist North Korea invaded its southern neighbour. The threat from both the Soviet Union and Communism, having been briefly eclipsed by Nazi Germany, had come back stronger than ever. Yet it was only after the defection of Guy Burgess and Donald Maclean in 1951, and the Conservative election victory in the same year, that Soviet espionage and Communist subversion formally became MI5's main priority once again.

M must have felt a wave of vindication. His overall sense of the threat posed by Moscow had proved to be accurate, as had his more specific concern about British sleeper agents recruited at university. He was in demand once more as a flotilla of new government agents was launched at British trade unions, student unions, left-wing charities, protest groups, the Labour Party and, of course, the Communist Party itself. The threat posed by the Party was no longer political – the Communist share of the vote was almost non-existent – but industrial, and it concerned the Party's ability to stage strikes. M was also called upon for his intimate historical understanding of the Communist Party as MI5 hastily raked over the pre-war activities of Burgess, Maclean and others to find evidence of any other Soviet moles.

One of M's most able recruits during this period has been described by Christopher Andrew, formerly the official MI5 historian, as probably 'the most successful penetration agent in the early Cold War'. Like Mona Maund, Olga Gray and M/C, this female agent of M's was a quick-witted typist who made herself 'part of the furniture' at the Communist Party headquarters on King Street. Perhaps she worked occasionally at the same desk that had been occupied by Olga or Mona. She devoted herself to her task, living the life of an impoverished secretary, taking few holidays and seeing few of her friends outside the movement, until she could stand it no more. For her own well-being, M agreed to end her agent career.

Another new recruit to M Section was David Cornwell, better known today as the novelist John Le Carré. He began to work as an officer under M in the late 1950s and, according to his biographer, Adam Sisman, looked up to M as 'the "Pied Piper", a romantic and heroic figure', and of course later used M as the inspiration for Jack Brotherhood in *A Perfect Spy*.

It is curious that a left-leaning young man like Cornwell should have been so taken by M, a person who had, after all, been a prominent member of the British Fascists in his youth. But this was M's great skill. Throughout his career a succession of young people, from a variety of backgrounds, were won over either by the force of M's personality, the romantic appeal of his exploits in MI5 or else they were looking for a father-figure and felt that in M they had found one.

Le Carré memorably described M's fictional alter ego as 'a tweedy, unscalable English mountain' and 'a handsome English warlord who served sherry on Boxing Day and had never had a doubt in his life'. He 'was country stock. His forebears were gypsies and clergymen, gamekeepers and poachers and pirates.' 'He was as broad as an old blockhouse and, when he wanted to be, as rough.' Brotherhood was angry about the changes inside 'the Firm' since the end of the war, 'its retreat into bureaucracy and semi-diplomacy, its pandering to American methods and example. By comparison his own hand-picked staff had only looked better to him.' He had little time for the 'desk jockeys' outside his section. 'Brotherhood was hardier than all of them and more or less they knew it.'

There is silence when Brotherhood speaks at meetings – which he presides over 'like an old grey bird glowering down on his prey'. He is 'the grand old man of covert operations', as M obviously was, 'with his reputation and his anger and his connections and with his section's record, in the modern jargon that he loathed, of low cost and high productivity'. 'The Firm should have retired him ten years ago,' one character says, which was possibly true of M by the late 1950s, yet he still had time for at least one final outing with his most long-serving agent.

On 11 February, 1956, a *Sunday Times* correspondent staying in the National Hotel in Moscow was summoned unexpectedly to Room 101 where he was introduced to Donald Maclean and Guy Burgess.

This was the first time that any Western journalist had been allowed to see the two British defectors. It would not be the last.

Over the weeks that followed, both men took on more public roles, and the possibility loomed that one of them – Burgess, who missed his mother back in Britain – might try to come home. A number of their friends and relatives wrote to Maclean and Burgess after it was revealed that they were at the National Hotel, including a man who had been a presenter on the BBC radio programme *The Week in Westminster* during the war, when Guy Burgess had been a producer. Now Tom Driberg had a favour to ask.

Guy Burgess and Tom Driberg had a great deal in common, and not only that they were both gay and went for the same type of man (which ruled out their going for each other). 'They shared a contempt for the bourgeoisie, and a romantic fondness for the aristocracy and the working class,' wrote Driberg's biographer, Francis Wheen. 'They were congenitally and self-destructively indiscreet, yet agile at eluding the retribution which their indiscretion seemed certain to provoke: Burgess had glided effortlessly through the Foreign Office and the secret service even though he seldom bothered to conceal his political sympathies, just as Tom's sexual adventures, of which he boasted so recklessly, never led to the nemesis that colleagues feared and predicted.'

Shortly after his dismissal from the Communist Party, in 1941, Tom Driberg had become a member of Parliament. After thirteen years in the House of Commons, most of them as a Labour MP, he had left to concentrate on journalism, as he explained to Burgess in his letter. Now he wanted to interview the former NKVD agent in Moscow.

For eighteen days there was no reply. Then a telegram arrived. Burgess had agreed to an exclusive interview. Driberg was delighted, and so was M.

Although it is unclear whether sending this letter had been

Driberg's idea or M's, newly released papers show that Driberg coordinated with MI5 from the start. After Guy Burgess made a telephone call to him, in June, to discuss his forthcoming trip, M immediately filed a summary of their conversation. Because Driberg's phone was not being tapped, this information could only have come to him from Driberg himself. An MI5 officer later confirmed that Driberg had received 'some preliminary briefing by us' before setting off for Moscow, which he did in August of that year.

Tom Driberg spent the next two weeks in the Russian capital with Burgess, interviewing him at length, plying him with gossip from London and, at one point, pointing out the best spots to pick up men despite having never been to Moscow before. 'When it came to "cottages",' wrote Francis Wheen, Driberg 'had the directional sense of a homing pigeon.' He also found time to carry out in Moscow the principal task he had been given by MI5.

Over the next few months Driberg wrote up his material into a book, and after another visit to Moscow to check several details with Burgess, and deliver socks and a leather bottle case, the manuscript was finished. The book was set to be published by Weidenfeld & Nicolson. The *Daily Mail* paid £5,000 for the serial. One of the advertisements for the forthcoming scoop declared: 'News that even MI5 could not get!' No doubt Driberg came up with that.

Tom Driberg's mission to Moscow had been a success. As well as earning him enough money to pay off his many debts, it provided MI5 with useful intelligence on Burgess's circle and a solution to a knotty problem. Shortly before Driberg had first gone to Moscow, MI5 had put together a summary of the legal case against the two defectors. Neither man had confessed to espionage and, as feared, there was not enough evidence to mount a successful prosecution if one or the other returned to Britain. Their defection had been embarrassing enough, yet this would be nothing next to the compound humiliation of the police being unable to arrest them if they returned.

This was where Driberg came in. During the course of their interviews, Guy Burgess did not confess to being a spy, yet by passing on details he had acquired during his government employment, he had committed an offence under the Official Secrets Act. MI5's legal adviser also pointed out, rather worryingly, that 'Driberg has committed another offence by receiving the information willingly.' Yet neither the Director of Public Prosecutions nor the Attorney General, he went on, was likely to authorise a prosecution against this MI5 agent.

Several weeks after the publication of Tom Driberg's book about Guy Burgess, an article appeared in the *Daily Express* by Chapman Pincher, a journalist famously described by the historian E. P. Thompson as 'a kind of official urinal in which, side by side, high officials of MI5 and MI6', among others, 'stand patiently leaking in the public interest'. On this occasion it was MI5's turn.

'BURGESS BURNS HIS BOATS,' ran the headline, 'NOW – AND ONLY NOW – THEY'VE GOT HIM.'

Inadvertently, they had also got one of their own agents. But it never came to that. Burgess did not attempt to return to Britain. Instead, he continued to invite Driberg to see him in Moscow, and over the months and years that followed M would file many more reports on Burgess based on what he had said to Driberg. Most of this intelligence was useful, some of it less so, like the fact that Burgess 'has a dog and a cat at his dacha. The dog is called Joe after Stalin.' This stream of intelligence did not change the course of the Cold War, but it was a small triumph for MI5 and M at a time when victories against Moscow were rare.

By the end of the 1950s, M was spending much less time running his MI5 section. Indeed, his interests seemed to be gravitating away from the world of intelligence and the more suspicious and close atmosphere that had taken hold within the Office. The foundations of British intelligence had been rocked by the exposure of so many

Soviet moles. The punishment for those in MI5 and MI6, it seemed, was to live in a world without coincidence. M had joined the service in 1931, hoping, perhaps, to step into the pages of a novel by John Buchan. By 1961, the year that he retired, it had become more reminiscent of a book by his officer John Le Carré. It was time for M to step into the other life he had been carefully building for himself over the last decade.

45

REBIRTH

The marmoset is a small South American primate that is usually found in the upper reaches of a rainforest canopy, not a well-lit television studio. In 1961, during the live recording of *Good Companions,* a popular BBC television programme about pets and unusual animals, one of the show's regular hosts began to tell the audience at home about the marmoset he had in his hands. Yet this creature was on edge, and the presenter knew why. The previous item had featured a number of dogs and the smell had proved to be unnerving. Before the presenter could finish his piece, the small primate drove its long incisors into his flesh. The bite was so deep that it reached his bone.

To be bitten live on air was a first for Maxwell Knight, and yet, at the same time, his reaction was familiar. He covered it up. He had spent most of his life erecting Chinese walls between what he thought and what he did, his life often resembling a drawn-out negotiation between who he was and how he came across, and few viewers at home registered what had happened. All they could see was a familiar and much-loved naturalist doing what he had done so many times before on the same programme. You could probably count on one hand the number of people watching him on television at that moment who knew that he had spent the last thirty years of his life working for MI5.

Max – he was no longer 'M' – was by 1961 one of the BBC's most prolific broadcasters. In the 1950s alone, he featured in at least 306 original radio broadcasts, he had no fewer than 20 books published in this one decade, he appeared on television more than 40 times, excluding repeats, he gave lectures throughout the country and he wrote numerous magazine articles, all on the subject of natural history. His rich, reassuring voice was synonymous by 1960 with radio programmes such as *The Naturalist, Country Questions, Nature Parliament* and *Naturalists' Notebook*. Max also popped up on *Woman's Hour,* did schools programming and featured on television programmes such as *Look* and the panel show *Animal, Vegetable, Mineral.* When children became junior members of the London Zoo in 1965, one of the advertised benefits was the chance to attend 'film shows and lectures given during the school holidays, when you can meet famous animal experts such as David Attenborough, Maxwell Knight, and Peter Scott'.

The name Maxwell Knight was so well known to the British public by the start of the 1960s, especially among children, that he was often invited to open schools or public natural history displays. When Max was absent from one of his regular radio slots, the audience feedback frequently included questions about when he would be back.

Max was also invited, in his new guise as a loveable naturalist, to be a castaway on *Desert Island Discs,* the long-running BBC radio programme in which public figures choose records relating to different parts of their lives. Almost all his choices were jazz recordings. He spoke about his childhood, his pets and his former clarinet teacher, Sidney Bechet, but that was it. The book he asked to take with him to the desert island was *The Cambridge Natural History*. His luxury was a microscope. This was not an interview with M, but with Maxwell Knight the popular naturalist, a public persona he had spent the past decade meticulously stitching together so that he could step into it when he finally left the Office.

What made this reinvention so remarkable was that most of it took place while he was still working for MI5. In 1956, two days after appearing on the BBC television programme *Countrywise,* in which he and another presenter performed an unrehearsed eight-minute piece to camera, Captain Knight of MI5, as he then was, passed on to a fellow officer a copy of a Guy Burgess letter that had been received by one of his agents. Having interviewed the former Soviet agent and journalist William Ewer, codenamed 'Trilby', part of MI5's ongoing attempt to find out whether 'there might still be persons in high Government position who would not be above giving information to the Russians', Max then went to chair an episode of *The Naturalist,* on the subject of how to tame animals.

Although he preferred to keep his life as a naturalist hermetically sealed off from his rival incarnation as an MI5 officer, there were times when the two overlapped. Max once told his readers about a clever pet otter of his that he had named 'Olga'. He christened a rather vain tawny owl that loved to bask in the sun 'Oswald'. There was a bush baby of his named 'Wee Jaikie', after a John Buchan character, and a Cairn terrier called 'Kim'. Occasionally, as a naturalist he encountered individuals he had known from his other line of work. The illustrations in two of Max's books were drawn by John Le Carré. The photographs in another were taken by Wolf Suschitzky, whose sister Edith Tudor-Hart had supplied Percy Glading with his camera (although Max was probably unaware of this when they collaborated). In April 1965, Max was one of five Fellows of the Zoological Society of London invited to fill a vacancy on its council. Another was Ivor Montagu, a Soviet agent who had been followed around London thirty-nine years earlier by Eric Roberts, acting on

Max's instructions. Now these former adversaries, one unknown to the other, found themselves working together on the management of London Zoo.

'The only time I realised there was something different about him,' recalled Desmond Morris, the zoologist and broadcaster, who frequently performed with Max, 'was when I saw an enormous, official-looking black car pull up and out stepped Max. The two didn't fit.'

The idea that a BBC national treasure was also a senior MI5 officer was unusual. Even more remarkable was just how prolific Max managed to be in his new guise. He wrote more books in the 1950s than most authors manage in a lifetime, to say nothing of his radio programmes, his television shows, his articles and his talks. In one sense this was testament to an intense work ethic. It also reflected his popularity. Max was certainly not invited back repeatedly and commissioned to write so many books because of his academic credentials. Desmond Morris remembered him as 'an avuncular, friendly old bloke, who loved animals and had written several books about how to keep pets', but one who 'wasn't, in my book, a serious scientist'.

What Max lacked in scientific qualifications he made up for with an almost endless supply of stories about the animals he had kept – and he had kept a great many. 'There are very few kinds of animal which it is possible for a private person to keep that I have not at some time had in my care,' he told his readers. 'On the whole casualties have not been heavy.' In his various books he referred to having kept sparrows, robins, thrushes, blackbirds, magpies, bantam hens, rabbits and a parade of different dogs, including 'Spaniels, Labradors, Great Danes, bulldogs and my favourites, bull terriers' as well as Haakon, an elkhound, who was 'an excellent house-dog' with 'a tiresome habit' of eating Max's pet rabbits. He also kept harvest mice as well as frogs, toads, snakes, more than a dozen parrots, tortoises, mongeese, civet cats, lemurs, monkeys, foxes, barbary ducks, almost 'all the species of crow which we have in this country', a pair of badgers, an otter, a bat, a bear, a baby hare, a White's tree frog and a number of tropical and cold water fish. 'I made it a rule to spend some period every day just sitting still and looking at them,' he wrote. 'I learned a great deal by doing so.' 'Spiders have always intrigued me,' he went on, 'and I have kept quite a number of these wonderful creatures', as well as beetles. 'I have even managed to get stag beetles to become tame and feed from sugar water from the tip of my finger.' 'It will be apparent that I have a weakness for spotted flycatchers,' he also confessed. 'I have had jackdaws, rooks, owls, starlings, and even a house martin and a cuckoo. The last of these was, perhaps, the most interesting bird pet I ever owned.'

Just as he took on agents from every walk of life, Max seemed incapable of sticking to one type of pet. Perhaps the only creature he could not abide was the cockroach. Nor was he very fond of cats, only because they interfered with his attempts to look after birds.

Yet his success as a broadcaster was about more than his experience of keeping pets. It was also down to his personality, the burr of his voice and his tone. He came across as warm-hearted, sensible and sturdy, if at times a little stern. The answer to little boys who harmed small animals was, he wrote, 'a good hiding – preferably from a parent'. He bemoaned 'the constant and usually ill-informed stream of propaganda against any kind of physical correction'. 'My views will be called old-fashioned or sadistic by a few of our wishy-washy reformers,' he wrote, 'but I can truthfully say that I have not formed my ideas in early senility – I have maintained them since I was a young man.' In some ways this lent to his appeal. It made him more familiar, more authentic, more of a 'type': a kindly, tweedy figure who knew a great deal about the natural world and seemed to enjoy passing it on in the grand tradition of an elderly storyteller.

What would also set him apart from the other big names in natural history, such as James Fisher and Peter Scott, both good friends of his, was that he urged his listeners to get out of the house after the programme and look for wildlife. Max coined the term 'nature detective', once telling his readers 'that field naturalists must be good detectives; and that the way to set about investigating the many exciting and interesting problems which all naturalists, young and old, encounter from time to time, is to model themselves on those officers of the law whose duty it is to solve crimes'. Just as his naturalism informed his espionage, the opposite was also true.

'His books emphasised the need for young people to get out into the field,' said the veterinarian John Cooper, who got to know Max around this time. 'He related natural history to ordinary people. As a listener, you felt that you could go out and do it, you could catch a beetle or a caterpillar, and I think we need more of that now.'

But what did Max get out of all this? This new career did not fall into his lap. He had to work hard to become a well-known presenter, and would always write to thank the BBC producers involved after appearing on a programme. He turned up well prepared, made himself available and, on at least one occasion, cheekily asked a producer whether he could appear on a prestigious television programme – 'if that doesn't sound impertinent!'

It would have been much easier for him to retire quietly to a suburban street with his collection of animals. Instead, this distinguished, decorated MI5 officer went out of his way to reinvent himself.

The main reason was money. Max's MI5 salary had never been large, he spent what little he had and, in 1961, he forfeited his full pension by retiring early due to ill health. This was largely because of his worsening angina. He needed to earn more in order to look after himself and his pets, and to support his new wife.

Max's marriage to Lois had been annulled during the war, on the grounds that it had not been consummated. Lois later blamed their physical incompatibility for the separation. Max had always said that he would see a doctor about his problem, but as far as she knew he never did. 'If only he could have been honest with me – about everything,' she told the author Anthony Masters, 'I'm sure we would have found the strength to face it together.'

Lois did not resent Max, and their separation in 1943 was largely amicable. Lois went on to remarry and have children and stayed in touch with Max and his sister, Enid. Many years later she would conclude that her former husband was simply someone who preferred the company of pets.

A similar sentiment crops up in other portraits of him, yet it never rings true. If this had been the case, in the years after his divorce Max would have become a recluse. Yet rather than hide himself away, he got married again and set out to become a famous broadcaster. This suggests an individual who not only enjoyed society but needed it, perhaps in ways that he did not recognise in himself.

Max's third wife was Susi Barnes, who was working in the MI5 Registry when they first met and was a little in awe of him as the grand old man of counterespionage. She was well-spoken, well-educated and discreet, as well as being fifteen years younger than him. She had also emerged recently from an unhappy relationship that had apparently put her off sex.

In one of Max's last books he referred, with some distaste, to 'human sex-maniacs', by which he meant people who thought too much about sex. For all the theories about Max's sexuality, that he was secretly gay or bisexual, it seems that most of his experiences in this department were simply unhappy, and that by this stage of his life sex was not something that interested him. In this sense, Susi Barnes was ideal. She offered love, companionship and care, and she probably demanded nothing of him physically.

Max and Susi were married at Windsor Register Office in 1944 and would remain together for the rest of their lives. Their marriage was not without difficulties. As Max began to suffer more from his angina and Susi spent an increasing amount of time looking after him, there were moments when he was unpleasant towards her and controlling. She sometimes resented the boundaries in their relationship. Like almost anyone married to an intelligence professional, she knew that there were parts of her husband's interior world that were shared with others but not her. Yet to most people who got to know the new Mr and Mrs Knight in Camberley, where Max had moved after the war, they came across as an attractive, glamorous and contented couple, two big fish in a small pond who were well suited to each other.

Providing for Susi and his pets was one of the reasons for Max's reinvention as a broadcaster. He had never owned a property, and when his broadcasting work dried up in the last few years of his life he and Susi were so short of funds that they had to move in with one of Max's former officers, Guy Poston.

Yet there was more to this reinvention than money. It was also for Max an escape. The natural world offered a respite from war, radical politics and the slow disintegration of the British Empire. The Frankenstein mutation of the Fascist movement to which he had belonged was saddening for him, it tore at parts of his identity and the way he remembered his past. By investing so much of himself in his new life as a broadcaster, Max was perhaps trying to create a different legacy and to leave behind some parts of his history.

In a different sense, Max's broadcasting allowed this intensely patriotic man to share with his listeners something of his own version of Britishness. 'I myself must plead guilty to having kept my share of foreign animals,' he wrote, 'but I have also made a point, wherever possible, of keeping British species', adding elsewhere that 'the British' are 'supposed to be people who are first and foremost in their love of birds and animals, and in their interest in natural history'.

His patriotism had always been rooted in a love of the British landscape and its wildlife. He wanted Britain to remain a nation of nature lovers, and he hoped to inspire the next generation of naturalists. He saw this as the first step towards slowing down man's destruction of the natural world, a subject that concerned him greatly by the end of his life. Rachel Carson's *Silent Spring,* an early classic of environmental writing, was a book that made a lasting impression on him.

Above all, Max's rebirth as a famous broadcaster was a chance for him to step into the spotlight after a lifetime spent in the shadows. Towards the end of his life, Max described how he liked to take his golden marmoset, Sadie, to local cafés where 'she would suddenly appear from under the table and would look up at me and chatter. I would chatter back, and then she would accept a piece of sweet cake or a currant or sultana. This performance was generally very popular.' There are many other stories of him taking out unusual pets in the hope of getting a reaction from passers-by. He clearly enjoyed all this. He liked being seen as an eccentric Dr Doolittle and all the 'friendly leg-pulling' that came with it, just as he had done many years ago as a boy. Indeed, throughout his life Max showed himself to be someone who craved recognition. His decision to tell Gwladys's friends on Exmoor about his secret work, those lunches with Colonel Carter of Special Branch and the publicity shots for his novel all suggest that a life of anonymity did not come easily to him. When he left the secret world, this spymaster needed to be in the public eye, just as a celebrity longs for anonymity. As one of the country's best-known natural history broadcasters he certainly achieved this.

Max did not imagine that his work for MI6 and MI5 would ever become public knowledge. Nor did he think that his moniker, 'M', would come to be associated all over the world with a pipe-smoking British spymaster.

In late 1962 Max may have visited one of the cinemas in Camberley to see the first James Bond film, *Dr No*. The audience would have been mostly teenage boys, all in love with the idea of being a spy – as Max had been at their age. Within the first ten minutes of the film, Bond's spymaster, 'M', appeared on-screen. Although Max would have known about this character from Fleming's books, which had begun to be published ten years earlier, the legend of the James Bond 'M' only really took off once the films came out.

Fleming never revealed who had inspired this character. Yet in manner, M was clearly based on Fleming's former boss, Admiral John Godfrey, who had been Director of Naval Intelligence. But Godfrey was never called 'M'. The name of this character was most likely a nod to Max. He and Fleming may have met each other either professionally during the war or socially through Ian Menzies. Otherwise Fleming would have heard of the MI5 spymaster. Max had been known as 'M' within MI5 and beyond since 1931. He ran 'M' Section. His agents had codenames such as 'M/1' and 'M/A'. He signed off all correspondence as 'M' and had dealings with individuals and organisations throughout the secret world. Although there was one other figure in wartime British intelligence who was briefly known as 'M' – Major-General Sir Colin Gubbins, the head of SOE – by the time Fleming began to write his James Bond novels the man with the greatest claim to the moniker 'M' in British intelligence was undoubtedly Maxwell Knight.

In the years after his retirement from MI5, if he was not performing on television or writing another book, Max was usually to be found outside watching cricket or roaming the fields and woods around his home, a landscape which reminded him of where he had grown up. It was on these expeditions that he was at his happiest. 'Those of us who had the privilege of going on field trips with him,' wrote one of his companions on some of these outings, Leo Harrison Matthews, Director of the London Zoo, 'are left with memories of many happy days full of interest, good talk, and deep enjoyment.'

He described him as 'the perfect friend, loyal, kind and gentle, full of fun and good companionship'.

Max cut a distinctive figure on these outings, not least because of the amount of gear he took with him. 'I must issue a word of warning about the very real danger of overloading yourself with bits and pieces that you probably won't use very much. I say this with real feeling,' he confessed, 'for I myself am a great sinner in this respect. In fact, my friends tease me unmercifully on this point and tell me that I look like the White Knight in *Alice Through the Looking-Glass*.'

During the 1960s, the 'White Knight' was a regular sight out in the environs of Camberley, in his old fishing coat with its capacious pockets, searching for wildlife. In some ways this is a familiar image to us, for this was how he had spent so much of his time as a boy. In old age, Maxwell Knight had returned to his childhood. His love of wildlife and the English landscape was the great constant throughout his life, from the time he was given his naturalist badge as a twelve-year-old Boy Scout through to his arrival as a popular broadcaster in his mid-fifties. Coming to the end of his life, Max was revisiting his youth and that golden age before the outbreak of the First World War, the years before the deaths of his father and brother or the advent of Communism and Fascism. It was during those days that Max had learned the most important lesson of his life: that if you watch an animal carefully, and if you study its behaviour, you might learn enough of its character to be able to tame it, and that if you can do that, you may be able to look after it. This was what he went on to do, in one way or another, for the rest of his life.

EPILOGUE

Maxwell Knight died of a heart attack on 24 January, 1968, at the age of sixty-seven, only seven years after retiring from MI5. His memorial service was held at St James's Church, in Piccadilly, west London, and brought together Max's many friends from the world of natural history as well as 'lots of men in brown felt hats who didn't really identify themselves,' his nephew recalled. In death, it seemed, the two parts of his life had come together. Yet the only references in the memorial address to his MI5 career were heavily veiled and meant little to those beyond the secret world.

A letter soon appeared in *Countryside* magazine from a list of British natural history luminaries, including James Fisher, Peter Scott, Johnny Morris and David Attenborough, calling for contributions to the Maxwell Knight Memorial Fund. This led to the creation of the Maxwell Knight Young Naturalists' Library, a collection of books housed initially at the Linnean Society and later the Natural History Museum, where it remains to this day. Royalties from the sales of his books continue to go to this library.

The actual details of his MI5 work, and the extent of his agent-running operation, would remain obscure for many years. With so little accurate information about his espionage career, the story of this part of his life came to be dominated by rumours, snippets of information and a fantastical memoir written by Joan Miller, one of Max's former secretaries. Miller argued that Max was secretly gay, and in the years that followed the publication of her book he was routinely described as both homosexual and homophobic, as well as neurotic, manipulative, anti-Semitic and obsessed by the Occult.

Only recently has it become possible to put together a fuller and more accurate account of Max's life and MI5 career. The Security Service Act of 1989 placed MI5 on a statutory footing, and after the collapse of the Soviet Union in 1991 attitudes within Thames House towards the service's history underwent a dramatic change. The following year came the 'Waldegrave Initiative', which led to the periodic declassification and release of material from the MI5 archive to the National Archives, a major turning point in the field of British intelligence history.

Ask MI5 today about Maxwell Knight and you will learn that he 'had a hugely significant impact in the success of our operations', even if he 'was clearly an unusual and talented character'. One retired senior MI5 officer has been more specific about Max's legacy, highlighting the way 'he demonstrated the importance in security intelligence work of agent-running'.

Another of Max's key contributions was that he changed the perception within MI5 of female agents. Olga Gray, Mona Maund, Hélène de Munck, Marjorie Mackie, Kathleen Tesch and Friedl Gaertner were just some of the women he turned into successful government spies. Max described 'a woman's intuition' as 'sometimes amazingly helpful and amazingly correct' and that, 'given the right guiding hand, this ability can at times save an Intelligence Officer an enormous amount of trouble'. Deep down he felt that women were more discreet than men and often made for better agents. There may have been MI5 officers before him who employed female agents, but none used so many for so long and to such good effect.

A full obituary of Max, including his intelligence work, might have mentioned all this. Also, it would have touched on his anticipation of Soviet moles in Whitehall and how he had correctly suspected Anthony Blunt of working for Moscow. His fundamental conviction that the main threat to British security came from Russia was accurate, indeed it seems prescient in today's political climate.

Max also played the key role in the great MI5 success story of the 1930s, the breakup of the Woolwich Arsenal spy ring, and the wartime infiltration of the Right Club. This led to the prosecution of Anna Wolkoff and Tyler Kent and prevented the public disclosure of highly sensitive material from the Churchill–Roosevelt correspondence. Yet beyond the headlines, and what made him such a respected figure within British intelligence, a spymaster's spymaster, was his unusual ability to recruit and run a large stable of agents and to keep them going for many years. Throughout the latter stages of his career, he was called upon to give lectures about his experiences or to get them down on paper, and in this way his methodology and outlook were passed on within MI5 and beyond.

Yet Max's greatest achievement was his contribution to the demise of British Fascism, made all the more poignant by the part he had played in the rise of this movement during the 1920s. Max ran agents deep inside the British Union of Fascists, he compiled reports on British Fascism, and pushed to have its leaders detained during the Second World War. Indeed, it is hard to think of anyone who did more to bring about the death of organised Fascism in Britain.

After seven years learning his craft, first at the Makgill Organisation and later with MI6, Max spent no fewer than thirty years as an MI5 spymaster. From 1931 until his retirement in 1961, he practised and ultimately perfected the art of identifying, recruiting and running undercover agents. Recently, he has been described as one of the twentieth century's 'most intuitive intelligence officers' and 'one of the great spymasters in British intelligence history'. Perhaps we can be more precise: it is unlikely that any other MI5 officer, either before his time or since, has run so many agents during his or her career, or displayed such a sensitive understanding of their craft. For this reason, it is fair to think of Maxwell Knight as the greatest spymaster in MI5's history.

What of his agents? Hélène de Munck became a naturalised British citizen, as Max had promised when he first took her on, and later ran a guesthouse with her sister in Devon. Mrs Mackie carried on her MI5 work for some years before taking the position of manciple at the Charterhouse almshouse in London, where she became famous for throwing lively soirées that ended with a séance. Little is known about the postwar lives of Kathleen Tesch, who returned to her life in a Home Counties village, or indeed Mona Maund, only that her brother became Bishop of Lesotho and she left all her money to a spiritualist charity. E. G. Mandeville-Roe joined the army, where he remained until retirement. Claud Sykes was briefly part of MI6 before returning to his first love – writing. Graham Pollard became a legendary bibliographer and towards the end of his life was known for his eccentric outfits and his love of pipes and long walks in the country, much like his former spymaster. Tom Driberg wound up as a life peer, Chairman of the Labour Party and an enthusiastic campaigner in the House of Lords for the legalisation of cannabis. Friedl Gaertner, the beautiful divorcée, married the Second Secretary at the US Embassy in London and became a diplomat's wife. Yet like many of Max's agents, she was never able to leave behind her MI5 work entirely. In the years after leaving Britain, she would be interviewed occasionally by MI5 molehunters as they tried to piece together the extent of Soviet penetration during her time in the service. As her son later recalled, she found these visits deeply unsettling.

Having been an agent for most of the 1930s, Vivian Hancock-Nunn became an MI5 officer during the war. As such, he was probably one of the first to be told, in 1944, that his brother-in-law, Gerald Hewitt, had been arrested for making Nazi broadcasts from France. It may well have been Hancock-Nunn who arranged for his fellow MI5 officer John Maude, KC, to defend Hewitt in court. Hewitt avoided execution and was sentenced to twelve years in jail. Hancock-Nunn left MI5 and spent the rest of his life trying to reclaim and then restore his family's estate in Sussex. Increasingly, he seemed to be a man out of step, depressed and unhappy in the world. 'I see no object in life whatever,' declares the hero in one of Hancock-Nunn's novels. 'If I had a child I would be compelled to say to it – "is your journey necessary?" It would certainly be a most unenjoyable journey.'

Harold Kurtz did valuable work for MI5 during the war before going on to be a translator at the Nuremberg trials, where he was given the unenviable task of taking down the final words of Nazi war criminals. Max helped to secure his British naturalisation, and Kurtz would spend the rest of his life in Oxford, mainly writing historical biographies. He was often seen playing draughts with college porters, 'a familiar, vast and unforgettable figure', but one who was also described as 'a lonely man who thrived in company' and who had been driven to drink by his wartime experiences.

Jimmy Dickson was another of Max's former charges who found it hard to adjust to life outside MI5. Although he was kept on after the war, Dickson was frozen out of the Office in the early 1950s and took early retirement. He got back to his writing, but the spark had gone. As his son recalled, he became reclusive after the death of his wife and began to smoke and drink considerably more.

Dickson's closest ally in the Office had been Eric Roberts, another of Max's comrades from the British Fascists to make the transition from MI5 agent to MI5 officer. Having always wanted to get behind the curtain and become part of the cosmopolitan urban elite, he began to miss his days as an agent almost as soon as he got his feet under the table at MI5. 'I looked on myself as a field operator who had the ability to get the news,' he later wrote. Roberts left MI5 in the mid-1950s to emigrate with his wife and children, including his son, Maxwell, named after his former spymaster, to Canada, where he chose to live as far away from the Office as possible on a small island on the west coast.

Canada had a particular hold on Max and those who worked for him. His two most talented operatives moved there – Eric and Olga – while Vivian Hancock-Nunn finished one of his novels with the hero emigrating to Canada. Max's protégé in MI5, John Bingham, also completed an unpublished book in which the protagonist escapes to Canada to be at one with nature. For those in M Section, it seems that Canada was an Edenic emblem of empire, a larger, younger and less threatening version of the country in which they had grown up, a promised land they could escape to once they had finished with their life in the shadows.

There were times when Olga Gray felt otherwise. After the war, she moved with her young family to Lindsay, outside Ontario, a small town with small-town values. Rather than let her considerable talents go to waste, she became a reporter for the local newspaper, but had to write under a pseudonym because the assumption in Lindsay at that time was that if a woman had a job it meant that her husband was unable to provide for her. After dinner the former MI5 agent was known to leave the women's conversation to join the men, who were usually talking about hunting or fishing, and tell them to start talking about something that mattered, like politics.

Olga's daughter remembers how her mother would often pick her up from school and take a detour on the way home to a dirt track on the outskirts of town. It ran parallel to a railroad. They would wait in the car with the engine running until a freight train came into view. Olga would honk at the driver. He would blow his whistle. Olga would rev the engine until the train came alongside, then they began to race.

Her daughter still recalls the look on her mother's face as she slammed down the accelerator, screamed with joy and began to race against the train. That was when she came alive, the adrenaline coursing through her as it had done during her days working for M. Then the road ran out, the train hived off and Olga returned to her new life as a housewife in a small town in Canada.

Olga was tracked down in the 1980s by Anthony Masters, who wrote up their interview as a feature in the *Mail on Sunday*. He was so pleased with the double-page spread that he sent a copy to Olga as a way of saying thank you. Yet after seeing the piece, she had a nervous breakdown and would spend the next month in a psychiatric ward. Olga convinced herself that the children of the men she had helped to put away would find her or one of her children. The panic attacks she had experienced intermittently over the last few decades came back.

Post-Traumatic Stress Disorder is usually associated with soldiers who have experienced warfare, or victims of traumatic accidents or disasters. Although it is often linked to a single event, it can also follow a period of acute and sustained tension, as it appears to have done for some of M's agents.

'Six years of work under conditions of constant anxiety and fear had made me suspicious of my own shadow and even of myself,' wrote Eric Roberts, after he was visited unexpectedly by an MI5 officer towards the end of his life. Years after retirement he confided in a friend, 'I still get nightmares.' Going back over his work as an agent, after 'deliberately suppressing the past' for so long, 'hurt like hell,' he wrote. 'I repeat, hurt like hell.'

Two days later 'fear returned in full force. Yes, fear,' he went on. 'I was ill. Very ill.'

Whereas some of Max's agents were relatively unaffected by their work, others experienced panic attacks or flashbacks and in other ways they paid a price for their service. By talking to the relatives of these agents and examining their death certificates, it is possible to put together a rough picture of what happened to at least ten of these agents after they retired. Two died of complications related to excessive consumption of alcohol. One became morbidly obese. Many of the others began to suffer from type 2 diabetes. During the 1960s, when most of Max's agents died, although less than one in fifty Britons had type 2 diabetes, its prevalence among Max's agents was more than twenty times worse and it was described as a cause of death for four of these ten agents. Without full medical histories it is impossible to make any precise causal link between their work and their subsequent health, but it does seem that the transition from high-pressure intelligence work to a life outside MI5 took a considerable toll on most of Max's agents.

We know a lot about the burden that soldiers bear in the years after their active service ends, and we celebrate their bravery and their sacrifice. Rightly so. But it is rare to hear the contribution of government agents described in similar terms. For some of Max's agents, that was part of the problem. Not only had they grown up in a society that emphasised self-discipline and personal restraint, making it unusual for them to seek professional help, but they understood that for some of their countrymen or -women the work they had done was not something to celebrate.

'In Great Britain, for some peculiar psychological reason, there has always been a stigma attached not only to the calling of secret agents, but also to the actual word,' wrote Max, in 1945. 'Even officials in Government Departments, on whose shoulders lies the burden of responsibility in connection with National Defence, have been – and in some cases, still are – prone to regard an "agent" as an unscrupulous and dishonest person actuated by unworthy motives.' And yet, he stressed, 'an honest and loyal agent, whether he is working for his country in foreign lands, or at home, has often to exhibit some of the highest human qualities. It would be a satisfactory reward to any person engaged in the operation of agents, if he could feel that his efforts had done something, by example, to raise the status of an agent.'

One of the ways to change how we think about these government agents and to celebrate their work is by knowing their names, the lives they led and therefore the nature of what they gave. This has been one of the aims of this book, to celebrate M and his agents. During his long career at MI5, Maxwell Knight wanted to elevate the standing of his operatives: individuals who lived, like him, in an age when extreme ideology was in the ascendant, yet who decided to worship at a different altar. They were brave men and women who chose to let go of a part of themselves – who gave over their lives, really, anonymously and for very little reward – to a spymaster they trusted, and for a country they believed in.

ACKNOWLEDGMENTS

For their help during the research of this book my thanks to Bernard Baverstock at the Camberley Natural History Society, Susan Benson at the Cumbria Archive and Local Studies Centre, Bernie Bickerton and Beryl Jones at the Society of Civil and Public Service Writers, Lynda Brooks at the Linnean Society, Bill Burnett of the Old Penwithians Association, Julie Carrington at the Royal Geographical Society, Lynette Cawthra and Jane Taylor at the Working Class Movement Library, Pam Champion at St Helen and St Katharine, Abingdon, Jackie Cheshire at Queen Square Library, Matthew Chipping at the BBC Written Archives, Tony Copsey at Suffolk Painters, Janet Dotterer at Millersville University, Elving Felix at the Library of Congress, Ruth Frendo at the University of London, Michael Frost at Yale University Library, Stewart Gillies in the News Reference Department of the British Library, Bill Gordon at Surrey Cricket Club, Jonathan Holmes at Queens' College, Cambridge, Jeff Howarth at the TUC Library Collections, Debbie Hunt at the Royal Microscopical Society, Gill Jackson at Robert Hale, Frances Johnson at Camden Local Studies and Archives Centre, Val McAtear at the Royal Entomological Society, Carole McCallum and Simon

Docherty at Glasgow Caledonian University, Owen McKnight at Jesus College, Oxford, Emma Milnes at the Zoological Society of London, Joanne Morgan at the Daily Mail, Kate Nivison at London Writer Circle, Jonathan Oates at Ealing Local History, Hellen Pethers at the Natural History Museum, Kieren Pitts at the Amateur Entomologists' Society, Anne-Marie Purcell at Hammersmith and Fulham Local Studies and Archives, Michael Riordan at St John's and The Queen's Colleges, Oxford, Karen Robson at University of Southampton, Chris Schuler at the Authors' Club, Rowena Siorvanes at Falmouth University, Laurence Spring at Surrey History Centre, John Squier at Normandy Historians, Richard Temple at Senate House Library, Darren Treadwell at the People's History Museum, Daniel Warren at Stamford Endowed Schools, Helen Wicker at Kent History and Library Centre, Claire Yelland and Sarah Jane at Camborne School of Mines, Robert Winckworth and Dan Mitchell at University College London, Andy Wood at the Royal Institute of Painters in Water Colours, Liz Wood and Helen Ford at the Modern Records Centre, University of Warwick, Oliver Wooller at Bexley Heritage and Archives Services, and all the staff at the National Archives in Kew and the British Library.

I am even more grateful to the relatives of the main characters in this book for taking the time to talk, or else pointing me in the right direction, in particular Harry Smith, for his many insights into the world of his uncle, as well as Ian Aitken, Charlotte Brady, Ian Calder, John Dickson, Dominic Dobson, Anne Dobson, Fiona Gray, Richard Gray, Carolyn Hirst, Valerie Lippay, Crista MacDonald, Stephen and Karen Mackie, Anne Maude, Belinda Mayne, Penny Parsley, Neil Roach, Tony Taylor, Caroline Thistlethwaite and Gregory Wolcough.

My thanks also to those who have corresponded with me or in other ways helped to shed light on the many lives of Maxwell Knight and his agents: Christopher Andrew, David Attenborough, Francis

Beckett, Barry Buitekant, Paul Connell, John Cooper, Margaret Cooper, David Cornwell, Ted Crawford, Stephen Dorril, Richard Dove, Tom Everard, Naresh Fernandes, Andy Goodall, Ben Gummer, George Hewson, Frank James, Neil Kent, Charles Knight, Thomas Linehan, Andrew Lownie, Andrew Lycett, Kate Marris, Lindsay Merriman, Nick Merriman, Rosie Merriman, Giles Milton, Desmond Morris, Peter Pugh, Kevin Quinlan, Scott Reeve, Richard Ritchie, Laurence Scales, Adam Sisman, Graham Stevenson, Willie Thompson, David Turner, William Tyrer, Sally Wade-Gery, Francis Wheen and Paul Willetts. I owe particular thanks to Rupert Allason, for his thoughts on the manuscript, and to Rob Hutton, for his insights into Eric Roberts and for many enjoyable evenings spent talking shop. Finally, I'd like to thank those former intelligence officers from both MI5 and MI6 who were able to enrich my understanding of Maxwell Knight and the art of recruiting and running agents.

At PublicAffairs, I am eternally grateful to both Clive Priddle, who first suggested the idea of this book, and to Ben Adams, for his consistently shrewd and imaginative input, as well as Melissa Raymond and Melissa Veronesi for all their help, and to Christina Palaia for her elegant and skilful copyediting. At Preface, I am indebted to Lizzy Gaisford for her assistance and to Trevor Dolby, for his excellent advice and friendship.

My agent, Jonathan Conway, has been involved at every stage of this book and I can't thank him enough for his expert judgement and the faith he has shown in this story. My thanks also to Gemma Hirst, Katie Snaydon and Jean Kitson for all their help on the film and television side of things.

Last of all my thanks to Dad and Bea, for taking the time to look at the manuscript and offer all sorts of useful advice, and to Helena, for her support, her inimitable sense of how to shape a story and her love. The last person to thank is my very own M, Matilda

Hemming, born at around the same time that I began to write this book, whose first words may not have been 'Max Knight' – but not far off. Like all the most interesting characters in this story, she strikes me as being one of life's watchers. This book is dedicated to her.

NOTES

In citing works in the notes, short titles have generally been used. Works frequently cited have been identified by the following abbreviations:

1369 – The Red Book in the Wiener Library

495-198-1267 – Glading Papers in the Russian State Archive of Social-Political History (RGASPI), Moscow

ADM – Records of the Admiralty and related bodies in the National Archives, Kew

CAB – Records of the Cabinet Office in the National Archives, Kew

COR – London Western Coroners District Collection in the London Metropolitan Archive

DOM – Domvile Papers in the National Maritime Museum, Greenwich, London

HO – Records created or inherited by the Home Office and related bodies in the National Archives, Kew (the first two numbers following HO indicate the record shelfmark, the third number refers to the document number, so HO 283/40/22 is the document numbered 22 in the record HO 283/40)

HS – Records of Special Operations Executive

IOR – India Office Records in the British Library, London

KV – Records of the Security Service in the National Archives, Kew (the first two numbers following KV indicate the record shelfmark, the third number refers to the item number, so KV 4/227/1a is the document labelled 1a in the record KV 4/227; 'History Sheet' refers to a non-indexed section found at the back of some older MI5 personal files)

MS 310 – Kent (Tyler Gatewood) Papers in the Yale University Library, New Haven, Connecticut

For any further help on tracking down a source or citation listed here, please contact the author via his website.

Chapter 1: A Man Adrift

8   **'except for an uncomfortable'**: John Baker White, *It's Gone for Good* (London: Vacher, 1941), 119.

9   **'promising young officer'**: ADM 240/49/4.

10   **'the inevitable tortoises'**: Maxwell Knight, *Some of My Animals* (London: G. Bell & Sons, 1954), 20.

11   **'I was brought up'**: Maxwell Knight, *How to Keep an Elephant* (London: Wolfe, 1967), 26.

11   **'more intelligent than'**: Knight, *Some of My Animals*, 13–14.

11   **'I got her to'**: Maxwell Knight, *Pets: Usual and Unusual* (London: Routledge & Kegan Paul, 1951), 78.

11   **'He handled them'**: Quoted in Anthony Masters, *The Man Who Was M* (London: Grafton, 1986), 15.

12   **'unfit for'**: Dennis Wheatley, *The Young Man Said* (London: Hutchinson, 1977), 136.

13   **'You can call off'**: *1924 Black's Dictionary of Music and Musicians* (London: A & C Black, 1924), 296.

13   **'London's first small'**: Tom Driberg, 'William Hickey', *Daily Express*, 27 September, 1934.

13   **'as they say love'**: Philip Larkin, 'For Sidney Bechet', in *The Whitsun Weddings* (London: Faber, 1971), 16.

13   **'did my best'**: *Desert Island Discs*, BBC Home Service, 28 June, 1965.

14   'Some ass': Ibid.

14   'fairly close': Maxwell Knight, *Reptiles in Britain* (Leicester: Brockhampton, 1965), 34.

14   'the most attractive bundle': Knight, *Pets: Usual and Unusual*, 78.

15   'In a world where': Ibid., 13.

17   'completely enamoured': Nigel Farndale, *Haw-Haw* (London: Macmillan, 2005), 59.

Chapter 2: The Makgill Organisation

18   'The whole of Europe': David Lloyd George, 'The Fontainebleau Memorandum of 25 March 1919', in *Breakdown and Rebirth: 1914 to the Present*, ed. Thomas G. Barnes and Gerald D. Feldman (Lanham, MD: University Press of America, 1982), 43.

19   'makes no secret': Quoted in Richard H. Ullman, *The Anglo-Soviet Relations 1917–1921* (London: Oxford University Press, 1972), 412.

20   'somewhat on Masonic lines': Christopher Andrew, *The Defence of the Realm* (London: Penguin, 2010), 123.

20   'If you talk': John Baker White, *True Blue* (London: Frederick Muller, 1970), 130.

21   'unique feature': Baker White, *It's Gone for Good*, 119.

Chapter 3: Bloody Fools

23   'superfluity of voluntary workers': KV 3/57/3a.

24   'the Roman genius': Quoted in Martin Gilbert, *Winston S. Churchill*, Vol. 5 (London: Heinemann, 1981), 226.

24   'persuade': Peter Martland quoted in Tom Kington, 'Recruited by MI5', *Guardian*, 13 October, 2009.

25   'decried my youthful': Baker White, *True Blue*, 123.

25   'The opinion of Headquarters': KV 3/57/3a.

26   'experience of intelligence work': HS 9/978/1.

26   'self-confident': Ibid.

26   **'Information will come to you'**: Maxwell Knight to Eric Roberts, 19 November, 1934, Eric Roberts Papers.

27   **'look of unutterable boredom'**: Maxwell Knight, *Gunmen's Holiday* (London: Philip Allan, 1935), 94.

27   **'breeding bears'**: Knight, *Pets: Usual and Unusual*, 79.

28   **'intensely keen'**: HS 9/978/1.

Chapter 4: The Razor's Edge

29   **'He saw battle'**: KV 2/245/1b.

32   **'Join the Fascisti'**: 'Class War', *Daily Herald*, 26 January, 1925.

32   **'crept like duck-weed'**: 'The "Reds" of Battersea', *The Times*, 29 November, 1923.

33   **'chose from among'**: KV 3/57/3a.

34   **'Pandemonium'**: 'Socialist Hooligans Wreck Opposition Meetings', *Daily Mirror*, 23 October, 1924.

34   **'Scenes of great disorder'**: 'Election Rowdyism', *The Times*, 23 October, 1924.

34   **'untiring in his efforts'**: KV 2/245/1a.

34   **'little short of'**: KV 2/245/331b.

35   **'It wasn't a Jewish'**: Hazel Barr quoted in Colin Holmes, *Searching for Lord Haw-Haw* (London: Routledge, 2016), 53.

35   **'These Fascist blackguards'**: Farndale, *Haw-Haw*, 55.

Chapter 5: Revenge

38   **'I was dragged'**: Quoted in John Mahon, *Harry Pollitt* (London: Lawrence and Wishart, 1976), 116.

39   **'gently, rather like'**: 'Pollitt Case', *The Times*, 24 April, 1925.

40   **'in a great state'**: 'Glasgow Communist Office Raided', *Scotsman*, 4 May, 1925.

41   **'a scene of desolation'**: 'Fascist Raid on "Sunday Worker" Offices', *Sunday Worker*, 24 May, 1925.

41   **'latent spark of aggression'**: Knight, *Gunmen's Holiday*, 42.

42 **'interested in patriotic work'**: Classified advertisement, *Sussex Agricultural Express,* 7 December, 1923; Tom Bower, *The Perfect English Spy* (London: Heinemann, 1995), 26.

42 **'secured information'**: KV 3/57/48a.

44 **'What we would like'**: KV 2/3874/1.

45 **'with a leaky'**: Eric Roberts to Harry, 10 February, 1969, Eric Roberts Papers.

45 **'set my mind'**: Ibid.

45 **'Pied piper nature'**: Bower, *Perfect English Spy,* 26.

46 **'personal magnetism'**: Eric Roberts to Harry, 10 February, 1969, Eric Roberts Papers.

46 **'an almost mystical figure'**: Ex-MI5 officer quoted in Andrew, *Defence of the Realm,* 132.

46 **'Every good agent'**: KV 4/227/1a.

46 **'He gave tremendous support'**: Masters, *The Man Who Was M,* 146–147.

47 **'In the strictest confidence'**: John Rowlandson quoted in Mahon, *Harry Pollitt,* 117.

48 **'a store of arms'**: KV 3/57/3a.

48 **'one of London's'**: J. G. Dickson (anonymously) in *Union Jack,* 7 March, 1925.

48 **'well organised'**: KV 3/57/3a.

48 **'members of H. M. Forces'**: KV 3/57/58.

48 **'desirable in this country'**: KV 3/57/6.

48 **'bring discredit'**: KV 3/57/48.

Chapter 6: The Freelance Spymaster

50 **'a shrewd old bugger'**: Dick White to Barrie Penrose, 15 July, 1985, quoted in Bower, *Perfect English Spy,* 27.

51 **'makes an excellent impression'**: Gill Bennett, *Churchill's Man of Mystery* (London: Routledge, 2007), 129.

51 **'clearly perfectly honest'**: Ibid.

52   'one of the most': Knight, *Some of My Animals,* 29.

53   'the best to be had': Constance Kell, *Secret Well Kept,* IWM, PP/MCR/120
      Reel 1.

Chapter 7: The Day

55   'I knew her': KV 2/1221/44a.

55   'as one of the county's': 'Went Christmas Shopping, Died', *Daily Express,*
      23 November, 1936.

57   'gentlemen with Eton ties': Cass Canfield, *Up and Down and Around*
      (London: Collins, 1972), 87.

57   'in silence': William Woodruff, *The Road to Nab End* (London: Hachette
      Digital, 1993).

58   'any attempt by': G. H. Q. Council of the British Fascists, 'The British
      Fascist Manifesto', *British Lion,* October–November 1927.

59   'I regret very much': Maxwell Knight, letter, *British Lion,* December,
      1927.

60   'Conservatism with knobs on': Arnold Leese, *Out of Step* (Guildford:
      Arnold Leese, 1951), 49.

Chapter 8: Exile

62   'a madly keen fisherman': *Desert Island Discs,* BBC Home Service, 28 June,
      1965.

64   'reasons of health': Maxwell Knight, letter, *British Lion,* December,
      1927.

64   'to have lived with': Guy Liddell Diaries, 28 March, 1944, KV 4/193.

Chapter 9: Morton's Plan

67   'ten years': KV 2/1016/1101a.

68   'International Leninism': Desmond Morton quoted in Bennett, *Churchill's
      Man of Mystery,* 71.

68   'typical old-fashioned': Unnamed friends quoted in ibid., 33.

69   'I have just heard': Morton quoted in ibid., 128.

70   **'With every passing month'**: Morton quoted in Andrew, *Defence of the Realm*, 128.

70   **'little ships'**: Bower, *Perfect English Spy*, 26.

71   **'whose personal honesty'**: KV 4/227/1a.

Chapter 10: 'I Can Make Things Bloody Unpleasant for You'

72   **'Was Major Morton'**: Quoted in Bennett, *Churchill's Man of Mystery*, 130.

73   **'a worm'**: Quoted in ibid.

74   **'This is going to be'**: Quoted in ibid.

74   **'make his life'**: Andrew, *Defence of the Realm,* 129.

74   **'We have a government'**: Quoted in Bennett, *Churchill's Man of Mystery*, 130.

74   **'outright warfare'**: Ibid., 128.

75   **'universal phenomenon'**: Quoted in Stephen Dorril, *Blackshirt* (London: Penguin, 2006), 199.

76   **'could not possibly'**: Keith Jeffery, *MI6* (London: Bloomsbury, 2011), 234.

76   **'the danger of'**: Ibid.

Chapter 11: Olga

83   **'I say, old thing'**: Angus Macpherson, 'Olga the Beautiful Spy', *Mail on Sunday*, 29 July, 1984.

84   **'Gosh, Doll'**: Ibid.

84   **'Any woman who'**: Bernard Newman, *Inquest on Mata Hari* (London: Robert Hale, 1956), 82.

Chapter 12: The M Organisation

88   **'should never be'**: Vernon Kell, Vernon Kell Papers, PP/MCR/120 Reel 1.

89   **'A showpiece for'**: 'Now You See It, Now You Don't', *The Times Magazine*, 7 August, 1993.

89   **'the amount of information'**: KV 4/227/1a.

90   **'a little leg-pulling'**: KV 2/1869/163a.

91   'she might stand': KV 4/227/1a.

91   'Women do not make': Vernon Kell, 'Security Intelligence in War. Lecture Notes', 1934, PP/MCR/120 Reel 1.

91   'It is frequently alleged': KV 4/227/1a.

Chapter 13: Watchers

92   'The agent must trust': KV 4/227/1a.

92   'A vivid imagination': Eric Roberts to Harry, 10 February, 1969, Eric Roberts Papers.

93   'best watcher': John Le Carré, *Tinker Tailor Soldier Spy* (London: Sceptre, 2009), 12.

94   'There are few': Maxwell Knight, *A Cuckoo in the House* (London: Methuen, 1955), 80.

94   'I have hand-reared': Knight, *Some of My Animals*, 89.

94   'deserted or stray': Maxwell Knight, *Bird Gardening* (London: Routledge & Kegan Paul, 1954), 3.

94   'fledglings fallen from': Maxwell Knight, *Animals After Dark* (London: Routledge & Kegan Paul, 1956), 92.

94   'I have reared many': Maxwell Knight, *Maxwell Knight Replies* (London: Routledge & Kegan Paul, 1959), 67.

94   'crawling on hands': Joan Miller, *One Girl's War* (Dingle: Brandon, 1986), 49.

95   'beating out a tune': Ibid., 50

95   'soothing words': Maxwell Knight, *Taming and Handling Animals* (London: G. Bell & Sons, 1959), 104.

95   'the tone of the human voice': Knight, *Pets: Usual and Unusual*, 33.

95   'hypnotic': Miller, *One Girl's War*, 16.

95   'dance, whistle': Maxwell Knight, *Talking Birds* (London: G. Bell & Sons, 1961), 58.

95   'I didn't have': Masters, *Man Who Was M*, 49.

Chapter 14: Cuckoo Eggs

96 **'like the den'**: Macpherson, 'Olga the Beautiful Spy'.

96 **'It would make the squeak'**: Maxwell Knight, *Keeping Pets* (Leicester: Brockhampton, 1971), 25.

97 **'the real "M" organisation'**: Dick Thistlethwaite, unpublished reminiscences.

98 **'I state unhesitatingly'**: KV 4/227/1a.

99 **'The great thing'**: Knight to Roberts, 5 November, 1934, Eric Roberts Papers.

99 **'The very best training'**: KV 4/227/1a.

100 **'should be disseminated'**: KV 5/72/341c.

101 **'H. G.'**: History Sheet, 4 December, 1934, KV 2/2021.

102 **'facility in mastering'**: Esther Potter, 'Graham Pollard at Work', *The Library* 11, no. 4 (December 1989).

102 **'Pollard did not often'**: Peter Quennell, *The Marble Foot* (London: Collins, 1976), 126.

103 **'like a bookseller's'**: A. L. Rowse, *A Cornishman at Oxford* (London: Jonathan Cape, 1965), 82.

103 **'A cuckoo is not'**: Knight, *A Cuckoo in the House*, 5.

Chapter 15: Trailing One's Coat

106 **'These people have'**: Quoted in Hugh Witford, *The Mighty Wurlitzer* (Cambridge, MA: Harvard University Press, 2008), 12.

106 **'an ordinary, interested'**: KV 4/227/1a.

107 **'very shortly after'**: Ibid.

107 **'she had any free time'**: Ibid.

107 **'speedily reduced'**: Ibid.

107 **'Form the habit'**: Maxwell Knight, *Be a Nature Detective* (London: Frederick Warne, 1968), 169.

108 **'a considerable amount'**: KV 4/227/1a.

108 **'Efforts are being made'**: 'Touts and Spies', *Daily Worker*, 29 March, 1932.

108   'an acute attack': KV 3/338/44b.

109   'an agent becomes': KV 4/227/1a.

109   'coming into local': History Sheet, 9 February, 1932, KV 2/1599.

109   'Bishop is not': History Sheet, 15 February, 1932, KV 2/1599.

109   'might be pumped': KV 2/2199/14x.

110   'very deaf': KV 5/2/51x.

111   'rather an odd fish': Barry Domvile Diary, 11 January, 1939, NMM, Dom 55.

111   'quite agreeable': Vivian Hancock-Nunn (as 'Lucien Francis'), *Two Worlds* (London: Talbot's Head, 1960), 78.

111   'haughty disdain': Ibid., 77–78.

112   'The increased efficiency': KV 4/227/1a.

112   'engaged in some': KV 2/3206/4a.

112   'anti-militarist work': KV 2/3206/8.

112   'It is an immense safeguard': KV 4/227/1a.

Chapter 16: An Author With Unpredictable Hours

113   'my hat': Knight, *Gunmen's Holiday*, 96.

114   'about as reliable': Maxwell Knight, *Crime Cargo* (London: Philip Allan, 1934), 1.

114   'a hundred similar ones': Ibid., 160.

114   'They amused me': *Desert Island Discs*, BBC Home Service, 28 June, 1965.

115   'You are not': Knight, *Crime Cargo*, 51.

115   'a decent, well-built': Ibid., 12.

115   'very violent temper': KV 2/245/1b.

117   'Order of the Fasces': 'Headquarter Orders', *British Fascism,* Summer 1933.

Chapter 17: Heart and Soul

119   'the usual joys': Glading Papers, RGASPI, 495-198-1267-015.

119   'from 6 a.m.': Ibid.

120   'a red-hot Communist': KV 2/1034/12.

120   'be dismissed at': KV 2/1020/9a.

120   'I refuse to renounce': 'Government Ban on Communists', *Manchester Guardian*, 23 October, 1928.

122   'We no longer': Quoted in Richard Crossman, ed., *The God That Failed* (New York: Bantam, 1970), 62.

123   'Moscow-sympathising': Macpherson, 'Olga the Beautiful Spy'.

123   'that she should rearrange': KV 4/227/1a.

124   'The tempo of her work': Ibid.

124   'Detective work': Knight, *Be a Nature Detective*, 2.

124   'Never make it up': John Le Carré, *A Perfect Spy* (London: Coronet, 1986), 234.

125   'position and prestige': KV 4/227/1a.

125   'John Dickson Carr': Masters, *Man Who Was M*, 52.

127   'initiated' into the 'illegal section': KV 2/2494/320a.

127   'specially trained': Ibid.

128   'all incriminating documents': History Sheet, 28 February, 1933, KV 2/2801.

128   'Vivian Hancock-Nunn': Wintringham papers, 4/3, Liddell Hart Centre Military Archive.

129   'grey people': Private telephone interview with author, January 2016.

129   'how very happy': Security Service Archives, quoted in Andrew, *Defence of the Realm*, 132.

130   'appear to be': History Sheet, 22 June, 1933, KV 2/1020.

130   'doggo': KV 2/1035/89a.

Chapter 18: Blackshirts

132   'a "hero" in an': Home Office report, quoted in Dorril, *Blackshirt*, 247.

133   'the greatest Englishman': Joyce quoted in Farndale, *Haw-Haw*, 81.

134   'You would not believe': KV 2/1221/44a.

135   'one of the dozen finest': Quoted in Farndale, *Haw-Haw*, 72.

135   'a psychopathic expression': Francis Selwyn, *Hitler's Englishman* (London: Penguin, 1993), 48.

136   'whether the time': HO 45/25386/54-9.

136   'MI5 should undertake': KV 4/140/1x.

136   'quite reliable': KV 3/53/1c.

137   'a motor salesman': Quoted in Liddell Diaries, 10 August, 1940, KV 4/186.

137   'there have undoubtedly been': KV 4/111.

138   'The Comintern remained': Andrew, *Defence of the Realm,* 190.

138   'insists on the common': KV 3/58/161a.

139   'the last of the great': Dorril, *Blackshirt,* 286

139   'in distinct opposition': KV 4/331/1z.

139   'no evidence whatsoever': KV 3/53/1c.

139   M's original spymaster, 'Don': KV 3/53/1c and KV 3/53/1e.

140   'a far more reliable source': KV 3/53/1e.

140   'It is considered': Ibid.

Chapter 19: Courier

141   'special mission': History Sheet, 25 January, 1938, KV 2/1022.

142   'With very becoming self-restraint': KV 4/227/1a.

142   'a time of the year': Ibid.

142   'themselves as being': Ibid.

143   'a secret agent': Ibid.

143   'drift along with': Knight to Roberts, 23 October, 1934, Eric Roberts Papers.

144   'Baldy McGurk': Knight, *Crime Cargo,* 195.

144   'long hand-made cigarettes': Miller, *One Girl's War,* 16.

145   'my ally': Knight, *Some of My Animals,* 16.

145   'encouraged me in': *Desert Island Discs,* BBC Home Service, 28 June, 1965.

145   'a keen naturalist': Maxwell Knight, *Pets and Their Problems* (London: Heinemann, 1968), 2.

145   'a good library': Ibid.

145   'a sensible and rather': Knight, *Pets: Usual and Unusual,* 76.

145   '**never threatened anything**': Maxwell Knight, *My Pet Friends* (London: Frederick Warne, 1964), 54.

145   '**tried almost too hard**': Quoted in Masters, *Man Who Was M*, 15.

146   '**of Sherlock Holmes**': 'First Edition Forgeries', *The Times*, 29 June, 1934.

146   '**a superb piece**': Robert Harling, *Ian Fleming*, Kindle ed. (London: Robson Press, 2015), chap. 1.

146   '**perhaps the most dramatic**': 'Mr Graham Pollard', *The Times*, 16 November, 1976.

146   '**first notorious**': 'Graham Pollard', *The Book Collector* (London), Spring 1977.

147   '**vile little boat**': Angus Macpherson, 'Olga the Beautiful Spy', *Mail on Sunday*, 29 July, 1984.

147   '**was the only single girl**': Masters, *Man Who Was M*, 34.

147   '**riotous mob**': Weekly Report, 19 May, 1934, IOR/L/PJ/12/137/50.

148   '**render all the aid**': Report of the Director, 9 June, 1934, IOR/L/PJ/12/137/62.

148   '**the first time**': Masters, *Man Who Was M*, 34.

149   '**I started my education**': Glading Papers, RGASPI, 495-198-1267-009.

Chapter 20: The Honeymooning Spy

151   '**the down to earth**': Roberts to Harry, 10 February, 1969, Eric Roberts Papers.

152   '**In all approaches**': Knight, *Pets and Their Problems*, 92.

152   '**I shall be very**': Knight to Roberts, 7 June, 1934, Eric Roberts Papers.

152   '**I am anxious**': Knight to Roberts, 16 August, 1934, Eric Roberts Papers.

153   '**Very many thanks**': Knight to Roberts, 5 October, 1934, Eric Roberts Papers.

153   '**How would that**': Ibid.

153   'no purely mercenary agent': KV 4/227/1a.

153   'We should like': Knight to Roberts, 22 October, 1934, Eric Roberts Papers.

154   'It is not necessary': Knight to Roberts, 23 October, 1934, Eric Roberts Papers.

154   'I cannot give': Ibid.

154   'Do not be disturbed': Knight to Roberts, 5 November, 1934, Eric Roberts Papers.

155   'Very many thanks': Ibid.

155   'an excellent report': Knight to Roberts, 13 November, 1934, Eric Roberts Papers.

155   'to be unduly': Ibid.

155   'May I again emphasise': Knight to Roberts, 19 November, 1934, Eric Roberts Papers.

156   'the sister-in-law of Miss H. B.': KV 2/1012/18c.

157   'the sister-in-law of Miss T-H': Rita Retallick to Eric Roberts, 31 May, 1935, Eric Roberts Papers.

157   'very tricky': Knight to Roberts, 24 January, 1935, Eric Roberts Papers.

158   'Up to date': Ibid.

158   'You're always saying': Le Carré, A Perfect Spy, 74.

159   'a novel for that large': Undated publicity material, Philip Allan.

159   'a real good': Ibid.

159   hailed as 'readable': M. W., 'Piracy in Bias Bay Style,' Straits Times, 1 March, 1935.

159   'thriller with a': Tom Driberg, 'William Hickey', Daily Express, 27 September, 1934.

159   'Knight – lean, long-beaked': Ibid.

160   'I rather liked': Roberts to Harry, 10 February, 1969, Eric Roberts Papers.

161   'I am always glad': Knight to Roberts, 11 February, 1935, Eric Roberts Papers.

161   'a rabid anti-Catholic': KV 2/245/1b.

161   **'one of the most'**: Mary Kenny, *Germany Calling* (Dublin: New Island, 2003), 122.

162   **'For your own private information'**: Knight to Roberts, 24 January, 1935, Eric Roberts Papers.

162   **'the impression that'**: History Sheet, 28 January, 1935, KV 2/245.

162   **'M. thought this remark'**: History Sheet, 20 February, 1935, KV 2/245.

Chapter 21: Olga Pulloffski

163   **'I was approached'**: History Sheet, 25 January, 1938, KV 2/1022.

163   **'No official or other'**: KV 4/227/1a.

164   **'was too much'**: Ibid.

164   **'The work was'**: History Sheet, 25 January, 1938, KV 2/1022.

164   **'stitching reports into'**: Macpherson, 'Olga the Beautiful Spy'.

164   **'most valuable information'**: KV 4/227/1a.

164   **'explained how the cipher'**: Nigel West, *Mask* (London: Routledge, 2005), 21.

165   **'an honest Communist'**: Macpherson, 'Olga the Beautiful Spy'.

165   **'was a very nice man'**: Masters, *Man Who Was M,* 35.

165   **'had been sleeping'**: Ted Crawford footnote in Harry Wicks, *An Unpublished Chapter from Harry Wicks's Autobiography,* ed. Ted Crawford, http://www.cix. co.uk/~jplant/revhist/supplem/wicksind.htm.

165   **'It is important to stress'**: KV 4/227/1a.

165   **'A clever woman'**: Ibid.

166   **'She's Olga Pulloffski'**: Written by Bert Lee and R. P. Weston. Lyrics accessed at http://lyricsplayground.com/alpha/songs/o/olgapulloffskithe beautifulspy.shtml on 10 September, 2012, and transcribed by Mark MacNamara in November 2003.

166   **'Some "superior" people'**: Knight, *Taming and Handling Animals,* 53.

167   **'looking over your shoulder'**: Valerie Lippay, telephone interview with author, May 2014.

168   'he was told': Sean Rayment, 'Traumatised MI5 Spy Fights Murder Verdict', *Sunday Times*, 13 March, 2016.

168   'I informed the officer': History Sheet, 25 January, 1938, KV 2/1022.

168   'As may be': KV 4/227/1a.

168   'in an agent context': Roberts to Harry, 10 February, 1969, Eric Roberts Papers.

169   'On instructions': History Sheet, 25 January, 1938, KV 2/1022.

Chapter 22: Mussolini's Man

170   'Mind Britain's Business': Dorril, *Blackshirt*, 354.

171   'the Fascist party in this country': Transcript of *Rex v. Tyler Gatewood Kent*, MS 310/1/1/10.

172   'grim determination': Quoted in Dorril, *Blackshirt*, 390.

172   'a genuine statement': Quoted in ibid., 368.

173   'an imitation strategist': Quoted in Farndale, *Haw-Haw*, 83.

173   'never before': Quoted in Ibid. p. 83.

173   'it is not thought': KV 2/245/1b.

Chapter 23: A Mysterious Affair

174   'very acute sciatica': Dr Boyall to Dr Warner, 21 November, 1936, COR/LW/1936/154.

174   'unwilling to accept': Ibid.

174   grey shirt studs for 'L': G. Knight Shopping List, COR/LW/1936/154.

175   death was called a 'riddle': 'Riddle of Dying Woman in Club', *Daily Mail*, 21 November, 1936.

175   'mysterious affair': 'Wealthy Woman Found Dying', *Dundee Courier*, 23 November, 1936.

175   'to elucidate if': 'Former Resident of Sherborne', *Western Gazette*, 25 December, 1936.

176   'Sweetheart': 'Death of Author's Wife', *The Times*, 18 December, 1936.

177   'was to be a prison governor': Masters, *Man Who Was M*, 79.

177   'an instant dislike': Bower, *Perfect English Spy*, 26.

Chapter 24: Percy's Proposal

179   'a devoted communist': File STEPHAN, No. 32826, Vol. 1, pp. 15–16, quoted in Nigel West, *The Crown Jewels* (London: HarperCollins, 1998), 123.

179   'bumptious': KV 2/804/2a.

181   'Percy Glading is the comrade': KV 2/2494/325b.

181   'seemed to be somewhat': KV 2/1021/202a.

182   'To be quite frank': KV 4/227/1a.

182   'the bravest girl': S. S. Birch, 'Britain's Bravest Girl Traps Russ Master Spy', *Telegram*, 23 April, 1949.

182   'M's ability to instil': Miller, *One Girl's War*, 16.

Chapter 25: Mr Peters

184   'very unscientific': Quoted in West, *Crown Jewels*, 149.

184   'was to put the whole': Roberts to Harry, 10 February, 1969, Eric Roberts Papers.

184   'polite conversation': KV 4/227/1a.

184   'Aged about 45': KV 2/1008/1a.

185   'The purpose of the meeting': KV 4/227/1a.

Chapter 26: Moscow Moves

189   'They were clearly foreigners': Masters, *Man Who Was M*, 45.

189   'very self-assured': KV 2/1004/1b.

189   'decidedly nervous regarding': KV 2/1004/1d.

189   'very jumpy': Quoted in Masters, *Man Who Was M*, 63.

190   'live on a volcano': Quoted in David Burke, *The Spy Who Came in from the Co-op* (Woodbridge: Boydell, 2008), 90.

190   'is obviously regarded': Ibid.

190   'a large oblong parcel': Masters, *Man Who Was M*, 45.

191   'active and dangerous': KV 2/1020/21b.

Chapter 27: Old Friends, New Agents

193   'for his deficiencies': KV 3/220/31a.

194   'there is strong evidence': Ellen Radley, email to author, 17 December, 2015.

195   'spy who goes alone': C. W. Sykes, *Secrets of Modern Spying* (London: John Hamilton 1930), 9.

196   'a very reliable informant': KV 3/59/241a.

197   'I was immediately attracted': Masters, *Man Who Was M,* 78.

197   'the charm this smiling man': Miller, *One Girl's War,* 16, 44.

197   'Be confident and unafraid': Knight, *Pets: Usual and Unusual,* 34.

197   'for your confidence': Ibid., 29–30.

198   'shattered': Masters, *Man Who Was M,* 79.

198   'thinks differently': A. P. Herbert, *Dolphin Square* (London: Haxwell, Watson & Viney, 1935), 4.

198   'I have myself felt': Maxwell Knight, *Animals and Ourselves* (London: Hodder and Stoughton, 1962), 16.

199   'Failure to do this': Knight, *Taming and Handling Animals,* 92.

199   'It was extremely': Harry Smith, interview with author, London, January 2016.

200   'Joyce, to my mind': KV 2/245/24a.

201   'from an informant': KV 2/2145/25a.

201   'Joyce has a well organised': Knight to Roberts, 24 January, 1935, Eric Roberts Collection.

201   'seriously handicapped': John Curry, *The Security Service 1908–1945* (Kew: Public Record Office, 1999), 393.

201   'was growing morose': KV 2/245/60a.

201   'I should not think': KV 2/245/1b.

Chapter 28: Reprieve

203   'aim and ambition': History Sheet, 17 January, 1938, KV 2/1022.

Chapter 29: Miss X

206   **'Sample of the tempting'**: 'Miss X', *Time Magazine*, 28 March, 1938.

206   **'Britain's counter-espionage'**: 'Foreigner Named by British Agent,' *Baltimore Sun*, 12 February, 1938.

206   **'stylish'**: 'Stylish "Miss X" Tells of Trapping British Arms Spy', *Washington Post*, 8 February, 1938.

206   **'black two-piece'**: 'Girl Tells of Net in British Spy Case', *Atlanta Constitution*, 8 February, 1938.

206   **'slim', 'blonde'**: 'Woman Turns Spy to Foil Plot to Steal British Arms Secrets', *Atlanta Constitution*, 4 February, 1938.

207   **'Fair-haired'**: 'Aircraft and Gun Plans', *Manchester Guardian*, 4 February, 1938.

207   **'exceptionally pretty'**: 'Miss X', *Time Magazine*, 28 March, 1938.

207   **'a real spy hunt'**: Sam Brewer, 'Joins with Red Plotters, Then Tips War Office', *Chicago Tribune*, 4 February, 1938.

207   **'many fictional trials'**: T. J. Hamilton, 'British Spy Case Tinged with Irony', *New York Times*, 13 February, 1938.

207   **'Was there ever'**: Editorial, 'Miss X', *Atlanta Constitution*, 12 February, 1938.

207   **'asked her if she'**: Quoted in Masters, *Man Who Was M*, 69.

208   **'Big, blue eyes'**: H. J. J. Sargint, 'Spy Fighters Guard Name of "Miss X"', *Atlanta Constitution*, 10 February, 1938.

208   **'would not be surprised'**: 23 March, 1938, KV 2/1793.

208   **'was whisked away'**: '"Miss X" Describes Capture of Spies', *New York Times*, 8 February, 1938.

208   **'I wanted to get'**: Masters, *Man Who Was M*, 72–73.

209   **'nasty fingers'**: S. S. Birch, 'Britain's Bravest Girl Traps Russ Master Spy', *Telegram*, 23 April, 1949.

209   **'Spy Fighters Guard'**: H. J. J. Sargint, 'Spy Fighters Guard Name of "Miss X"', *Atlanta Constitution*, 10 February, 1938.

210   **'Miss G'**: KV 2/2159/52a; *Washington Post*, 4 February, 1938.

210   **'the comparatively small'**: 'Charges Under Official Secrets Act', *Manchester Guardian*, 15 March, 1938.

210   **'with the sole and vulgar'**: Ibid.

211   **'I do not propose'**: Ibid.

211   **'the closest enquiries'**: KV 2/2159/52a.

211   **'leading pre-war penetration'**: Andrew, *Defence of the Realm*, 220.

Chapter 30: Mona

214   **'An organised "spy hunt"'**: KV 3/391/217a.

214   **'the most exhaustive investigations'**: KV 3/234/11a.

216   **'Honours'**: Speech Day, Stamford Girls' High School, 1907 and 1910.

218   **'This girl is a rather'**: Security Services Archive quoted in Andrew, *Defence of the Realm*, 182.

218   **'it is also certain'**: Ibid.

218   **'Party work' was so important**: Ibid., 183.

218   **'Suppose you can draw'**: Knight, *Be a Nature Detective*, 16.

218   **'very small feet'**: Geoffrey Elliott, *Gentleman Spymaster* (London: Methuen, 2011), 73.

219   **'I've been rather'**: Burke, *The Spy Who Came in from the Co-op*, 2.

Chapter 31: 'What a Very Beautiful View'

220   **'sooner or later'**: Quoted in Martin Pugh, *We Danced All Night* (London: Vintage, 2009), 441.

221   **'Though willing to work'**: KV 2/1280/1.

221   **'an extremely level-headed'**: KV 2/1280/6.

222   **'as a sort of'**: KV 2/1280/8.

222   **'financial starvation'**: KV 4/227/1a.

222   **'the Ghetto descendants'**: E. G. Mandeville-Roe, *Financiers* (London: Steven Books, 2002), 4–5.

222   **'no officer can efficiently'**: KV 4/227/1a.

222   **'I shall always endeavour'**: Knight to Roberts, 12 November, 1934, Eric Roberts Papers.

222 'be at the beck-and-call': KV 4/227/1a.

222 'The officer will': Ibid.

223 'Joyce's loyalty can be': KV 2/245/62x.

224 'but I am convinced': Ibid.

224 'For God's sake': KV 2/245/96e.

225 'personal introductions to': KV 5/2/51x.

225 'I must admit': 15 August, 1939, KV 5/2/135b.

226 'Hitler seemed': Ibid.

227 'very honoured one': Ibid.

Chapter 32: Crisis

229 'like waiting a doctor's verdict': Virginia Woolf, 28 August, 1939, *The Diary of Virginia Woolf*, Vol. 5, ed. Anne Olivier Bell (London: Hogarth, 1985), 231.

229 'excellent work': KV 2/1280/113.

230 'highly regarded by the Germans': B1a to SIS, 7 January, 1944, KV 2/1278.

230 'I have been able to': KV 3/393/327d.

231 'very clear': William Joyce, *Twilight Over England* (Berlin: Internationaler Verlag, 1940), 11.

231 'Defence Regulations would': J. A. Cole, *Lord Haw-Haw* (London: Faber, 1987), 86.

231 'the biggest danger': Bill Grieg quoted in Farndale, *Haw-Haw*, 180.

232 'secret service' officer: KV 2/245/179x.

233 'did not rate democracy': Christopher Lee, 'M Is for Maxwell Knight', BBC Radio 4, broadcast on 27 January, 2009.

233 'if I had to choose': E. M. Forster, 'What I Believe', *Two Cheers for Democracy* (London: Edward Arnold, 1951), 68.

Chapter 33: Mrs Mackie Investigates

237 'Gloomy, darkened and lifeless': Gabriel Gorodetsky, ed., *The Maisky Diaries* (New Haven, CT: Yale University Press, 2015), 225.

238 'One begins to wonder': Liddell Diaries, 1 December, 1939, KV 4/185.

239 'called upon to show': Liddell Diaries, 30 August, 1939, KV 4/185.

239 'old-fashioned liberalism': Liddell Diaries, 25 May, 1940, KV 4/186.

239 'Our tradition is that': F. H. Hinsley and C. A. G. Simkins, *British Intelligence in the Second World War,* Vol. 4 (London: Her Majesty's Stationery Office, 1990), 57–58.

239 'laughable': Guy Liddell, Memorandum, 1942, KV 4/170.

239 'The liberty of the subject': Liddell Diaries, 25 May, 1940, KV 4/186.

243 'I telephoned to Mrs Ramsay': KV 2/902/62a.

243 'If you could help': Ibid.

243 'I made no promise': Ibid.

244 'that instructions have now': KV 3/393/327c.

244 'there was no question': KV 2/245/179x.

Chapter 34: The Fashion Designer

246 'Yes, I think when': KV 2/677/141a.

247 Duke of Wellington, Lord Carnegie: The Red Book, 1369/1.

247 'a staunch Nazi': KV 2/840/76x.

247 'displaying pro-Nazi': KV 2/840/4c.

249 'a fine example': Quoted in Bryan Clough, *State Secrets* (Hove: Hideaway, 2005), 109.

250 'suddenly immobilised': Miller, *One Girl's War,* 50.

250 'there was little difference': KV 2/1343/84a.

Chapter 35: The Mystic

252 'ludicrous': HO 283/40/22.

252 'several aristocratic Russian': KV 2/2258/92b.

253 'I noticed that': KV 2/902/62a.

253 'the Hon. John': Adam Sisman, *John Le Carré* (London: Bloomsbury, 2015), 200.

253 'set himself the task': KV 4/227/1a.

253 'a thing much to be desired': KV 4/331/9.

254   'in the throes of': Miller, *One Girl's War*, 52.

254   'It is difficult to imagine': KV 4/227/1a.

254   'practically three hours': KV 2/677/141a.

254   'the little Storm Trooper': KV 2/841/140c.

254   'Anna Wolkoff used to tell': KV 2/8839/36a.

255   'as it was considered': KV 2/1212/19a.

255   'Anna Wolkoff claims': Ibid.

255   'a certain subject': KV 2/840

255   'Wolkoff is in contact': KV 2/840/14a.

256   'If by any chance': KV 2/840/11x.

256   'the character and temperament': KV 4/227/1a.

256   'Wolkoff, like many Russians': Ibid.

257   'to a remarkable degree': KV 4/227/1a.

257   Now he planned to harness: Ibid.

257   'suitably edited and embellished': Ibid.

258   'This is not necessarily due': Ibid.

Chapter 36: A Smokescreen

259   'No war was being': Quoted in Pugh, *We Danced All Night*, 443.

259   'our time is approaching': HO 45/24895/3-4.

259   Fellowship of the Services: Liddell Diaries, 11 March, 1940, KV 4/186.

259   'that Geary was trying': HO 45/23775.

260   'young man employed': KV 4/227/1a.

260   'that this man is': KV 2/840/20d.

260   'It was a real pleasure': KV 2/840/20a.

261   'with thanks for': Ibid.

261   'I hope I am right': Ibid.

261   'Dear Captain King': KV 2/840/20cdd.

262   'pedigree': KV 2/902/79a.

262   'She had some idea': KV 2/543/38x.

262   'John Kent': KV 2/543/1ab.

Chapter 37: A Letter to an Old Friend

263 'one of those intensely': Malcolm Muggeridge, *Chronicles of Wasted Time,* Vol. 2 (London: Collins, 1973), 108.

264 'The sooner you shoot': KV 2/543/37d.

264 'actively taking part': *Rex v. Kent,* MS 310/1/1/10.

264 'Part of my function': Interview with Robert Harris, BBC *Newsnight,* 3 December, 1982.

265 'bulky': KV 2/543/1z.

266 'do incalculable harm': KV 4/227/1a.

266 'were not being adequately informed': *Rex v. Kent,* MS 310/1/1/10.

267 'a smart woman': Quoted in John Costello, *Ten Days to Destiny* (New York: William Morrow, 1991), 111.

267 'pleasant, politically stupid': KV 2/840/69a.

268 'if she would like': Ibid.

268 'Herr W. B. Joyce': KV 2/543/43x

269 'Why didn't you tell': KV 2/902/62a.

269 'I replied that I': Ibid.

269 'I explained that I': Ibid.

269 'I replied that it might': Ibid.

269 'a single sheet of quarto': Ibid.

270 'She resealed the letter': Ibid.

270 'Certain arrangements were then': KV 4/227/1a.

Chapter 38: Carlyle

272 'May I have this?': Rex v. Kent MS 310/1/1/10

273 'our principal agent': KV 4/227/1a.

273 'confidential information about': KV 2/840/29b.

273 'information which [he] had': KV 4/227/1a.

273 'It seems urgently necessary': Ibid.

274 'close to collapse': Andrew, *Defence of the Realm,* 222.

274 'strongly of the opinion': Liddell Diaries, 7 May, 1940, KV 4/186.

Chapter 39: Victory at All Costs

275   **'It will be interesting'**: Liddell Diaries, 11 May, 1940, KV 4/186.

275   **'An elephant keeper'**: Liddell Diaries, 12 May, 1940, KV 4/186.

275   **'the slightest doubt'**: Ibid.

276   **'very concerned'**: Ibid.

276   **'severely strained'**: Hinsley and Simkins, *British Intelligence in the Second World War,* 39.

277   **'It was a joke'**: *Rex v. Kent,* MS 310/1/1/10.

277   **'name like a tin'**: KV 2/841/140c.

277   **fifty 'of your older destroyers'**: Quoted in James Leutze, 'The Secret of the Churchill–Roosevelt Correspondence: September 1939–May 1940', *Journal of Contemporary History* 10 (1975): 465–491.

278   **'It is understood'**: May 16, 1940, KV 2/840/49a.

278   **'unimpeachable source'**: Hans Georg von Mackensen quoted in Strix, 'The Golden Egg', *The Spectator,* 26 October, 1956, 17.

278   **'We said that as a'**: Liddell Diaries, 17 May, 1940, KV 4/186.

279   **'Action should also be'**: CAB 65/7, (40) 139.

279   **'During wartime'**: KV 4/227/1a.

279   **'profoundly shocked'**: *Rex v. Kent,* MS 310/1/1/10.

280   **'will act with great care'**: KV 2/543/8a.

Chapter 40: The Raid

281   **'Captain M. King'**: Quoted in Paul Willetts, *Rendez-vous at the Russian Tea Rooms* (London: Constable, 2015), 471.

281   **'the news had been'**: Liddell Diaries, 22 May, 1940, KV 4/186.

282   **'old-fashioned poacher'**: Maxwell Knight, *The Senses of Animals* (London: Museum Press, 1963), 106.

283   **'M certainly never minded'**: Miller, *One Girl's War,* 106.

283   **'examined' 'many'**: KV 2/545/128a.

285   **'in the event of its being'**: KV 2/840/57c.

285   **'one would not expect you'**: KV 2/543/22a.

286   **'what the suspect says'**: Knight, *Gunmen's Holiday,* 258.

Chapter 41: The Meeting

289 **'M. explained that this'**: Liddell Diaries, 21 May, 1940, KV 4/186.

289 **'M explained to him'**: Ibid.

289 **'considerably shaken'**: Ibid.

290 **'our policy with regard to'**: Liddell Diaries, 12 June, 1940, KV 4/186.

291 **'It seems that the Prime Minister'**: Guy Liddell quoted in Hinsley and Simkins, *British Intelligence in the Second World War*, 52.

291 **'mortified' by the extent**: Hugh Trevor-Roper, *The Secret World* (London: I. B. Tauris, 2014), 133.

291 **'great contact'**: Ex-MI5 officer quoted in Masters, *Man Who Was M*, 162.

294 **'I'd like to impress on you'**: KV 2/1221/44a.

Chapter 42: The Trial

295 **'almost a major catastrophe'**: Fred L. Israel, ed., *The War Diary of Breckinridge Long* (Lincoln, NE: University of Nebraska Press, 1966), 113.

295 **'might implicate the chief'**: Ibid., 114.

296 **looking 'dapper'**: 'Diplomat and Woman on Secrets Charges', *Daily Sketch*, 25 October, 1940.

296 **'complimented each of the two'**: KV 4/227/1a.

296 **'congratulated all the agents'**: Ibid.

298 **'The lawyer told me'**: KV 2/839/36a.

299 **'The real reason why'**: KV 2/2474/142.

299 **'The agent provocateur'**: Quoted in Nicholas Hiley and Julian Putkowski, 'A Postscript on P. M.S.2', *Intelligence and National Security* 3, no. 2 (April 1988).

299 **'In a very mild sense'**: Liddell Diaries, 4 October, 1943, KV 4/192.

300 **'The duties of a Security Service'**: Vernon Kell, Vernon Kell Papers, PP/MCR/120 Reel 1.

Chapter 43: Knight's Black Agents

303 **'actively ran and controlled'**: J. C. Masterman, *The Double-Cross System* (Guilford, CT: Lyons, 2000) 3.

304 'was acquired in the school': KV 4/88/2a.

304 'The only thing to do': Liddell Diaries, 8 August, 1940, KV 4/186.

304 'I was given permission': KV 4/227/1a.

304 'deplorable, both from the sex': Liddell Diaries, 28 March, 1944, KV 4/193.

304 'M's attitude to paperwork': Miller, One Girl's War, 66.

304 'laxity of control': Liddell Diaries, 25 March, 1944, KV 4/193.

304 'tremendous leader': Quoted by Masters, Man Who Was M, 101.

304 'We adored him': Ibid., 146–147.

305 'clucked round like a mother': Ibid., 147.

305 'held in some awe': Nigel West, MI5 (London: Triad Granada, 1983), 154.

305 'an explorer of world-wide': KV 4/227/1a.

307 'present as a treasonable conversation': Liddell Diaries, 18 January, 1942, KV 4/189.

307 'had become very uneasy': Quoted in Jeremy Lewis, Shades of Greene (London: Vintage, 2011), 297.

307 'what is fatal in': Knight, Be a Nature Detective, 7.

307 'if you are going to tell': Miller, One Girl's War, 34.

308 'a low point': Ex-MI5 officer, email correspondence with author, January 2016.

309 'I have unlimited trust': KV 2/899/54b.

310 'were the favourite topic': W. J. West, Truth Betrayed (London: Duckworth, 1987), 216–217.

311 'That boy will either do': Quoted in Farndale, Haw-Haw, 48.

Chapter 44: The Comintern Is Not Dead

313 'In dealing with Communism': KV 4/227/1a.

313 'The Russians are very patient': Derek Tangye, The Way to Minack (Bath: Cedric Chivers, 1979), 247.

314 'perhaps the best informed': KV 3/397/454a.

314 'He was convinced': Harry Smith, interview with author, London, January 2016.

315 'Neither Hollis nor I': Liddell Diaries, 6 October, 1942, KV 4/190.

316   'In our insularity': Trevor-Roper, *Secret World*, 80–81.

316   'bewildered when faced by': Tangye, *Way to Minack*, 183.

318   'the old cloak and dagger': Liddell Diaries, 24 October, 1944, KV 4/195.

319   'the most successful penetration agent': Andrew, *Defence of the Realm*, 401.

319   'part of the furniture': Security Service Archive quoted in Andrew, *Defence of the Realm*, 401.

319   'Pied Piper': Quoted in Sisman, *John Le Carré*, 130.

320   'a tweedy, unscalable English': Le Carré, *A Perfect Spy*, 273.

320   'a handsome English warlord': Ibid., 277.

320   'was country stock': Ibid., 212.

320   'He was as broad as': Ibid., 72.

320   'its retreat into bureaucracy': Ibid., 214.

320   'desk jockeys': Ibid., 236.

320   'like an old grey bird': Ibid., 306.

320   'the grand old man': Ibid., 295.

320   'with his reputation': Ibid., 214.

320   'The Firm should have': Ibid., 212.

321   'They shared a contempt': Francis Wheen, *Tom Driberg* (London: Fourth Estate, 1990), 309.

322   'some preliminary briefing by us': KV 2/4116/791a.

322   'when it came to "cottages"': Wheen, *Tom Driberg*, 311.

322   'News that even MI5': *Daily Mail* advertisement, *Evening News*, 19 September, 1956.

323   'Driberg has committed': KV 2/4117/826b.

323   'a kind of official urinal': Quoted in Peter Gill and Mark Phythian, *Intelligence in an Insecure World* (Cambridge: Polity, 2006), 11.

323   'BURGESS BURNS HIS': Chapman Pincher, 'Burgess Burns His Boats', *Daily Express*, 23 November, 1956.

323   'has a dog and a cat': KV 2/4117/871z.

Chapter 45: Rebirth

326 'film shows and lectures': Quoted from *Look and Learn,* accessed at http://www.lookandlearn.com/childrens-newspaper/CN650410-012.pdf on 8 June, 2016.

327 'there might still be persons': KV 2/1017/1105a.

327 he had named 'Olga': Knight, *Some of My Animals,* 43–44.

328 'The only time I realised': Desmond Morris, telephone interview with author, February 2015.

328 'an avuncular, friendly old': 'Desmond Morris: Oral History Transcription,' interview by Christopher Parsons, 6 September, 2000, transcript, WildFilmHistory, Bristol.

328 'There are very few': Knight, *My Pet Friends,* viii.

328 'Spaniels, Labradors': Ibid., 24.

328 'an excellent house-dog': Knight, *Some of My Animals,* 94.

329 'all the species of crow': Ibid., 90–91.

329 'I made it a rule': Maxwell Knight, *Field Work for Young Naturalists* (London: G. Bell & Sons, 1966), 173.

329 'Spiders have always': Knight, *Some of My Animals,* 128.

329 'It will be apparent that': Knight, *Bird Gardening,* 69.

329 'I have had jackdaws': Maxwell Knight, *Letters to a Young Naturalist* (London: Collins, 1955), 56.

329 'a good hiding': Knight, *Animals and Ourselves,* 20.

329 'the constant and usually ill-informed': Ibid.

330 'that field naturalists must': Knight, *Be a Nature Detective,* 2.

330 'His books emphasised': John Cooper, interview with author, London, December 2015.

330 'if that doesn't sound': Maxwell Knight to Nancy, 24 November, 1958, BBC Written Archives.

331 'If only he could have': Quoted in Masters, *Man Who Was M,* 163.

331 'human sex-maniacs': Knight, *How to Keep an Elephant,* 61.

332 'I myself must plead': Knight, *Some of My Animals,* 37.

332   'supposed to be people': Knight, *Bird Gardening,* 1–2.

333   'she would suddenly appear': Knight, *Some of My Animals,* 51.

333   'friendly leg-pulling': Knight, *Pets: Usual and Unusual,* 13.

334   'Those of us': Leonard Harrison Matthews in Knight, *Pets and Their Problems,* vii.

335   'I must issue a word': Maxwell Knight, *The Young Field Naturalist's Guide* (London: Richard Clay and Co., 1952), 39.

Epilogue

336   'lots of men in brown felt hats': Harry Smith, interview with author, London, January 2016.

337   'had a hugely significant impact': T. Denham for the Director General, letter to the author, 28 September, 2015.

337   'he demonstrated the importance': Ex-MI5 officer, email correspondence with author, January 2016.

337   'a woman's intuition': KV 4/227/1a.

339   'most intuitive intelligence officers': Lee, 'M Is for Maxwell Knight', BBC Radio 4.

340   'I see no object in life': Hancock-Nunn (as 'Lucien Francis'), *Two Worlds,* 190.

340   'a familiar, vast and unforgettable': 'R. C.C.', Letters, *The Times,* 30 December, 1972.

341   'I looked on myself': Roberts to Harry, 10 February, 1969, Eric Roberts Papers.

342   'Six years of work': Roberts to Harry, October 1967, Eric Roberts Papers.

342   'I still get nightmares': Ibid.

343   'In Great Britain': KV 4/227/1a.

SELECT BIBLIOGRAPHY

Archives

BBC Written Archives, Caversham
Maxwell Knight Papers

British Library, London
IOR – India Office Records

Christ Church Archives, Oxford
John Maude Papers

Imperial War Museum, London
Vernon Kell Papers

Liddell Hart Centre Military Archive, King's College London
Tom Wintringham Papers

London Metropolitan Archive
COR – London Western Coroners District Collection

National Archives, Kew
ADM – Records of the Admiralty and related bodies
CAB – Records of the Cabinet Office
HO – Records created or inherited by the Home Office and related bodies
HS – Records of Special Operations Executive
KV – Records of the Security Service

National Maritime Museum, Greenwich, London
DOM – Domvile Papers

Russian State Archive of Social-Political History (RGASPI), Moscow
495-198-1267 – Glading Papers

Wiener Library
1369 – The Red Book

Yale University Library, New Haven, Connecticut
MS 310 – Kent (Tyler Gatewood) Papers

Unpublished Material

Eric Roberts Papers
Dick Thistlethwaite, unpublished reminiscences

Books by Maxwell Knight

Crime Cargo (London: Philip Allan, 1934).
Gunmen's Holiday (London: Philip Allan, 1935).
Pets: Usual and Unusual (London: Routledge & Kegan Paul, 1951).
Keeping Reptiles and Fishes, illus. Gretel Dalby and Kerry Dalby (London: Nicholson & Watson, 1952).
The Young Field Naturalist's Guide (London: Richard Clay and Co., 1952).
Some of My Animals, illus. by E. M. Mansell (London: G. Bell and Sons, 1954).
Bird Gardening, illus. by Jean Armitage (London: Routledge & Kegan Paul, 1954).

Letters to a Young Naturalist, illus. by Patricia Lambe (London: Collins, 1955).

A Cuckoo in the House (London: Methuen, 1955).

Instructions to Young Naturalists, No. 1: British Amphibians, Reptiles and Pond-Dwellers (London: Museum Press, 1956).

Animals After Dark (London: Routledge & Kegan Paul, 1956).

How to Observe Our Wild Mammals, illus. Eileen Soper (London: Routledge & Kegan Paul, 1957).

Taming and Handling Animals (London: G. Bell and Sons, 1959).

Maxwell Knight Replies, illus. Rona Cloy (London: Routledge & Kegan Paul, 1959).

Talking Birds, illus. D. Cornwell (London: G. Bell and Sons, 1961).

Animals and Ourselves, illus. D. Cornwell (London: Hodder & Stoughton, 1962).

Frogs, Toads and Newts in Britain, illus. John Norris Wood (Leicester: Brockhampton, 1962).

With Leonard Harrison Matthews, *The Senses of Animals* (London: Museum Press, 1963).

Birds as Living Things, illus. R. A. Richardson (London: Collins, 1964).

Tortoises and How to Keep Them, illus. John Norris Wood (Leicester: Brockhampton, 1964).

My Pet Friends (London: Frederick Warne, 1964).

Reptiles in Britain, illus. by John Norris Wood (Leicester: Brockhampton, 1965).

Field Work for Young Naturalists, illus. Caroline Lees (London: G. Bell, 1966).

The Small Water Mammals, illus. Barry Driscoll (London: Bodley Head, 1967).

How to Keep an Elephant (London: Wolfe, 1967).

How to Keep a Gorilla (London: Wolfe, 1968).

Pets and Their Problems (London: Heinemann, 1968).

Be a Nature Detective, illus. R. B. Davies (London: Frederick Warne, 1968).

Published Material

Christopher Andrew, *The Defence of the Realm* (London: Penguin, 2010).

———. *The Mitrokhin Archive* (London: Allen Lane, 2006).

John Baker White, *It's Gone for Good* (London: Vacher, 1941).

———. *True Blue* (London: Frederick Muller, 1970).

SELECT BIBLIOGRAPHY

Gill Bennett, *Churchill's Man of Mystery* (London: Routledge, 2007).

Genrikh Borovik, *The Philby Files* (London: Little, Brown, 1994).

Tom Bower, *The Perfect English Spy* (London: Heinemann, 1995).

David Burke, *The Spy Who Came in from the Co-op* (Woodbridge: Boydell, 2008).

Miranda Carter, *Anthony Blunt* (London: Macmillan, 2001).

J. A. Cole, *Lord Haw-Haw* (London: Faber, 1987).

John Curry, *The Security Service 1908–1945* (Kew: Public Record Office, 1999).

Stephen Dorril, *Blackshirt* (London: Penguin, 2006).

William Duff, *A Time for Spies* (Nashville, TN: Vanderbilt University Press, 1999).

Geoffrey Elliott, *Gentleman Spymaster* (London: Methuen, 2011).

Nigel Farndale, *Haw-Haw* (London: Macmillan, 2005).

Lucien Francis, *Two Worlds, or, A Story of Frustration* (London: Talbot's Head, 1960).

Peter Gill and Mark Phythian, *Intelligence in an Insecure World* (Cambridge: Polity, 2006).

Gabriel Gorodetsky, ed., *The Maisky Diaries* (New Haven, CT: Yale University Press, 2015).

F. H. Hinsley and C. A. G. Simkins, *British Intelligence in the Second World War,* Vol. 4 (London: Her Majesty's Stationery Office, 1990).

Colin Holmes, *Searching for Lord Haw-Haw* (London: Routledge, 2016).

Keith Jeffery, *MI6* (London: Bloomsbury, 2011).

William Joyce, *Twilight Over England* (Berlin: Internationaler Verlag, 1940).

John Le Carré, *A Perfect Spy* (London: Coronet, 1986).

———, *Tinker Tailor Soldier Spy* (London: Sceptre, 2009).

Jeremy Lewis, *Shades of Greene* (London: Vintage, 2011).

Ben Macintyre, *For Your Eyes Only* (London: Bloomsbury, 2009).

E. G. Mandeville-Roe, *The Corporate State for Britain* (London: Alexander Ouseley, 1934).

———, *Financiers* (London: Steven Books, 2002).

J. C. Masterman, *The Double-Cross System* (Guilford, CT: Lyons, 2000).

Anthony Masters, *The Man Who Was M* (London: Grafton, 1986).

Joan Miller, *One Girl's War* (Dingle: Brandon, 1986).

Malcolm Muggeridge, *Chronicles of Wasted Time,* Vol. 2 (London: Collins, 1973).

SELECT BIBLIOGRAPHY

Graham Pollard and John Carter, *An Enquiry into the Nature of Certain Nineteenth Century Pamphlets* (London: Constable, 1934).

Francis Selwyn, *Hitler's Englishman* (London: Penguin, 1993).

Adam Sisman, *John Le Carré* (London: Bloomsbury, 2015).

Derek Tangye, *The Way to Minack* (Bath: Cedric Chivers, 1979).

Hugh Trevor-Roper, *The Secret World* (London: I. B. Tauris, 2014).

Nigel West, *Crown Jewels* (London: HarperCollins, 1998).

——, *Mask* (London: Routledge, 2005).

——, *MI5* (London: Triad Granada, 1983).

Dennis Wheatley, *The Young Man Said* (London: Hutchinson, 1977).

Francis Wheen, *Tom Driberg* (London: Fourth Estate, 1990).

Paul Willetts, *Rendez-vous at the Russian Tea Rooms* (London: Constable, 2015).

Philip Ziegler, *London at War* (London: Pimlico, 2002).

INDEX

INDEX

bird watchers 93
Birmingham: Conservative garden
party (1931) 81, 82–3
Birrell and Garnett bookshop 103
Bishop, Reg 109
Black and Tans 29, 30, 35
Blackmore, R. D. 9, 61; *Lorna Doone* 61
Bletchley Park 318
Blunt, Anthony ('Tony') 128, 137, 179,
184, 314–15, 316, 338
Board of Deputies of British Jews 222
Boddington, Con 53, 90
Borovoy, Mikhail, and wife (Willy
and Mary Brandes/'Mr and Mrs
Stephens') 189–92, 203
Bramley, Lieutenant-Colonel 52
Briscoe, Norah 309
Bristol, Arnold 252
British Council for a Christian
Settlement in Europe 306
British Empire Union 8, 9, 10, 17, 20
British Fascism (BF paper) 117, 194
British Fascisti/British Fascists (BF)
23–5, 26; infiltration by Max 22–3,
25–8, 30, 31, 33, 37–42, 52, 55,
57–8, 59–60, 75, 117–18, 223, 232–4,
320; joined by Joyce 30; 'K' unit
31, 32, 33, 34, 35, 39–40, 47–8, 51,
60, 116–17, 126, 259; Lambeth Baths
rally (1924) 32–5, 37; joined by
Roberts 44–5; and MI5 48, 51;
Women's Units 55, 117; 'The Day'
57, 58; after the General Strike
58–9; death throes 116–18; and
British Union of Fascists 139
British Lion (BF journal) 59, 64
British Loyalists 58
British National Socialist League 200
British Non-Ferrous Metals Research
Association 219
British People's Party 306

British Union of Fascists (BUF) 118;
earliest recruits 118; Joyce's rise in
132, 133–5; relationship with
foreign Fascist regimes 135–6, 154,
162; and MI5 136, 137; membership
rockets 138–9; investigated by M
139–40; infiltrated by Roberts
152–5, 157–8, 159, 160–61, and
Joyce 161–2, 201; supports
Mussolini 170; receives payments
from him 139–40, 171, 172;
attitudes change towards 171, 172;
infiltrated by M's agents 193–5, 241,
228; and outbreak of war 238, 245,
251–2, 259, 275–6, 288, 289; and
mass internment 289–93; *see also*
Mosley, Sir Oswald
Brixton Prison 310
Brocklehurst, Henry 305
Brooke, General Sir Alan 288
Brown, Isobel 112
Buchan, John 16, 45, 324, 327
BUF *see* British Union of Fascists
Bullitt, William C. 264
Burgess, Guy 128, 179, 272, 318, 319,
320–23, 327
Burn, Sir Charles 25

'C' *see* Sinclair, Sir Hugh; Menzies, Stewart
Cable Street, Battle of (1936) 172
Cairncross, John 179
Camberley, Surrey 310, 332, 333, 335
'Cambridge Spies' 128, 210, 313; *see also*
Blunt, Anthony; Burgess, Guy;
Maclean, Donald; Philby, Kim
Canning, Albert 278
Carnegie, Lord Charles (*later* 11th Earl
of Southesk) 247
Carr, John Dickson 125
Carson, Rachel: *Silent Spring* 333
Carter, Lt-Colonel John 72–4, 75, 77